READINGS IN LANGUAGE STUDIES

VOLUME 5

LANGUAGE
AND
SOCIETY

INTERNATIONAL SOCIETY FOR LANGUAGE STUDIES

READINGS IN LANGUAGE STUDIES

VOLUME 5

LANGUAGE AND SOCIETY

EDITED BY
PAUL CHAMNESS MILLER
HIDEHIRO ENDO
JOHN L. WATZKE
MIGUEL MANTERO

A PUBLICATION OF THE
INTERNATIONAL SOCIETY FOR LANGUAGE STUDIES, INC.

Copyright © 2015

International Society for Language Studies, Inc.
2885 Sanford Ave SW, #21186
Grandville, MI 49418
USA

All rights reserved.

ISBN 978-0-9779114-9-3

Library of Congress Control Number: 2008927091

Text layout by Julie Wernick Dallavis

Cover art comes from the original watercolor on paper entitled "A Way of Communication" by Hiromi Endo. Mr. Endo is retired and an amateur watercolor artist living in Ibaraki, Japan.

This book was printed on acid-free paper.

Printed in the United States of America.

For my siblings, Lora, Susan and David – PCM

For my parents, Hiromi and Takako Endo – HE

To friends and colleagues at the University of Portland – JLW

Para Sara y Miri – MM

CONTENTS

Introduction ix

LANGUAGE TEACHING PRACTICES, PEDAGOGY, AND SOCIETY

1 Classroom as Society: Using Peer Review to Teach an Unfamiliar Writing Style in Foreign Language Writing Instruction 3
   Brian G. Rubrecht

2 A Critical Examination of Foreign-Language Individuality: Choices, Conflicts, and Dilemmas 23
   Gerrard Mugford

3 Reading the Community Critically in the Digital Age: A Multiliteracies Approach 45
   Rosa Alejandra Medina-Riveros, Luz Maribel Ramírez-Galindo, and Amparo Clavijo-Olarte

4 Examining the Role of Critical Pedagogy in Japanese University Students' Desire to Learn English 67
   Takayo Kawabe

5 Challenges and Transformations: Using Narratives to Forefront Writing Pedagogy 83
   Nancy Wasser

6 Evaluative Expressions in Persuasive Essays Produced by L2 Learners of Japanese 107
   Kazumi Matsumoto

LANGUAGE, POLICY, AND SOCIETY

7 Linguistic Implications That Aid or Undermine National Unification: In France and the Former Yugoslavia 133
   Anton Vegel

8 "Policy Borrowing'" and Compatibility: Critical Discourse Analysis on the CEFR, CEFR-J, and JF Standard 151
   Shinji Kawamitsu

9 The "Others" Fight Back: Struggles for Language Rights in Japan 169
   Tamara M. Chung Constant

10 War, Peace, and Language 199
   Charles Kowalski

LANGUAGE, CULTURE, AND SOCIETY

11	Identifying and Identified—in Vain: Autoethnographic Inquiry into Language, Gender, and Identity *Aya Kitamura*	219
12	Desired Communities and Conflicting ESL Identities: Negotiating Identities Across Composition Classes *Heejung Kwon*	233
13	What Makes Students' Lives Challenging? Major Educational Issues Facing Japanese Sojourner Students in the Midwestern United States *Reiko Akiyama*	249
14	Evaluating Concepts of Face *Lin Tao*	269

Index	291
About the Editors	295
About the Contributors	297

INTRODUCTION

Introduction

The International Society for Language Studies has its origins in a grassroots effort to bring together multiple disciplines around issues of language, power and identity. In 2002, a group of international scholars began planning a conference that would eventually grow to forty papers, representing such diverse fields as medicine, law, education and linguistics, presented the following year in St. Thomas, Virgin Islands. This fledging "society" was further advanced through its incorporation as a 501c(6) non-profit with the vision of founding a volunteer-based organization of scholars and practitioners committed to critical, interdisciplinary, and emergent approaches to language studies. Fast forward to 2015. We are well into our second decade as an organization, as well as the twelfth volume of the society's official journal, *Critical Inquiry in Language Studies* (published by Taylor & Francis) is being published this year. Our first conference in Asia was successfully organized last year in Akita, Japan, and we are currently planning our ninth conference to be held at the University of Hawai'i in 2016. International membership continues to grow, and throughout this period of growth the society has remained focused on providing a means to disseminate the important scholarship of its membership. This fifth volume of the *Readings in Language Studies* series, focused on language and society, represents ISLS's continued efforts to provide peer-reviewed fora as a reflection of its mission.

Readings in Language Studies, Volume 5: Language and Society presents international perspectives in several thematic sections. The book's first section focuses on Language Teaching Practices, Pedagogy, and Society (Chapters 1-6). In Chapter 1, Rubrecht initiates the section by presenting research that was conducted with Japanese university English majors enrolled in mandatory freshman English writing classes. The research explored if students' writing would improve when taught a specific and unfamiliar type of writing (i.e., academic English writing) via peer review as a method of teaching and learning and simultaneously sought to determine students' views on peer review. Results showed students to find peer review to be overwhelmingly beneficial, a fact that holistic writing assessment confirmed. Mugford maintains in Chapter 2 that linguistic power and opposing discourses and social practices often limit the foreign-language learners' potential to come across in their own way in a target-language (TL). All too often they are expected to adopt TL social and cultural practices while disregarding first-language beliefs and experiences. To identify how foreign-language users can be encouraged to interact with a socio-culturally identifiable personality, 84 Mexican speakers of English as a Foreign Language (EFL) were interviewed regarding their use of interpersonal politeness practices in the TL. The results indicate that students employ Mexican concepts of solidarity and respectfulness but frequently fail to come across appropriately. Medina's chapter (Chapter 3), details a pedagogical and research experience in which young adult EFL learners in an online based program at a public university in Colombia engaged in a critical reading of their surrounding community by recognizing human, linguistic, cultural, ideological and social assets; acknowledging issues of inequality and power; raising awareness and proposing strategies to transform their shared reality. The study refurbishes Freire and Macedo's (1987) ideas on reading the world and the word and Freire's problem posing method (1993) in technological times. Furthermore, it nurtures from community-based pedagogies (Clavijo & Sharkey, 2012), a socially situated understanding of literacy (Gee, 2000), critical applied linguistics (Pennycook, 1999), multimodality (New London Group, 1997) and technology (Warschauer, 2004) to make sense of a critical reading of the world in the digital age. Following a qualitative approach and an online ethnography methodology, learners' artifacts, surveys and interviews evidence the multimodal literacy practices learners developed while working on the critical reading of the community using technological tools. Aside from learning language by using it for meaningful purposes, reading the community critically triggered students' and teacher's change of perspectives and pushed them to engage in actions to transform their immediate world. Chapter 4, by Kawabe, investigates the role of pedagogy in Japanese university students' desire to learn English. Utilizing Positioning (Bamberg, 2003; Davies & Harre, 1990) theory, the participants' discourse was analyzed, based on the notion that discourse is where speakers produce particular words in the pattern of word usages that demonstrate how they understand themselves and their relationship to their social surroundings. The study confirmed that the students' identity appears as language socialization, as well as positioning influences the students' desire to learn English. Wasser's discussion in Chapter 5 treats challenges to writing pedagogy forefronting personal narrative that pre-service teachers encountered during this study and transformations they experienced as a result of it. She used Teacher Action Research as a framework to explore narrative writing as deep pedagogy, and to promote social justice by applying these authentic funds of knowledge as classroom texts. Additionally, she looked for places of transformation where, through collaborative and evolutionary classroom discourse, participants evolved a new Discourse about teaching writing. Her aim was to explore with preservice teachers, through narrative, the pedagogical question of "whose knowledge counts" (Delgado Bernal, 2002; Delgado Bernal, & Yosso, 2005). In Chapter 6, Matsumoto investigates how evaluative expressions were employed in Japanese persuasive essays and how language proficiency groups affected the usage of the evaluative expressions. The investigation used the Appraisal Framework (Martin & White, 2005) in examining persuasive essays written by three language proficiency groups. This study focused on only Attitude, one of the three sub-systems within the framework. The study found that Japanese persuasive essays had similar characteristics to English ones, and language proficiency affects the resources. Successful writers could use affectual resources to interconnect with other Attitude resources to successfully express their personal stance in their persuasive essays.

The second section of the volume focuses on Language, Policy, and Society (Chapters 7-10). Chapter 7 presents Vegel's study where he posits that literacy initiatives, linguistic establishment, and linguistic isolationism are elements that have the potential to both aid or undermine national ideology by investigating implications of the nation-state oriented contexts, France and the former Yugoslavia. Both contexts' constituents, Slovenia and the southern region of France, demanded national tolerance through cultural and linguistic establishment and strove towards autonomy although they resulted in distinctly different national outcomes. Slovenia, through linguistic isolationism and established educational administrations, was able to secede from Yugoslavia. However, France was abled to maintain its regional constituents, despite isolationist like movements striving for cultural and linguistic autonomy. Kiwamitsu offers, in Chapter 8, an analysis of the Common European Framework of Reference and its impact on the particular language approaches introduced at the university level in Japan. Drawing on Fairclough's critical discourse analysis and Halliday's systemic functional linguistics, this chapter raises issues for educational policy practices and national development of language ideology. Chapter 9 presents Chung Constant's examination of grassroots movements at the local level as part of the people's daily material life which is affecting their conditions in society. Moreover, it aims to explore modes of action for education are being used by local communities for language minorities in Japan. In the past, the Japanese government has used assimilation policies in the public education system to strip ethnic minorities of their language and cultural heritage. Today, Japan seems to have no policies in place to preserve the ethnic origins of marginalized groups that are living within its borders, either by maintaining or reviving their language and cultural practices. Kowalski's chapter (Chapter 10) questions that while most language teachers would probably affirm that language learning and multilingualism contribute to world peace, is there any way to prove this assertion? The chapter starts by examining the inverse, that suppression of language increases violence, and exploring some ways in which violence can also result from misinterpretation or intentional distortion of language. It then goes on to examine how language learners, using their special skill and perspective to persuade and mediate, have worked as agents of peace in times of conflict.

The final section of the volume focuses on Language, Culture and Society. In Chapter 11, Kitamura, through turning an analytical gaze at herself as an ethnographer—a bilingual Japanese woman researching other bilingual Japanese women—this chapter explores the representation politics of ethnography. The analysis of her own field experiences, including predicaments, failures and dilemmas that stem from being a learner, teacher and researcher all at once, sheds light on the tensions within herself and between herself and her research participants. This self-reflexive analysis reveals how ethnographic "epiphanies" (Denzin, 2001; 2014) involve not merely personal troubles but also sociopolitical issues, and points toward the connected nature of the two. Kwon's Chapter 12 explores international students' linguistic identity labels, their perceptions and feelings toward the label, "ESL," and their own self-identification of linguistic ability in an American higher education setting. The author interviewed and observed two international Chinese students who registered for mainstream composition courses at first, and came back to ESL writing classes after attending two weeks of mainstream composition courses. Using semi-structured interviews and classroom observations, the author investigated students' own perceptions and attitudes toward the label, "ESL", as well as how they negotiated identities in the process of placing themselves in a variety of composition courses. Akiyama, in Chapter 13, reports on Japanese sojourners in the Midwest of the U.S., where the population is predominantly white, while Asian and/or Japanese students are considered an ethnic minority in school environments. Thus, students in the racial majority group (i.e., white) and school teachers may not have sufficient experiences integrating with these ethnic minority students. In this chapter, she discusses the major educational issues faced by Japanese sojourner students in this homogeneous educational environment. The final chapter in this volume, Chapter 14 by Tao, presents a study that focuses on the results of a questionnaire that sought opinions on the concepts of 'face' in verbal communication from Chinese and Japanese university students. The study aimed to answer a set of four research questions in order to clarify the conceptualizations of 'face' by Chinese and Japanese university students. The study also discussed in relation to Brown and Levinson's (1987) perspectives on 'face.' The results suggest that face is a universal construct in Chinese and Japanese interaction. Both positive face and negative face exist in Chinese and Japanese culture, and university students appear to consider positive face more important than negative face. The findings offer insight into cultural and linguistic differences in emic conceptualizations of face. The paper ends with a call for more research on emic conceptualizations of face.

Since its inception, ISLS has had as its mission the bridging of disciplines around language studies with a particular emphasis on critical theory. With few venues, the Society, with its conference, journal and publications initiative, now stands as a major advocate for this paradigm. *Readings in Language Studies, Volume 5,* represents contemporary issues, theory, and practices in language studies around issues of language and society. Volume 6, scheduled for publication in 2016 will continue to focus on emergent international perspectives on the intersection of language and community, and Volume 7, scheduled for publication in 2018, will focus on the intersection of language and peace. These forthcoming volumes, as well as future volumes will further the Society's core mission and the work of its membership.

Paul Chamness Miller
Hidehiro Endo
John L. Watzke
Miguel Mantero

LANGUAGE TEACHING PRACTICES, PEDAGOGY, AND SOCIETY

CHAPTER 1

CLASSROOM AS SOCIETY:
Using Peer Review to Teach an Unfamiliar Writing Style in Foreign Language Writing Instruction

Brian G. Rubrecht
Meiji University

The act of writing has traditionally been defined as composing text by marking coherent words on paper. This act, even if its purpose is for transmission to a readership, is at base an individual endeavor. Yet, in second language (L2) or foreign language (FL) learning contexts, the writer/learner must, by necessity, relinquish some of what makes the act of writing individualistic and seek collaboration with others, especially when the writing style being learned is either unfamiliar or specialized. In typical classroom situations, this collaboration comes primarily in the form of students' first accepting instruction from others (i.e., the teacher) and then making alterations in writing based on teacher feedback and further instruction (either in subsequent drafts or in new writing assignments).

However, the teacher is not the only one capable of providing instruction and feedback. Collaboration may also come by means of partnerships with other writer/learners, that is, by the use of peer review between students. It was the educational reformer John Dewey (1916/2009) who took the position that schools and classrooms are microcosms of communities and society as a whole, as they are, ideally, places where participants learn and grow together. Peer review fits well into Dewey's view, as he believed that classrooms should be constructed to be collaborative in nature, which means abandoning the typical teacher-centered educational approach by allowing knowledge and authority to be shared among all classroom participants. More currently, those who favor social constructivist educational approaches also find peer review to be a powerful tool in the classroom.

Even so, questions remain about whether peer review is effective in the teaching and learning of all writing genres or when teaching all types of learners, as positive research results found from collaborative learning procedures could be mitigated by unique difficulties posed by the chosen genre or by writer/learner idiosyncrasies. In order to fill in our knowledge gaps related to genre, learners, and peer review, a study was conducted with a group of Japanese university freshmen English majors. The research meant to ascertain if the peer review method would improve students' writing abilities when they were taught a generally new and unfamiliar style of English writing and if the use of such a method would be viewed by the typically collectivistic learners as beneficial and viable as a means of teaching and learning writing.

The Literature

Peer review (at times also called peer assessment, peer correction, peer editing, or collaborative writing) is a long-established technique for teaching writing. With its roots established in the late 1960s (see Byrd, 2003; Hoogeveen & van Gelderen, 2013), peer review is, put simply, the act by which learners assess their fellow learners' written work by providing feedback via critique and suggestions for improvement. Peer review emerged from a paradigm shift in teaching composition that emphasized stages (i.e., pre-writing, writing, and revision) and the rhetorical principle of audience (DiPardo & Freedman, 1988) alongside the trend to include constructivist approaches and interactive and cognitively reflective activities in language learning endeavors (van Lier, 2007, as cited in Diab, 2011).

Being at its core a collaborative effort between one or more learners, peer review is seen as a pedagogical activity where student writers work together to discover what they wish to say (Zamel, 1982). It has been described as "an arrangement for peers to consider the level, value, worth, quality or successfulness of the products or outcomes of learning of others of similar status" (Topping, Smith, Swanson, & Elliot, 2000, p. 150). By engaging in this activity, writer/learners are meant to gain feedback that informs them about their current state of learning or performance (Narciss, 2008, as cited in Gielen, Peeters, Dochy, Onghena, & Struyven, 2010), though this is not always the case (Gielen et al., 2010).

John Dewey

The very nature of the peer review classroom that sees students engaged in learning not as individuals but as equal cooperative members who share knowledge is very much in line with Dewey's thinking. Dewey recognized the relationship between culture and the creation and maintenance of democratic communities in the classroom. In such classroom communities, students work together to construct knowledge, and their engagement with others in problem-solving tasks not only lends itself to better and more diverse answers but also stands as a classroom learning resource. As Dewey (1916/2009) himself stated, for equity and democracy to come about, all group members must be able to equally give to and take from others and share in the variety that comes from sharing undertakings and experiences. Education that is meant to empower rather than classify students must draw upon students' multiple abilities, varied perspectives, and all forms of personal and cultural knowledge.

The Social Constructivist View

Those holding social constructivist views of learning often embrace the collaborative classroom ideal championed by Dewey. Largely attributed to Russian psychologist Lev Vygotsky, this theoretical perspective was revived in the 1970s (see Hoogeveen & van Gelderen, 2013, for other perspectives) and posits that individuals only truly learn and master higher mental functions when involved in social interaction that is mediated by communicative language. Vygotsky's thoughts on learning offer strong support for the utilization of peer review in writing instruction and are "particularly applicable to the kind of collaborative instructional activity that occurs during peer revision" (Villamil & de Guerrero, 1996, p. 54), even to the point where Jacobs, Curtis, Braine, and Huang (1998) insist that social constructivist views of learning be added to any list of peer review advantages (see below).

Within this perspective, writing is seen as a social learning process whereby writer and reviewer interact to build meaning. Because "instruction usually precedes development" (Vygotsky, 1986, p. 184), a more capable participant (i.e., the teacher) scaffolds the pieces and processes of writing within the learners' zone of proximal development (ZPD), or within their ability to learn (Vygotsky, 1978). Scaffolding also occurs between peers and allows them to work together by pooling resources and performing in ways that surpass their individual abilities (see Diab, 2011; Kaneko, 2011). Thus, the social constructivist view of learning explains well why, as a "total communicative experience" (Villamil & de Guerrero, 1996, p. 66) whereby students engage in all four skill areas, the act of providing peer feedback "may be the most beneficial aspect of peer review" (Lundstrom & Baker, 2009, p. 38).

Peer Review Advantages
The literature is replete with peer review advocates, with many providing detailed lists (which often overlap) of its advantages. Nearly 40 years ago, Witbeck (1976) claimed that peer review provides students with extensive practice in developing editing skills, allows for student-student and student-teacher communication, and reinforces and expands an understanding of writing rules when errors are corrected, among other benefits. Two decades later, Zhang's (1995) list included the benefits of peer social support, feedback from peers of the same ability level as being informative, learning that occurs via the exchange of feedback, and peers acting as an additional audience base. Berg (1999) noted that peer review aids students in identifying incongruities in their writing, provides valuable learning and affective benefits, mimics how experienced writers rely on colleagues for feedback in the writing process, engages students' knowledge of writing pieces and process, allows for discussion that can lead to alternative writing options for any unclear writing, and encourages students to recognize and develop a sense of audience.

Others have found it to develop in learners an awareness of their own mistakes and a stronger sense of text ownership (Tsui & Ng, 2000), for it often encourages students to read and revise their own writing more critically (Rollinson, 2005). Since students have been found to respond both appropriately and helpfully in peer review activities (Rinnert & Kobayashi, 2001), peer feedback may be seen as more specific and hence more valuable than teacher feedback (Caulk, 1994). Peer review also forces L2 learners to become active agents in their learning, as their considering and questioning peer feedback spurs them to apply their learning, as they no longer simply make corrections to mistakes pointed out by their teachers (Berg, 1999; Mendonca & Johnson, 1994; Mittan, 1989).

Peer Review Disadvantages
This is not to say that peer review is without its criticisms. Writer/learners may lack trust in their peers as competent reviewers (Mendonca & Johnson, 1994; Nelson & Carson, 1998; Nelson & Murphy, 1993; Tsui & Ng, 2000), sometimes justifiably so (see Hovardas, Tsivitanidou, & Zacharia, 2014; Villamil & de Guerrero, 1996). Peers' questionable language proficiency may potentially play a role in L2 learning situations (Carson & Nelson, 1996; Coomber & Silver, 2010; Nelson & Murphy, 1993), as limited language abilities may hamper reviewers' attempts to provide useful feedback and keep writer/learners from being able to differentiate good feedback from bad (Tsui & Ng, 2000). As such, some students may be willing to primarily or exclusively accept teacher feedback (see Connor & Asenavage, 1994; Mendonca & Johnson, 1994; Nelson & Carson, 1998; Paulus, 1999; Tsui & Ng, 2000; Yang, Badger, & Yu, 2006; Zhang, 1995), as the teacher is the one considered to be more experienced, authoritative, and in possession of expertise and superior knowledge (Taferner, 2008; Tsui & Ng, 2000), not to mention the one who ultimately must evaluate their work (Amores, 1997).

Negative or skeptical views toward peer review can hinder the peer review process (Coomber & Silver, 2010) and lead to peer hostility and overly critical feedback (Nelson & Murphy, 1992). However, skepticism can also lead to writers making deeper-level changes in content, organization, and vocabulary (Paulus, 1999; Shehadeh, 2011) because the feedback, being "pitched more at the learner's level of development or interest" (Tsui & Ng, 2000, p. 148), stimulates discussion, reflection, and searches for confirmation. Teacher comments, on the other hand, are often taken "as is" without question, even if they are not fully understood (Yang, Badger, & Yu, 2006). Regardless, it is often suggested that teacher and peer feedback be regarded as complimentary rather than contradictory (see Caulk, 1994; Rollinson, 2005).

Writer and Reviewer Benefits
Due to the shared and collaborative nature of peer review settings, research has revealed that all participants can benefit from the peer review process. Writers who have had their compositions peer reviewed have improved their writing abilities (Berg, 1999; DiPardo & Freedman, 1988; Dobao, 2012; Gielen et al., 2010; Paulus, 1999) and have developed genre knowledge (Lewis & Wray, 1995, as cited in Hoogeveen & van Gelderen, 2013), with

students' success being attributed directly to the qualities and extent of their collaborative interactions (Hedgcock & Lefkowitz, 1992; Mendonca & Johnson, 1994). Reviewers have been found to learn more than writers (Amores, 1997; Lundstrom & Baker, 2009), improve their understanding of writing criteria (Althauser & Darnall, 2001), and produce better writing (Diab, 2011; Lundstrom & Baker, 2009), the latter because reviewers' additional engagement encourages them to think more deeply about their own writing while editing (Rouhi & Azizian, 2013).

The Research

Considering the potential benefits to learners participating in collaborative writing instruction settings, mentioned above, research into the use of peer review was conducted with Japanese university EFL (English as a foreign language) learners. These learners were selected for participation in the current study for reasons that include their being unfamiliar with peer review, their being collectivistic learners, and their general lack of experience and knowledge about English writing, particularly the style of English writing taught in their university writing classes (see below).

The two research questions in this study were:

1. Would the students improve in their writing when taught a generally new and unfamiliar writing style (i.e., academic English writing) that includes peer review in the learning method?
2. How do the students perceive the use of the peer review method when learning this specific, new, and unfamiliar writing style?

The first research question is grounded in the theoretical perspective known as genre theory. The early work of Halliday (1975, 1978) laid the foundation for the need to view how language expresses meaning in different contexts (Halliday & Matthiessen, 2004). If texts are structured according to their purpose, then texts with similar purposes should share similar structures (Martin, Christie, & Rothery, 1987). Thus, in the genre approach to writing instruction, learners "succeed" in writing a text only so long as it complies with the linguistic and structural requirements of that genre, but learners can only accomplish this product via the process of exploring the social relations between the writer and the reader (Hoogeveen & van Gelderen, 2013).

The genre of writing chosen for the present study was academic English writing (hereafter, AEW). For the purposes of this study, AEW is defined as forms of expository and argumentative writing in English meant to convey information about a particular subject. It is taken to be a concept that embodies process as well as product. That is to say, in the teaching of this style of writing, the students are taught and allowed to practice not only English grammar and sentence construction, but they are also instructed on the steps that take them to increasingly complex stages and forms of writing (i.e., from the sentence and paragraph level to the essay and finally to the research paper or thesis level). In this style, writers are expected to introduce a topic and a controlling idea, provide reasons and examples in support of that idea that come from having (ideally) conducted research on the topic, and ultimately draw conclusions that produce new observations, recommendations, and/or predictions.

This style was selected because, first, as students of a prestigious university in Tokyo, many were expected to continue their studies after graduation and later work in international careers. Learning the pieces and process to AEW via peer review would teach them the various writing norms of American academic writing (LoCastro, 2000) as well as provide them with the knowledge and skills necessary to clearly state and support thoughts and positions. Second, the students were taught a writing style they were not likely to have encountered previously. Japanese students receive little formal expository or academic writing instruction in their L1, as they are mainly taught expressive writing (Hirose, 2003). Furthermore, pre-tertiary level English writing instruction is often little more than Japanese-to-English translation (Kitao & Kitao, 1995) where even the basic concepts of topic sentences and support in paragraph construction go untaught (Gilfert & Croker, 1997). Third, the students were expected to write graduation theses during their senior year. As English majors who receive two years of mandatory English writing instruction, it made sense to teach AEW, which is an appropriate style for theses written in English.

There were also several reasons for asking the second research question. First, as stated previously, negative or skeptical views about peer review can hinder its efficacy (Coomber & Silver, 2010). Even with its known advantages, peer review should only be utilized if students find it acceptable (Yang, Badger, & Yu, 2006). Additionally, course developers must take into account students' views on learning since their views affect their learning. Even if a teaching method is found to be effective in certain cases, if students are overly averse to it, its benefits are negated (see Leki & Carson, 1994). Thus, knowing students' perceptions about using peer review to learn AEW would likely prove insightful when assessing the research results obtained by asking the first research question.

Second, as Japanese and other East Asians are often broadly classified as collectivists who tend to identify themselves via group membership rather than as individuals (see Triandis, Bontempo, Villareal, Asai, & Lucca, 1988), there was some concern that the participants would not only be averse to peer review on the grounds that peer critique could disrupt group harmony (thereby negating that which is beneficial about peer review), but also that a student-centered teaching approach rather than the deeply entrenched teacher-centered learning style that is the norm in Japan might make them uncomfortable. When examining the case of peer review and collectivistic language learners (such as those from China and Japan), the research is somewhat divided, as some find group dynamics and cultural factors to influence the effectiveness of peer review (e.g., Carson & Nelson, 1994; Nelson & Murphy, 1993), while others essentially find such concerns to be nonissues (e.g., Braine, 2003; Coomber & Silver, 2010; Kaneko, 2011; Taferner, 2009; Yang, Badger, & Yu, 2006).

The Participants and Classes
The participants were Japanese university English majors ($n = 65$) who were enrolled in three separate mandatory freshmen English writing classes at a private university in the Tokyo metropolitan area. Background information gathered from the pre-test sampling questionnaire revealed that all were native Japanese with Japanese being their first language. Only four students (6%) mentioned having previously learned writing that included the typical pieces of topic, supporting, and concluding sentences.

The research period for the present study spanned the entire 14-week spring (first) semester of the students' freshman year at university. Each class met for 90 minutes once a week. During the first class, the teacher (who was also the researcher) explained the research to the students, and all consented to study participation. Some students initially voiced their embarrassment upon learning that they would be doing peer review, as they remarked that they might be ashamed that others would see their mistakes or that because they lacked ability in English they would not only be unable to find others' writing mistakes but also be unable to give appropriate and useful feedback. Such trepidation at doing peer review echoes the reactions Taferner (2008) encountered. In following Amores' (1997) example, it was stressed to the students in the first class that peer review "is but one aspect of the larger process of composing and communicating a message" (p. 520).

Method

As Lundstrom and Baker (2009) state, there are many choices available when setting up a course that utilizes peer review. In order to answer the first research question, writing samples were collected from the students pre- and post-academic term. Pre-term sampling, which occurred during the second class in mid-April prior to any writing instruction, contained three sections: (1) a student background information section, (2) a sentence writing section where students were asked to translate Japanese sentences into sentences that sounded and looked natural in English, and (3) a paragraph writing section that asked the students to write a paragraph on a single topic (in this case, a good hobby to have) that followed what they considered AEW should look like. The post-term sampling, which occurred during the first class of the second term (i.e., after the summer break), consisted of the exact same sentence and paragraph writing sections that were found in the pre-term sampling.

The sentence and paragraph writing sections were used to directly assess the students' writing. Because it was unclear what types of sentences the students would write (e.g., simple sentences, compound sentences) and because there was no guarantee the students would write sentences with more involved structures, the sentence writing sections in the samplings were used to see if students were more apt to conduct direct translations and maintain parity in their translations or if they would indeed attempt to write more natural-sounding English sentences. Translated sentence writing quality was assessed by the teacher-as-researcher holistically using a 0-3 point scale in terms of grammar, vocabulary, mechanics, and accuracy.

For the paragraph writing, samples were assessed using the writing scale Hedgcock and Lefkowitz (1992) adapted from the scale originally developed by Jacobs, Zinkgraf, Wormuth, Hartfiel, and Hughey (1981). The 0-100 point scale, used by Shehadeh (2011) for purposes similar to the current study, assesses the following:

- content (i.e., subject knowledge, thesis development, topic coverage, quantity and relevance of details, and substance)
- organization (i.e., fluency of expression, clarity in idea statements, support, idea organization, and the sequencing and development of ideas)
- grammar (i.e., correctness and accuracy in agreement, number, tense, word order, articles, pronouns, prepositions, and negation, as well as use of sentence structures and constructions)
- vocabulary (i.e., range, accuracy of word and idiom choice, mastery of word forms, register appropriateness, and effectiveness of meaning transmission)
- mechanics (e.g., conventions of spelling, punctuation, capitalization)

In order to answer the second research question, the students were given a separate Peer Review Questionnaire, which asked them a range of open-ended questions about their perceptions of peer review and the peer review process. Their responses were categorized and tallied. They completed this questionnaire just prior to the post-term sampling.

Although providing peer review training sessions to students is ideal (see Berg, 1999; Diab, 2011; Rahimi, 2013; Rollinson, 2005), time constraints dictated that full training could not be done. At the beginning of the school year when the peer review process was explained, the students were instructed to focus on the three areas their teacher would assess when grading students' compositions when they conducted peer reviews: grammar, content, and organization.

No textbook was used for the course. Instead, the students were given two packets. The first packet consisted of 17 handouts that explained and allowed for the practice of the pieces (e.g., titles, topic sentences, concluding sentences, transitions) and the process (e.g., brainstorming, prewriting, writing, proofreading and editing, multiple draft writing) necessary for the expected style of AEW. These handouts were explained and practiced during class time. The second packet consisted of 10 activity sheets that allowed for additional pieces and process practice (e.g., capitalization, punctuation, grammar). Some activities were completed in class, but a majority of the sheets were assigned as homework.

Once most of the handouts were explained and completed, the students were assigned three writing tasks in turn throughout the semester. All three tasks required argumentative writing because the students were taught how to provide reasons and examples that both persuaded the reader to accept their side of an argument and provided factual information rather than restating opinions. The writing tasks all began with prewriting that involved brainstorming activities and ended with proofreading, editing, and peer review. After peer review, the instructor collected and graded each draft (see Mendonca & Johnson, 1994) for course grading and feedback purposes. Each draft was returned the next class, when students could check and ask about the instructor's comments. Two drafts were expected for each task, as multiple drafts have been found to improve final products (Paulus, 1999; Zhang, 1999).

The Peer Review Sessions
When pairing the students for peer review, the advantages and disadvantages of pairing students by friendship status, by language ability, or by random means were considered. Because the students in this class were (according to the university) of the same high language ability level, students were allowed some freedom in selecting a peer review partner. They were encouraged to change partners frequently because, as was explained to them, different peer review partners would present them with different perspectives.

The instructor walked around the classroom during the peer review sessions, silently observing but interjecting only to urge students to return to using English if they spoke in Japanese. Because the feedback was supposed to be peer feedback (rather than teacher feedback during the peer review process), the instructor took a "guide" approach (see Moffett, 1968, as cited in Jacobs et al., 1998). If questions arose (e.g., about grammar or word choice), the instructor then guided the students to an answer rather than giving them the answer directly. By saying things like "I think there might be a problem here. What do you think?" students were given indirect yet nevertheless useful feedback (see Ferris & Roberts, 2001, regarding the positive nature of indirect feedback; see also Gascoigne, 2004).

Results

Research Question 1
Because the first research question meant to determine whether or not the students would improve in their writing when that writing was new and was

taught via the utilization of the unfamiliar peer review method, comparisons were made between the writing the students produced prior to and after instruction that included peer review sessions. These comparisons examined the pre- and post-instruction samples of the students' sentence writing (i.e., translations) and paragraph writing.

Paired t-tests were conducted on the translated sentences to see if there was any statistically significant improvement in the students' writing between the testing times. Results revealed such improvement in all four areas.

- Grammar: $t(389) = -5.625, p < 0.0001$
- Vocabulary: $t(389) = -3.85, p = 0.0001$
- Mechanics: $t(389) = -4.765, p < 0.0001$
- Accuracy: $t(389) = -3.182, p = 0.002$

These results indicate that the students' ability to write what they intended to say in English (i.e., accuracy) improved, as did the manner in which they conveyed their intended meanings on paper (i.e., via grammar, vocabulary, and mechanics) in English.

Paired t-tests were also used to make comparisons between pre- and post-instruction paragraphs, with results indicating statistically significant improvement in all areas except for vocabulary.

- Content: $t(64) = -5.005, p < 0.0001$
- Organization: $t(64) = -3.976, p = 0.0002$
- Grammar: $t(64) = -3.873, p = 0.0003$
- Vocabulary: $t(64) = -0.683, p = 0.497$
- Mechanics: $t(64) = -6.842, p < 0.0001$

Much like the sentence-level translations, these results indicate student ability improvement when peer review was utilized as part of the method of instruction, although improvement in vocabulary was not found (see below).

Research Question 2
The second research question, which sought to reveal students' perceptions of peer review while learning AEW, was answered via the students responding to the Peer Review Questionnaire. Because of the questionnaire's many open-ended questions, the students offered a large number and wide variety of

responses. Due to space limitations, only the top five responses to questions will be given here.

When asked to reveal and explain their reactions at the beginning of the semester upon hearing that peer review would be used in the teaching and learning of AEW, their responses were categorized as "good or helpful" (33 students, 51%), "embarrassing" (22, 34%), "collaborative" (17, 26%), "necessary" (6, 9%), and "interested in doing" (5, 8%). When asked what their opinion was of peer reviewing at semester's end, their responses were categorized as "good or helpful" (46, 71%), "collaborative" (30, 46%), "necessary" (4, 6%), "interesting" (4, 6%), and "embarrassing" (3, 5%).

The 65 students provided 79 reasons regarding the positive aspects of peer review, with the top reasons including "peers find your (simple) mistakes" (11, 17%), "can know how others write" (7, 11%), "share opinions, knowledge, or ideas" (7, 11%), "it improves your own writing" (7, 11%), and "get a different perspective" (6, 9%). The 58 responses to the negative aspects of peer review included "nothing negative about it" (10, 15%), "embarrassing" (8, 12%), "cannot find all errors" (8, 12%), "peers are afraid to criticize friends" (7, 11%), and "it takes a long time" (6, 9%). Finally, when asked who benefits more, either the writer or the reviewer, 18 students (28%) believed the writer did while 21 students (32%) thought it to be the reviewer. Twenty-six students (40%) responded—without it being given as a possible option—that *both* parties benefited. A variety of explanations as to why they believed as they did were proffered.

Discussion

In the current study, statistical significance was found in the students' sentence translation grammar, vocabulary, mechanics, and accuracy and in paragraph writing grammar, mechanics, content, and organization, but not vocabulary. In answering the first research question, on the whole, it can be stated that the students' writing improved when peer review was included as a method of instruction when learning the new and unfamiliar AEW style. Vocabulary's exclusion can be explained by stating that throughout the semester, all areas minus vocabulary specific to the sampling's prompt were explicitly taught in the lessons. In other words, students were taught and expected to produce writing in a specific genre (i.e., AEW) by applying correct grammar to paragraphs that required specific mechanics, content, and organization. Not conforming to this writing genre was unacceptable, as it would have meant that the students would not be applying their learning, with the result being lower student grades. The particular vocabulary terms required in the samplings were the only things never explicitly taught, as they never became topics for discussion or feedback in the lessons or during peer review sessions. Because word choice in writing depends to a large degree on the writing topic, with the variety of writing task prompts given to the students throughout the semester, vocabulary instruction occurred on a case-by-case (i.e., topic-by-topic) basis. Without the aid of the instructor or dictionaries during sampling time, the students were left to utilize their own current vocabulary knowledge.

These results are somewhat contrary to those of Shehadeh (2011), who found peer review to influence to a statistically significant degree writers' content, organization, and vocabulary but not grammar or mechanics. Nevertheless, Shehadeh's research as well as the current research (especially with the sentence translations) indicate that students may be able to pick up linguistic aspects like vocabulary and grammar throughout their university experience, but not necessarily things like content and organization in writing unless they are taught them as a means to conform to a genre, which they were in both research cases. This is important to realize, as Hyland (2003) notes that freshmen university students in Japan, being novice writers, may focus too much on sentence-level grammar and vocabulary problems, thereby overlooking issues related to content or organization.

In answering the second research question of determining how the students perceived the use of peer review in learning a new writing style, it appears that although the students were not unanimous in their opinions, they generally found it to be an incredibly helpful and engaging endeavor that was advantageous to their learning and producing writing. Indeed, the Peer Review Questionnaire collected comments such as "We write not only for ourselves but also for readers," "If (a) friend teaches you, that sticks in your head more than if your teacher gives you feedback," and "We can grow our ability of thinking. We don't have to keep thinking after writing if the teacher checks all the paper(s). We can think together with (the) peer reviewer." The fact that 26 students believed both the writer and reviewer benefit from the peer review process, without being given that possibility as a prompt, indicates that the value of peer review and the merits to including others in the "individual" act that is writing were not lost on them.

Most of their apprehension about peer review arose from their perceived linguistic deficiencies, that is, some students were embarrassed to make public their "poor" English abilities, which, according to them, would cause them to either write inferior compositions or be unable to locate problems or mistakes in their peers' writing. However, at the time of questionnaire administration, most students found definite merit to the conducting of peer review and expressed their desire to continue using it, which is a finding similar to that revealed in other research (e.g., Kaneko, 2011; Jacobs et al., 1998). Being native Japanese learners new to university, it was almost assured that the students would not possess perfect English. However, much like the participants in Taferner's (2008) study, the students generally found the pointing out of others' errors to be, in the long run, helpful for them to discover their own.

Conclusions, Implications, and Future Directions

Dewey would no doubt agree that much education found in classrooms worldwide today falls short of the goal—which is either stated or otherwise implied—of empowering students with the necessary tools to allow them to continue learning on their own for the rest of their lives. While it may be granted that teachers have experience and knowledge that make them qualified to instruct students, students relying solely on teachers for information and feedback gives them the impression that their peers have little, if anything, to contribute to their education.

As made apparent from this and other research, this is clearly not the case. Peer review is but one potentially viable method that allows learners to engage in learning that mimics how learning happens after graduation: by consulting with peers, by networking with others, and even taking initiative to seek answers rather than wait to have those answers imparted by others. Answers to life's questions do not come from a single person. Living in a democratic society means becoming aware of the opinions of others as well as freely exchanging knowledge. Classrooms should be set up to prepare students for living in such a society.

The results of the current study indicate the potential benefits of introducing student-centric activities in wholly teacher-centric Japan, as instructors, in their pursuit of effective instruction, must make "informed pedagogical adjustments" (Zhang, 1999, p. 323) to lessons based on student perceptions. Taking a "more is more" approach by utilizing peer review in composition classes could not only provide non-instructor-based feedback that is "effective with different beneficial effects" (Rouhi & Azizian, 2013, p. 1350), but also help promote students' development of their critical evaluation skills (see Braine, 2003), an important asset for future workers in a global society.

In addressing the limitations of the study, I follow Kaneko's (2011) lead in advising caution when interpreting and generalizing findings. In the current study, the language the students used during the peer review process (e.g., register, politeness), the amount of peer feedback given, and the extent to which peer feedback was applied were not assessed. Additionally, the teacher-as-researcher method raises objectivity concerns, but the method has been used elsewhere to positive service (cf. Paulus, 1999). Furthermore, the present study only analyzed peer review as used across the span of one semester, and only for paragraph writing. Although data analyses were also conducted in the second semester when peer review was utilized as the students engaged in AEW at the essay level (see Rubrecht, forthcoming), truncated research as found in the current chapter is not unheard of (see Rahimi, 2013; Taferner, 2008). Lastly, peer review training was not conducted. As Rahimi's (2013) research found that trained reviewers address more than simply the formal aspects of writing, further research should ideally include training, but realistically, diverse educational environments coupled with the dual concerns of time and student interest make training unlikely for all but a few cases, for instance, when teachers questionably offload their grading assignments onto the students.

In closing, the acceptance of Dewey's beliefs on education that stress equality, the sharing of knowledge, and ample opportunities for students to take part in their own learning have led to the implementation of pedagogical practices like peer review that put more responsibility to learn—and to share in learning—into the hands of the learners themselves. Students engaged in peer review, beyond being able to receive additional feedback that is likely more comprehensible to them since it originates from peers with similar abilities and who are engaged in the same writing assignments, can come to see others in their environment as valuable sources of learning (Hovardas,

Tsivitanidou, & Zacharia, 2014). This looking to and sharing with others is precisely what can transform the classroom into the truest microcosm of society, a microcosm that should be created now and, in the instances where it is lacking, should be expanded to the world at large.

References

Althauser, R., & Darnall, K. (2001). Enhancing critical reading and writing through peer reviews: An exploration of assisted performance. *Teaching Sociology, 29*(1), 23-35.

Amores, M. (1997). A new perspective on peer-editing. *Foreign Language Annals, 30*(4), 513-522. doi:10.1111/j.1944-9720.1997.tb00858.x

Berg, E. C. (1999). The effects of trained peer response on ESL students' revision types and writing quality. *Journal of Second Language Writing, 8*(3), 215-241. doi:10.1016/S1060-3743(99)80115-5

Braine, G. (2003). From a teacher-centered to a student-centered approach: A study of peer feedback in Hong Kong writing classes. *Journal of Asian Pacific Communication, 13*(2), 269-288. doi:10.1075/japc.13.2.05bra

Byrd, D. R. (2003). Practical tips for implementing peer editing tasks in the foreign language classroom. *Foreign Language Annals, 36*(3), 434-441. doi:10.1111/j.1944-9720.2003.tb02125.x

Carson, J. G., & Nelson, G. L. (1994). Writing groups: Cultural issues. *Journal of Second Language Writing, 3*(1), 17-30. doi:10.1016/1060-3743(94)90003-5

Carson, J. G., & Nelson, G. L. (1996). Chinese students' perceptions of ESL peer response group interaction. *Journal of Second Language Writing, 5*(1), 1-19. doi:10.1016/S1060-3743(96)90012-0

Caulk, N. (1994). Comparing teacher and student responses to written work. *TESOL Quarterly, 28*(1), 181-188. doi:10.2307/3587209

Connor, U., & Asenavage, K. (1994). Peer response groups in ESL writing classes: How much impact on revision? *Journal of Second Language Writing, 3*(3), 257-276. doi:10.1016/1060-3743(94)90019-1

Coomber, M., & Silver, R. (2010). The effect of anonymity in peer review. In A. M. Stoke (Ed.), *JALT2009 Conference Proceedings* (pp. 621-631). Tokyo: JALT.

Dewey, J. (2009). *Democracy and education.* New York: Wilder Publications. (Original work published 1916)

Diab, N. M. (2011). Assessing the relationship between different types of student feedback and the quality of revised writing. *Assessing Writing, 16,* 274-292. doi:10.1016/j.asw.2011.08.001

DiPardo, A., & Freedman, S. W. (1988). Peer response groups in the writing classroom: Theoretical foundations and new directions. *Review of Educational Research, 58*(2), 119-149. doi:10.3102/00346543058002119

Dobao, A. F. (2012). Collaborative writing tasks in the L2 classroom: Comparing group, pair, and individual work. *Journal of Second Language Writing, 21*(1), 40-58. doi:10.1016/j.jslw.2011.12.002

Ferris, D., & Roberts, B. (2001). Error feedback in L2 writing classes. How explicit does it need to be? *Journal of Second Language Writing, 10*(3), 161-184. doi:10.1016/S1060-3743(01)00039-X

Gascoigne, C. (2004). Examining the effect of feedback in beginning L2 composition. *Foreign Language Annals, 37*(1), 71-76. doi:10.1111/j.1944-9720.2004.tb02174.x

Gielen, S., Peeters, E., Dochy, F., Onghena, P., & Struyven, K. (2010). Improving the effectiveness of peer feedback for learning. *Learning and Instruction, 20*(4), 304-315. doi:10.1016/j.learninstruc.2009.08.007

Gilfert, S., & Croker, R. (1997). Dialog performances: Developing effective communication strategies for non-English majors in Japanese universities. *The Aichi Gakuin Research Journal, General Education Faculty, 45*(2), 33-49.

Halliday, M. A. K. (1975). *Learning how to mean*. London: Arnold.

Halliday, M. A. K. (1978). *Language as social semiotic*. London: Arnold.

Halliday, M. A. K., & Matthiessen, C. M. I. M. (2004). *An introduction to functional grammar* (3rd ed.). London: Arnold.

Hedgcock, J., & Lefkowitz, N. (1992). Collaborative oral/aural revision in foreign language writing instruction. *Journal of Second Language Writing, 1*(3), 255-276. doi:10.1016/1060-3743(92)90006-B

Hirose, K. (2003). Comparing L1 and L2 organizational patterns in the argumentative writing of Japanese EFL students. *Journal of Second Language Writing, 12*(2), 181-209. doi:10.1016/S1060-3743(03)00015-8

Hoogeveen, M., & van Gelderen, A. (2013). What works in writing with peer response? A review of intervention studies with children and adolescents. *Educational Psychology Review, 25*(4), 473-502. doi:10.1007/s10648-013-9229-z

Hovardas, T., Tsivitanidou, O. E., & Zacharia, Z. C. (2014). Peer versus expert feedback: An investigation of the quality of peer feedback among secondary school students. *Computers & Education, 71*, 133-152. doi:http://dx.doi.org/10.1016/j.compedu.2013.09.019

Hyland, K. (2003). *Second language writing*. Cambridge: Cambridge University Press.

Jacobs, G. M., Curtis, A., Braine, G., & Huang, S.-Y. (1998). Feedback on student writing: Taking the middle path. *Journal of Second Language Writing, 7*(3), 307-317. doi:10.1016/S1060-3743(98)90019-4

Jacobs, H., Zinkgraf, S., Wormuth, D., Hartfiel, V., & Hughey, J. (1981). *Testing ESL composition: A practical approach*. Rowley, MA: Newbury House.

Kaneko, T. (2011). Japanese college students' perceptions of peer editing activities. In A. Stewart (Ed.), *JALT2010 Conference Proceedings* (pp. 378-386). Tokyo: JALT.

Kitao, K., & Kitao, S. K. (1995). *English teaching: Theory, research, practice*. Tokyo: Eichosha.

Leki, I., & Carson, J. G. (1994). Students' perceptions of EAP writing instruction and writing needs across the disciplines. *TESOL Quarterly, 28*, 81-101. doi:10.2307/3587199

Lewis, M., & Wray, D. (1995). *Writing frames: Scaffolding children's non-fiction writing in a range of genres*. Exeter, UK: EXEL. doi:10.1111/j.1467-9345.1996.tb00161.x.

LoCastro, V. (2000). Evidence of accommodation to L2 pragmatic norms in peer review tasks of Japanese learners of English. *JALT Journal, 22*(2), 245-270.

Lundstrom, K., & Baker, W. (2009). To give is better than to receive: The benefits of peer review to the reviewer's own writing. *Journal of Second Language Writing, 18*(1), 30-43. doi:10.1016/j.jslw.2008.06.002

Martin, J., Christie, F., & Rothery, J. (1987). Social processes in education: A reply to Sawyer and Watson (and others). In I. Reid (Ed.), *The place of genre in learning: Current debates (Typereader Publication 1)* (pp. 58-82). Geelong, Victoria: Deaking University Press.

Mendonca, C. O., & Johnson, K. E. (1994). Peer review negotiations: Revision activities in ESL writing instruction. *TESOL Quarterly, 28*(4), 745-769. doi:10.2307/3587558

Mittan, R. (1989). The peer review process: Harnessing students' communicative power. In D. M. Johnson & D. H. Roen (Eds.), *Richness in writing: Empowering ESL students* (pp. 207-219). White Plains, NY: Longman.

Moffett, J. (1968). *Teaching the universe of discourse*. Boston: Houghton Mifflin.

Narciss, S. (2008). Feedback strategies for interactive learning tasks. In J. M. Spector, M. D. Merrill, J. V. Merrienboer, & M. P. Driscoll (Eds.), *Handbook of research on educational communications and technology* (3rd ed., pp. 125-143). New York: Erlbaum.

Nelson, G. L., & Carson, J. G. (1998). ESL students' perceptions of effectiveness in peer response groups. *Journal of Second Language Writing, 7*(2), 113-131. doi:10.1016/S1060-3743(98)90010-8

Nelson, G. L., & Murphy, J. M. (1992). An L2 writing group: Task and social dimensions. *Journal of Second Language Writing, 1*(3), 171-193. doi:10.1016/1060-3743(92)90002-7

Nelson, G. L., & Murphy, J. M. (1993). Peer response groups: Do L2 writers use peer comments in revising their drafts? *TESOL Quarterly, 27*(1), 135-141. doi:10.2307/3586965

Paulus, T. M. (1999). The effect of peer and teacher feedback on student writing. *Journal of Second Language Writing, 8*(3), 265-289. doi:10.1016/S1060-3743(99)80117-9

Rahimi, M. (2013). Is training student reviewers worth its while? A study on how training influences the quality of students' feedback and writing. *Language Teaching Research, 17*(1), 67-89. doi:10.1177/1362168812459151

Rinnert, C., & Kobayashi, H. (2001). Differing perceptions of EFL writing among readers in Japan. *The Modern Language Journal, 85*(2), 189-209. doi:10.1111/0026-7902.00104

Rollinson, P. (2005). Using peer feedback in the ESL writing class. *ELT Journal, 59*, 23-30. doi:10.1093/elt/cci003

Rouhi, A., & Azizian, E. (2013). Peer review: Is giving corrective feedback better than receiving it in L2 writing? *Procedia: Social and Behavioral Sciences, 93*, 1349-1354. doi:10.1016/j.sbspro.2013.10.0

Shehadeh, A. (2011). Effects and student perceptions of collaborative writing in L2. *Journal of Second Language Writing, 20*(4), 286-305. doi:10.1016/j.jslw.2011.05.010

Taferner, R. H. (2008). Toward effective EFL writing revision: Peer review. *OnCUE Journal, 2*(2), 76-91.

Taferner, R. H. (2009). Attitudes toward peer collaboration within the EFL writing context in Japan. In A. M. Stoke (Ed.), *JALT2008 Conference Proceedings* (pp. 1117-1125). Tokyo: JALT.

Topping, K. J., Smith, E. F., Swanson, I., & Elliot, A. (2000). Formative peer assessment of academic writing between postgraduate students. *Assessment & Evaluation in Higher Education, 25*(2), 149-169. doi:10.1080/713611428

Triandis, H. C., Bontempo, R., Villareal, M. J., Asai, M., & Lucca, N. (1988). Individualism and collectivism: Cross-cultural perspectives on self-ingroup relationships. *Journal of Personality and Social Psychology, 54*(2), 323-338. doi:10.1037/0022-3514.54.2.323

Tsui, A. B. M., & Ng, M. (2000). Do secondary L2 writers benefit from peer comments? *Journal of Second Language Writing, 9*(2), 147-170. doi:10.1016/S1060-3743(00)00022-9

van Lier, L. (2007). Action-based teaching, autonomy and identity. *Innovation in Language Learning and Teaching, 1*(1), 46-65. doi:10.2167/illt42.0

Villamil, O. S., & de Guerrero, M. C. M. (1996). Peer revision in the L2 classroom: Social-cognitive activities, mediating strategies, and aspects of social behavior. *Journal of Second Language Writing, 5*(1), 51-75. doi:10.1016/S1060-3743(96)90015-6

Vygotsky, L. S. (1978). *Mind in society: The development of higher psychological processes.* M. Cole, V. John-Steiner, S. Scribner, and E. Souberman (Eds.). Cambridge, MA: Harvard University Press.

Vygotsky, L.S. (1986). Thought and language (A. Kozulin, Trans.). Cambridge, MA: MIT Press. (Original work published 1934)

Witbeck, M. C. (1976). Peer correction procedures for intermediate and advanced ESL composition lessons. *TESOL Quarterly, 10*(3), 321-326.

Yang, M., Badger, R., & Yu, Z. (2006). A comparative study of peer and teacher feedback in a Chinese EFL writing class. *Journal of Second Language Writing, 15*(3), 179-200. doi:10.1016/j.jslw.2006.09.004

Zamel, V. (1982). Writing: The process of discovering meaning. *TESOL Quarterly, 16*(2), 195-209. doi:10.2307/3586792

Zhang, S. (1995). Reexamining the affective advantage of peer feedback in the ESL writing class. *Journal of Second Language Writing, 4*(3), 209-222. doi:10.1016/1060-3743(95)90010-1

Zhang, S. (1999). Thoughts on some recent evidence concerning the affective advantage of peer feedback. *Journal of Second Language Writing, 8*(3), 321-326. doi:10.1016/S1060-3743(99)80119-2

CHAPTER 2

A CRITICAL EXAMINATION OF FOREIGN-LANGUAGE INDIVIDUALITY:
Choices, Conflicts, and Dilemmas

Gerrard Mugford
Universidad de Guadalajara, Mexico

Introduction

When entering the foreign-language (FL) classroom, adult learners will have their own perceptions regarding interpersonal language use, which will often mirror first-language (L1) practices, emerge from actual FL experiences and reflect their perception and understanding of the target-language (TL). However, students often find out that target-language social practices may limit their potential to come across in their own way, and since "learners' sense of identity is intertwined with how they use the language ... they sometimes choose not to behave in a native-like fashion" (Ishihara & Cohen, 2010a, p. 76). Language learners are frequently expected to adopt a docile and conforming role in the classroom, whilst at the same time forgoing their own L1 language beliefs, practices and experiences. Choice should be seen as a key dimension in target-language interpersonal interaction where FL users have choices in that they can follow prescribed target-language conventions offered by teachers and/or course textbooks, adhere to existing first-language structures (for example by using *tú/vosotros* (T/V) forms of address), or attempt to be creative and individualistic by employing existing and new resources in novel ways. In order to facilitate interpersonal language use, interactants need to attend to the other participants' *face* (Goffman, 1967), and consequently there is a need for "acting politely where politeness is a way of doing, not a doing in itself: a means of maintaining rapport while getting on with the real business at hand" (Aston, 1988, p. 61). To examine how FL students can be polite in their own ways, I first of all review a growing body of work on politeness in the foreign-language classroom (e.g., Ishihara & Cohen, 2010b; LoCastro, 2012; O'Keeffe, Clancy & Adolphs, 2011). Subsequently, I present the results of a series of written interviews with 84 undergraduate students at a public university in Guadalajara, Mexico, aimed at identifying student-teacher greeting practices, the intentions behind such practices, and the use of L1 Mexican politeness strategies in the TL. The results of this research indicate that students often employ existing Mexican concepts of solidarity and respectfulness in the TL, but frequently lack the necessary pragmatic resources to come across appropriately. This chapter explores the teaching implications behind linguistic politeness that may also be relevant to other FL contexts and other aspects of interpersonal language use.

Literature Review

In this section, I review how classic, discursive and relational approaches to (im)politeness (Culpeper, 2011) can provide an understanding of the practices that English as a Foreign Language (EFL) students bring from their L1. I then focus on Mexican Spanish politeness patterns (Curcó, 2007, 2011; Félix-Brasdefer, 2009), and particularly on the use of T/V forms of address to express *politic behaviour* and *confianza* (expression of familiarity) and *respeto* (valuing the other's personal integrity) to reflect *polite behaviour*. Finally, I examine the pragmatic resources, in terms of the pragmalinguistic and sociopragmatic knowledge, which students bring to the classroom and, following Rose and Kasper (2001) and Ishihara and Cohen (2010b), the pragmatic competence that may have to be taught by the foreign-language teacher.

Politeness Theory and EFL

In discussing politeness in the EFL context, I will not undertake a comprehensive review of definitions and models of (im)politeness since this has been ably carried out by Eelen (2001), Culpeper (2011) and Watts (2003), among others. Adopting an emic view, I study how students engage in EFL politeness practices in terms of *politeness1* and *politeness2* (Eelen, 2001). Politeness1 reflects how the layperson understands polite behaviour and "refers to the way politeness actually manifests itself in communicative behaviour, that is, politeness as an aspect of communicative interaction" (p. 32). It also refers to the layperson's concept of politeness in that "it is concerned with the way people *talk about* and provide accounts of politeness" (p. 32). Politeness2 reflects an analytical approach and focuses on "the scientific conceptualization of the social phenomenon of politeness in the form of a theory of politeness1" (p. 43). From an ELT point of view it is important to understand politeness1 (what FL users are trying to achieve) and whether politeness2 can help understand how politeness1 works.

Classic approaches to (im)politeness (e.g., Brown & Levinson, 1987; Lakoff, 1973; Leech, 1978) are relevant to the EFL context because they deal with the universality of politeness phenomena and the interrelationship of politeness practices across languages. Brown and Levinson (1987) argue that interactants support each other's face wants through the use of positive (solidarity) and negative (respect for territory) politeness strategies and through largely trying to tone down Face Threatening Acts (FTAs). Their distinction between positive and negative politeness strategies can be seen in the Mexican positive politeness terms of *confianza* and *respeto* (Curcó, 2007; Félix-Brasdefer, 2008). Meanwhile, Lakoff's politeness rules—*Don't Impose, Give Options*, and *Make A(dresee) feel good, be friendly* (1973, p. 298)—also highlight contrasts between languages, as Mexicans may prioritise Make A(ddresee) feel good, be friendly (i.e., show closeness), whilst British speakers may be characterised through Don't Impose (i.e., show distance). Brown and Levinson and Lakoff offer identifiable politeness strategies for FL users that allow them to compare practices between their L1 and the TL. Furthermore, classic approaches help those language users who want to be polite in conventionally acceptable ways since they provide identifiable patterns and norms regarding polite behaviour. Therefore they offer an option for the FL user who just wants to come across as conforming to target-language norms.

Whilst Brown and Levinson and Lakoff largely see (im)politeness in terms of avoiding conflict, Leech takes a proactive view and identifies the politeness principle in interpersonal language use whose aim is "to maintain the social equilibrium and the friendly relations which enable us to assume that our interlocutors are being cooperative in the first place" (1983, p. 82). Whilst Leech has been criticised for potentially opening the door to a myriad of interpersonal dicta, his politeness maxims of tact, generosity and approving of others offer practical courses of action for FL users.

Although classic approaches view (im)politeness in terms of conventions, norms and maxims, discursive models focus more on the interactants themselves and their communicative contexts. Distancing themselves from universalistic approaches, discursive models tackle the problems of negotiation and conflict. This is an attractive model for the FL users who struggle to come across in the TL as individuals, perhaps trying to reconcile first-language and target-language practices, and wanting to be polite in their own way. A particularly relevant discursive model is Watts's politic behaviour and polite behaviour. Politic "is that behaviour, linguistic and non-linguistic, which the participants construct as being appropriate to the ongoing social interaction" (Watts, 2003, p. 20). Meanwhile, polite behaviour "is perceived to be beyond what is expectable, i.e. salient behaviour" (Watts, 2003, p. 19). The distinction allows FL users to decide whether to be polite in a conventional TL way or to adopt a more individualistic and personalised manner, perhaps by using strategies adopted from his/her first language. Therefore first-language knowledge allows FL users to explore Watts' polite behaviour and develop their own way of interacting.

As I have discussed in this section, classic and discursive models offer choices in the target language. Classic models provide FL learners with a structure for use whilst discursive approaches allow the language user to express his/her individuality. Nevertheless, politeness theory needs to be situated in a specific context and related to aims and motivations of the participants, in this instance, the EFL classroom.

Politeness in the EFL Classroom
Examining the nature of politeness in foreign language education is fraught with difficulty as pointed out by LoCastro (1997), since theorists disagree on a common definition. Politeness in the EFL classroom has been studied in terms of formulaic behaviour and motivation (e.g., LoCastro, 2012), positive and negative politeness strategies (e.g., O'Keeffe, Clancy & Adolphs, 2011) and speech acts (e.g., Ishihara & Cohen, 2010b). In studying how FL students can be polite by adopting their own strategies in a foreign language, I consider them to be authentic language users in their own right who have their own histories, attitudes and values regarding politeness, which Bourdieu (1972) describes in terms of *habitus*.

Watts' (2003) terms of politic behaviour and polite behaviour are especially useful in identifying Mexican FL users' politeness practices. Politic behaviour can be seen through conventional greetings, predictable leave-taking routines and standard classroom interactional practices between teachers and students may reflect politic behaviour. Polite behaviour is often expressed through the creative and individualistic use of Mexican interpersonal practices such as *confianza, afiliación* (group identity) and *respeto* as FL users may try to use such practices in the target language (Curcó, 2007; Félix-Brasdefer, 2008). As language users engage in politic and polite practices in the TL language context, a potential problem arises if L1 understandings and practices are at variance with TL norms, and teacher intervention may be required.

Starting with the assumption that FL interactants want "to be perceived as being polite in the target-language", LoCastro (2012, p. 154) outlines a two-step approach for promoting politeness in the ELT classroom. At the beginners' stage, learners can be encouraged to develop a range of formulaic expressions, and at intermediate/advanced levels, students can be given the opportunity to identify instances of Watts's politic and polite behaviour. The two-step approach activities reflect production and recognition tasks and help learners develop pragmalinguistic and sociopragmatic knowledge (Leech, 1983; Thomas, 1983). Pragmalinguistic knowledge gives learners a range of communicative options (e.g., forms of address), whilst sociopragmatic knowledge helps students achieve the right level of communicative appropriateness (e.g., solidarity/distance or formality/informality). Kasper and Rose (2001) differentiate between the two terms in the following way: "pragmalinguistics is, in a sense, akin to grammar in that it consists of linguistic forms and their respective functions, sociopragmatics is very much about proper social behaviour" (p. 3).

Meanwhile O'Keeffe, Clancy and Adolphs (2011) examine the development of politeness behaviour through activities that promote pragmatic competence (i.e., the ability to get things done in socio-culturally appropriate ways). Whilst maintaining that positive and negative politeness cannot be taught overtly in theoretical terms, O'Keeffe et al. argue that classroom instruction should consistently focus on: 1) Showing people that we respect and value them (positive politeness); and 2) Making what you say or write less direct so as not to sound too forceful (negative politeness). In practical terms, O'Keeffe et al. offer a list of positive politeness formulae that include greetings such as *Hi* and *Hello* and by doing so, encourage learners to focus on social relationships when engaging in politeness practices.

Teaching politeness in terms of speech acts has an extensive literature in ELT (see Ishihara & Cohen, 2010b; Kasper & Blum-Kulka, 1993; Kasper & Rose, 2001). Whilst not referring directly to politeness *per se*, Ishihara and Cohen (2010b) focus on speech acts because they allow easy comparisons between the L1 and the FL. With respect to greetings, for instance, Cohen argues:

> For learners, the presumably easy task of performing greetings and leave-takings may be difficult. In fact, learners may simply translate what they would say in their native language in such a situation. It is easier than trying to determine how best to say it in a way that conforms with patterns for the target language and culture, given the respective ages, social status, and roles of the speaker and listener in that situation. (Cohen, 2010, p. 7)

Even though Cohen argues that interactional choices should be made based on contextual choices, I argue that the results of the present study indicate that FL learners may not have sufficient pragmatic knowledge regarding the available resources in the TL Therefore the use and teaching of politeness in the ELT classroom needs to focus on developing students' awareness of what they are producing and examine its appropriateness in the target-language context.

Mexican Politeness

In this section, I will not conduct an overview of Mexican politeness practices, since such efforts have already been exhaustively carried out by Curcó (2007) and Félix-Brasdefer (2009, 2012). However, in order to prepare the ground for an examination of Mexican EFL politeness practices (including the learners' use of L1 resources in the target language), I start by examining the linguistic resources available in the learners' L1.

With regards to Mexican FL users, the Spanish language employs negative politeness strategies such as T/V address forms to express formality and informality. Brown and Gilman (1960) describe the difference in forms of address as between "the T of intimacy and the V of formality" (p. 257). Meanwhile, positive politeness strategies use *confianza* and *afiliación* to convey interpersonal solidarity and closeness. Consequently, I argue that Mexican EFL students show both individual considerations when speaking in English through their attempts to find the equivalents of *tú* and *usted* in the TL and positive politeness as they attempt to express *confianza* and *afiliación*.

Since I am interested in the use of *tú* or *usted* as local practice among university students in Guadalajara, Mexico, I examine how they attempt to use T/V pronouns from their point of view rather than through conducting a broader examination of Mexican-Spanish politeness2. The use of *tú* and *usted* reflect Watts's politic behaviour as interactants focus on the individual. Another important aspect of forms of address is that they are often carried out in Mexican Spanish through the use of appellations such as *doctor, ingeniero* (engineer) and *maestro* (teacher). This observation is important for the EFL classroom where the utilisation of appellations is very common in Mexican Spanish as a way of showing respect, especially towards teachers as students will often address their teachers as *teacher* or *professor* rather than using an honorific title such as Mr., Mrs., or Ms. accompanied by a last name. Parallels can be drawn between the use of Mexican T/V forms of address and Brown and Levinson's negative politeness strategies since they aim to recognise and show deference to an addressee's status.

Mexican positive politeness strategies often reflect what Curcó (2007) has described as "the extreme preoccupation with safeguarding the positive face of an interlocutor which, in my view, pervades Mexican verbal interaction" (p. 105). Mexican interlocutors use a range of pragmatic resources to make an addressee welcome and to feel part of the group. These resources include showing *confianza*, seeking *familiaridad* (interpersonal closeness), expressing *afiliación* (group identity) and demonstrating *respeto*. *Confianza* can develop very quickly in emerging positive politeness relationships and places a new acquaintance in the position of feeling like a confidante. *Familiaridad* reflects both physical and emotional closeness as interactants share life experiences and views of the world. *Afiliación* reinforces the importance of group *face*, as argued by Félix-Brasdefer who characterises Mexicans as "collectivistic and more related to membership in a group such as a family, friends, or a work group" (2008, p. 4). Finally, *respeto* is the active attention and consideration given to a participant because of his/her hierarchical, personal or professional standing. Mexican positive politeness strategies reflect Watts's polite behaviour because they attempt to successfully reinforce interpersonal relationships and go well beyond what is required, or even expected, with politic behaviour.

In conclusion, Mexican politeness practices reflect Watts's politic behaviour and polite behaviour and Brown and Levinson's positive and negative politeness strategies. They offer contrasting ways of expressing politeness in Mexican Spanish which Mexican EFL users may consider to be lacking in the target language.

Methodology

The theoretical framework of this study is based on the work of Béal (1994) and Scollon and Scollon (1990), particularly since the focus is to understand the choices, conflicts and dilemmas involved in trying to be polite in one's own way in a foreign language. First of all, Béal begins with Brown and Levinson's (1987) observation that "even minor differences in interpretive strategies carried over from a first to a second language ... can lead to misunderstanding and cross-group stereotyping of interactional style" (p. 37). Therefore, Beale examined how FL students can be polite in their own ways in their first language. This was achieved through a qualitative study, where students were asked in a written questionnaire about how they addressed teachers in Spanish. *Béal* emphasised the importance of taking the participants' first-language knowledge and experiences into consideration. Rather than looking for politeness universals, she argued for a "systematic comparison of the performance of L2 speakers in English with their performances in their own language" (p. 36) in terms of looking for insights, understanding diverging linguistic behaviour and cultural values and identifying problems in cross-cultural communication. It is based on these ideas that the present study sets out to uncover how foreign-language users negotiate and project themselves in target-language situations.

Research Questions

In order to understand how Mexican EFL students interact politely in their own ways in the TL, I began with the students themselves and examined what they brought to the target-language context. Therefore, I asked the following overarching research question: *What first-language resources and knowledge do Mexican EFL students employ in order to be polite in the target language?*

To answer this overarching research question, I wanted to explore, following Béal (1994), the politeness patterns and practices that the students brought into the classroom. My first specific research question asked: *How do students greet teachers in the English-language classroom?* I asked the 84 students to reflect on how they greet teachers in the classroom. I wanted to know whether the students engage in different politeness practices when addressing a teacher in English taking into consideration whether they were Mexican or non-Mexican nationals. Given that gender, age and professional status are important considerations in Spanish when addressing another participant, I designed four contexts where the students were expected to address teachers characterized as belonging to the same age group (30-50), with the same qualification (all have MA degrees), but of different genders previous sections not discussed nationhood and as the type of language these bilingual individual use.ond group, or viceversa usgenders and nationalities (Mexican or American). For all scenarios the student is informed that he or she has been studying in the teacher's class for one month and that they have a good relationship. The language of the questionnaire was English and can be viewed in Appendix 1.

Subsequently, I wanted to know the intentions behind the use of particular forms of address in the TL and how students aimed to present themselves (Scollon & Scollon, 1990). Therefore, my second specific research question asked: *Do students use tú or usted forms (or search for English-language substitutes) with their teachers in English?* First of all, I asked the respondents how they addressed Mexican teachers in Spanish and in English. I then asked the students how they addressed their non-Mexican teachers in Spanish and English, because I wanted to find out whether the nationality of the addressee was a factor when using forms of address. The discourse completion tasks were applied in English and can be viewed in Appendix 2.2.

The third specific research question asked: *Do students use Mexican politeness practices when interacting with teachers in the target language?* The respondents were asked whether they attempt to express *confianza, familiaridad, afiliación, respeto* in English. The questions were applied in English and can be viewed in Appendix 2.3.

Participants

All 84 participants in the research were middle-class Mexican undergraduates studying for a BA degree in English language teaching and were aged between 18 and 24. They were students at a public university in a large city in Mexico. The students were asked to participate voluntarily in the study and were offered total anonymity and confidentiality regarding their answers.

Data Collection

The data was collected quantitatively through the use of three questionnaires: Classroom greeting practices, Mexican EFL politic behaviour and Mexican EFL polite behaviour. Questionnaire 1 (Classroom greeting practice), aimed at identifying students' English-language greeting practices towards Mexican and English native-speaking teachers, and to establish whether nationality plays a role in determining greeting practices. In questionnaire 2 (Mexican EFL politic behaviour*)*, interactants were asked whether they used equivalents of *tú* and *usted* when interacting in English, with the intent of determining whether the participants engaged in Mexican EFL politic behaviour (Watts, 2003) when engaging in the target language. The focus of questionnaire 3 (Mexican EFL polite behaviour) was on whether the participants went beyond the expected norms of behaviour, (Watts' polite behaviour) and attempted to be polite in Mexican ways with their teachers when interacting in English.

The data was collected by eight student interviewers from the same programme. They were in a closer relationship with their classmates than I was as a researcher and therefore it was easier for them to explain the purpose of the study. They further shared the same socio-economic profile as their classmates. I explained the purpose of the study to the interviewers, who in turn explained the objectives to their classmates (i.e., to examine interactional practices with their teachers).

Following Watts' (2003) distinction between politic and polite behaviour (as discussed in the Literature Review), I carried out the data analysis in three stages. First of all, I identified students' greeting practices to determine whether they adhered to Watts' politic behaviour (i.e., that they reflected standard norms of address teachers). I then analysed whether interactants used Mexican *tú* and *usted* politic behaviour in English. Finally, I analysed whether interactants employed Mexican politeness practices such as *confianza, familiaridad, afiliación* and *respeto* in English. These results helped me to determine whether the interactants came across in their own way in the target language.

Presentation of Results

In an initial study, students were asked how they greeted teachers in Spanish. The results were as follows: *usted* (84 replies); *tú* (3 replies); and depends (5 replies). The participants who chose 'depends' argued that the form of address depends on the relationship (3 replies) or age (1 reply). One participant gave no reason. The overwhelming majority of greetings were therefore formal (e.g., *¡Buenos días, profesor!*, *¡Buenos días maestro! ¿Cómo está usted?* and *¡Buen día maestra! ¿Cómo se encuentra?*) When asked why they greeted teachers formally, participants offered explanations such as:

- I use usted because I consider it disrespectful to use tú to an adult.
- My way of greeting is influenced by the value of respect.
- It shows or proves that I have respect for adults.
- I use usted because it shows respect to those who are older than me
- I usually use usted because it represents respect.
- It is a sign of respect and I'm used to addressing my teacher in this way.
- Well, one has to be respectful of the teachers and by using usted one show respectfulness to the professors.
- They need respect.

Questionnaire 1 (Classroom Greeting Practices)

In order to ascertain classroom greeting patterns, questionnaire 1 asked students to write down how they greet teachers in English. The results are presented in Table 2.1.

Table 2.1
Student-teacher greeting practices in the classroom

Addressee	Mexican female teacher	Mexican male teacher	Native speaking female teacher	Native speaking male teacher
Good morning/afternoon/etc.	29 (35%)	26 (31%)	24 (29%)	28 (33%)
Hello	35 (42%)	37 (44%)	38 (45%)	40 (48%)
Hi... / Hey	17 (20%)	20 (24%)	15 (18%)	15 (18%)
Other	3 (3%)	1 (1%)	7 (8%)	1 (1%)

The results reveal few differences between addressing Mexican and native speaking teachers. This suggests that nationality does not play a significant role in determining forms of address. The results also indicate that teachers are usually greeted with an informal hello rather than with the more formal good morning/afternoon/evening. Saying hello reflects a positive politeness strategy (O'Keeffe, Clancy & Adolphs, 2011), as opposed to the more formal good morning/afternoon/evening. I am not making any judgements regarding appropriateness in the FL class since this will depend on each classroom as a local context (Pennycook, 2010). What will be significant is whether these results correlate with how students are trying to come across, which is the objective of questionnaire 2.

Questionnaire 2 (Forms of Address: Motivation)
Results from questionnaire 2 (summarized in Table 2.2) show whether respondents wanted to come across formally by using *usted* or informally by employing *tú*. Answers to the first question regarding whether they address Mexican teachers in Spanish, show that the overwhelming reply was *usted* (76 replies), while *tú* (3 replies) was hardly chosen at all. Some students said that it depended on the relationship/age of the teacher (4 replies) and one respondent gave no answer. These answers indicate that the base form for greeting is *usted* in the Mexican classroom and show respect in terms of negative politeness.

The second question examined how students saw themselves addressing their Mexican teachers in English in terms of T/V. The answers were not quite so straightforward. The V-form dominated (31 replies) and the T-form increased marginally from the first question (6 replies). In order to express the V-form in English, students said that they tried to show distance with the use of formal phrases such as good morning, and terms of address such as Teacher, Miss, or Doctor. Significantly, a large number of students said that they avoid using the T/V distinction (20 replies). This is achieved by employing first-person pronouns or through using impersonal structures. A number of respondents who did not give an answer increased (13 replies). Meanwhile, there were respondents who said that there was no way of expressing the T/V distinction in English (8 replies). Other respondents said that they use equivalents (5 replies) without specifying exactly what they were. One respondent said that the choice between using the T or V form depends on the situation. These results indicate that students are conscious about how they express politeness in English.

In the third question, when it came to addressing English-speaking teachers in Spanish, the V-form dominated (61 replies) compared to the T-form (8 replies). In contrast with Mexican teachers, the V-form is employed less frequently with English-speaking teachers. There were respondents who said that they avoided using either *tú* or *usted* (5 replies), others said that it depends on the situation (5 replies) and other students gave no answer (4 replies). One student said that she did not talk to her teacher in Spanish. In the final question, students were asked if they used English-language equivalents of the T/V form when addressing native English-speaking teachers in English. Revealingly, most respondents said no (39 replies). This may indicate that they do not have the necessary pragmalinguistic and sociopragmatic resources to express solidarity/distance in the target language. In terms of usage of address forms, the results revealed that respondents claimed to use the V-form (28 replies), the T-form (7 replies) and others said that they used target-language equivalents (4 replies) (e.g., informal address forms). Meanwhile, some respondents said there were no equivalents to T/V forms of address in Mexican Spanish (4 replies), whilst others said that their usage depended on the specific situation (2 replies).

Table 2.2
Student-teacher use of T/V practices in the classroom

Question	1	2	3	4
Usted	76	31	61	28
Tú	3	6	8	7
No / Not answer question	1	13	4	39
Avoid using *tú* and *usted*		20	5	
No T/V forms in English		8		4
Depends (age / status relationship)	4	1	5	2
Use English equivalent		5	4	
Does not use Spanish w/teacher			1	

Questionnaire 3 (Mexican Politeness in English)

Questionnaire 3 asked whether students tried to be polite in Mexican ways with their teachers in English. The results are summarized in Table 2.3.

Table 2.3
Mexican positive practices with EFL teachers

Mexican politeness category	Answer	Replies	%
Confianza: Expression of trust in the teacher	Yes	39	46%
	No	31	37%
	No answer	13	16%
	Don't understand the question	1	1%
Familiaridad: Close sense of friendliness with the teacher	Yes	29	35%
	No	42	50%
	No answer	12	14%
	Don't understand the question	1	1%
Afiliación: Teacher is part of your social group	Yes	18	21%
	No	50	60%
	No answer	15	18%
	Don't understand the question	1	1%
Respeto: Respect for your teacher as a person	Yes	66	79%
	No	9	11%
	No answer	8	9%
	Don't understand the question	1	1%

The answers indicate that students try to show *respeto* (79% of replies) in the classroom. This aim arguably explains the attempts to use the V-form and/or English-language equivalents. To a lesser degree, *confianza* (46% of replies) is also important—a finding which reflects the often close relations between teachers and students in Mexico. However, it is notable that a considerable number of students are against showing *afiliación* (60% of replies) and *familiaridad* (50% of replies). The results show that students often actively try to express concepts of positive politeness (*confianza* and *respeto*) with their teachers. Therefore, students frequently report making a positive effort to present themselves in their own way and by employing Mexican politeness practices. It would appear that students are following Lakoff's (1973) politeness rule: Make A feel good—be friendly and Leech's (1983) maxim of approving of others. The study was less successful in uncovering the exact structures students use as many students thought that informal forms of address alone helped achieve Mexican positive politeness goals. Interestingly only one student said that she did not understand such terms as *confianza*, *afiliación* and *respeto* terms. In conclusion, the findings from Questionnaire 3 indicate that students enter the classroom with their own experiences, attitudes and values which often come from their first language *habitus* (Bourdieu, 1972) and they want to express them in the target language.

Discussion

Classroom greeting practices need to be seen in close relationship with intentions in order to ascertain whether students are achieving their desired politeness strategy. The majority of students greet teachers using positive politeness terms such as *hello* and *hi/hey* when addressing their teachers: Mexican female teachers (62%); Mexican male teachers (68%); English native-speaking female teachers (63%); and English native-speaking male teachers (66%). The figures show more formality is shown to female teachers. Table 1 illustrates that few students want to use the informal *tú* address form with teachers in the classroom whether it be in English or Spanish. Answers indicate that students try to use *usted* form (or equivalents). Pedagogical intervention is needed to assess how students think they are interacting. Secondly, teachers need to raise the students' awareness regarding pragmalinguistic resources available so that students, if they wish, are able to express equivalents of *usted* in the target language.

The findings reveal that students attempt to express Mexican politeness when interacting in English especially with regards showing *respeto* (79% of replies) and engaging in *confianza* (46% of replies). However, the findings indicate that Mexican politeness patterns are not carried out indiscriminately in the local context, in that students were aware that teachers are not part of their social group, where only 21% of the students were in favour of demonstrating *afiliación* (with) and 35% wanting to show *familiaridad*.

Nevertheless the results do show that students actively carry out Mexican positive politeness strategies in the target language.

Conclusion

This research is beneficial and relevant to foreign-language teaching and learning because it examines how students attempted to come across in their own way in the target-language when engaging in interpersonal politeness. Far from expecting their students to unthinkingly adhere to TL norms, teachers need to provide opportunities for their students to interact with a socio-culturally identifiable personality as was the case with these Mexican EFL students who wanted to express Mexican concepts of solidarity and respectfulness in the target language.

The major contribution of this study is that teachers and researchers need to understand linguistic politeness, especially Watts' (2003) politic and polite behaviour, from the point of view of both students' L1 use as well as that of the target-language utilisation. I have shown the importance of taking the participants' first language knowledge and experiences (Béal, 1994) as a starting point for understanding FL users' politeness practices, especially since students try to use Mexican politeness practices to make conscious decisions about how they want to come across in English. However, it appears that students do not have the necessary resources to convey the *tú/ usted* distinction of solidarity/distance in the target language when greeting and coming across in the way that they want to.

The use of Mexican politeness strategies indicate that students are not particularly interested in being polite in conventional TL ways. In the final analysis, the use of Mexican politeness strategies allows students to come across in much more individualistic ways rather than merely following target-language conventions and norms.

References

Aston, G. (1988). *Learning comity: An approach to the description and pedagogy of interaction speech*. Bologna, Italy: Cooperativa Libraria Universitaria Editrice Bologna.

Béal, C. (1994). Keeping the peace: A cross-cultural comparison of questions and requests in Australian English and French. *Multilingua, 13*(1/2), 35-58.

Bourdieu, P. (1972). *Outline of a theory of practice*. Cambridge: Cambridge University Press.

Brown, R., & Gilman, A. (1960). Pronouns of power and solidarity. In T. A. Sebeok (Ed.), *Style in language* (pp. 253-276). Boston: MIT Press.

Brown, P., & Levinson, S. (1987). *Politeness: Some universals in language usage.* Cambridge: Cambridge University Press.
Cohen, A. (2010). Coming to terms with pragmatics. In N. Ishihara & A. Cohen (Eds.). *Teaching and learning pragmatics* (pp. 3-20). Harlow, UK: Longman.
Culpeper, J. (2011). Politeness and impoliteness. In G. Andersen & K. Aijmer (Eds.), *Pragmatics of society* (pp. 393-438). Berlin: De Gruyter Mouton.
Curcó, C. (2007). Positive face, group face, and affiliation: An overview of politeness studies on Mexican Spanish. In M. E. Placencia & C. García (Eds.). *Research on politeness in the Spanish-speaking world* (pp. 105-120). London: Laurence Earlbaum.
Curcó, C. (2011). *El papel de la imagen positiva en la expresión de la cortesía en México* [Paper on the positive image of the expression of politeness in Mexico]. Paper presented at the Conferencia magistral, Segundo Coloquial Regional del Programa EDICE-México, Monterrey, Mexico.
Eelen, G. (2001). *A critique of politeness theories.* Manchester: St. Jerome.
Félix-Brasdefer, J. C. (2008). *Politeness in Mexico and the United States: A contrastive study of the realization and perception of refusals.* Amsterdam/Philadelphia: John Benjamins.
Félix-Brasdefer, J. C. (2009). El estado de la cuestión sobre el discurso de la (des)cortesía y la imagen social en México: Perspectivas teóricas y metodológicas [The state of affairs of politeness discourse and the social image in Mexico: Perspectives, theories and methodologies]. In L. Rodríguez Alfano (Ed.), *La (des)cortesía y la imagen social en México: Estudios semióticos-discursivos desde varios enfoques analíticos* [Politness and social image in Mexico: Semiotic-discourse studies from various analytical approaches] (pp. 15-45). Monterrey, Mexico: Universidad Autónoma de Nuevo León.
Félix-Brasdefer, J. C. (2012). Pragmatic variation in market service encounters in Mexico. In J. C. Félix-Brasdefer & D. A. Koike (Eds.), *Pragmatic variation in first and second language contexts: Methodological issues* (pp. 17-48). Amsterdam: John Benjamins.
Goffman, E. (1967). *Interactional ritual: Essays on face-to-face behaviour.* New York: Double Day Books.
Ishihara, N., & Cohen, A. (2010a). Learners' pragmatics: Potential causes of divergence. In N. Ishihara & A. Cohen (Eds.), *Teaching and learning pragmatics* (pp. 75-96) Harlow, UK: Longman.
Ishihara, N., & Cohen, A. (2010b). *Teaching and learning pragmatics.* Harlow, UK: Longman.
Kasper, G., & Blum-Kulka, S. (Eds.) (1993). *Interlanguage pragmatics.* New York: Oxford University Press.
Kasper, G., & Rose, K. (2001). Pragmatics in language teaching. In K. Rose & G. Kasper, *Pragmatics in language teaching* (pp. 1- 9). Cambridge: Cambridge University Press.
Lakoff, R. (1973). The logic of politeness: Or minding your p's and q's. *Papers from the Ninth Regional Meeting of the Chicago Linguistic Society, 9,* 292-305.
Leech, G. (1983). *Principles of pragmatics.* London: Longman.
LoCastro, V. (1997). Politeness and pragmatic competence in foreign language education *Language Teaching Research, 1,* 239-267.
LoCastro, V. (2012). *Pragmatics for language educators: A sociolinguistic perspective.* Routledge: New York.
O'Keeffe, A., Clancy, B., & Adolphs, S. (2011). *Introducing pragmatics in use.* Oxford: Routledge.
Pennycook, A. (2010). *Language as local practice.* London: Routledge.
Rose, K., and Kasper, G. (2001). *Pragmatics in language teaching.* Cambridge: Cambridge University Press.

Scollon, R., & Scollon, S. (1990). Athabaskan-English interethnic communication. In D. Carbaugh (Ed.), *Cultural communication and interactional contact* (pp. 261-290). Hilldsdale, N.J.: Erlbaum.

Thomas, J. (1983). Cross-cultural pragmatic failure. *Applied Linguistics, 4*(2), 91-112.

Watts, R. (2003). *Politeness.* Cambridge: Cambridge University Press.

Appendix 2.1
Questionnaire 2 (Classroom greeting practices)

1. How would you greet the following Mexican teacher in English on entering the classroom? The class is in English. Her name is Edith Avalos. She is between 30 and 50 years old and has an MA. You have been studying in her class for one month and feel you have a good relationship. What would you say?
2. How would you greet the following Mexican teacher in English on entering the classroom? The class is in English. His name is Pedro Garcia. He is between 30 and 50 years old and has an MA. You have been studying in his class for one month and feel you have a good relationship. What would you say?
3. How would you greet the following American teacher in English on entering the classroom? The class is in English. Her name is Sarah Carter. She is between 30 and 50 years old and has an MA. You have been studying in her class for one month and feel you have a good relationship. What would you say?
4. How would you greet the following American teacher in English on entering the classroom? The class is in English. His name is Paul Wright. He is between 30 and 50 years old and has an MA. You have been studying in his class for one month and feel you have a good relationship. What would you say?

Appendix 2.2
Mexican EFL politic behaviour

1. When you address your Mexican teachers in Spanish, do you use *tú* or *usted*? What influences your decision to use one term or the other?
2. When you address your Mexican teachers in English, do you use English-language equivalents *tú* or *usted*? If so, what terms do you use?
3. When you address your native English-speaking teachers in Spanish, do you use *tú* or *usted*? What influences your decision to use one term or the other?
4. When you address your native English-speaking teachers in English, do you use English-language equivalents *tú* or *usted*? If so, what terms do you use?

Appendix 2.3
Mexican EFL polite behaviour

Do you try to express the following ways when speaking English to your teachers? If you answer, yes, please give the exact words you use:

1. Mutual sense of trust between yourself and your teacher: *Confianza* (expression of familiarity)
2. Close sense of friendliness between yourself and the teacher: *Familiaridad* (interpersonal closeness):
3. That the teacher is part of your social group: *Afiliación* (group identity)
4. Respect for your teacher as a person: *Respeto* (respect):

CHAPTER 3

READING THE COMMUNITY CRITICALLY IN THE DIGITAL AGE: *A Multiliteracies Approach*

Rosa Alejandra Medina-Riveros
University of Massachusetts-Amherst

Luz Maribel Ramírez-Galindo
Amparo Clavijo-Olarte
Universidad Distrital Francisco Jose de Caldas

> The learning process is a process of self-mastery, self-consciousness and thus–liberation. (Gramsci, 1916/1935, p. 54)

Why read the community critically in the digital age? Why use a multiliteracies approach? Since literacy is used as a tool in society to make sense of the world (Freire & Macedo, 1987), in this chapter we share the experience of using three frameworks: critical literacy, community-based pedagogies and multiliteracies to engage online English as a Foreign Language (EFL) students in multimodal literacy practices, with the aim of increasing their awareness and leading to the transformation of themselves and their community.

Why read the *community*? From an asset-based perspective, communities offer resources for language learning and literacy (Sharkey & Clavijo, 2012). Why read the community *critically*? Drawing on Butler (2002) we understand critique as the virtue of "a critical interrogation of the present and ourselves" (p. 50). Reading the community critically means questioning reality, raising awareness, transforming self and rewriting the world. It entails drafting an understanding of the power relations that subjugate our students and communities, and using language and literacy tools to initiate very specific transformations in the intricate fabric of power (Foucault, 1984).

Why use a *mulitiliteracies* approach in the digital age? Multiliteracies pegadogy offers a conceptual platform that fits the needs of students in digital times: combined modes and genres and a critical framing (New London Group, 1997). We consider that multiliteracies and digital tools are suitable for drawing or at least drafting the first letter of a re-writing of the world starting by transforming ourselves and by micro-transforming our communities.

This chapter reveals the findings of a qualitative research study conducted in an online EFL course at a public university in Bogota, Colombia. The main idea underlying the research study is that situating English language learning in community exploration offers possibilities for learners to develop critical literacy practices, raise awareness and propose transformations of their communities. The foundations of the study are critical approaches to literacy, community-based literacies and pedagogies, and multiliteracies.

Community and Critical Literacy
This study focuses on using the community as a resource to promote critical literacy with EFL students. Their immediate learning community serves as a place to learn, raise awareness and propose changes by studying social and cultural issues critically. Inspired by Freire and Macedo's (1987) pedagogy, EFL learners and their teacher explored the community and shared stories, descriptions and images in the online classroom; then they reflected upon what they observed and designed multimodal texts to report their critical insights.

Freire and Macedo's (1987) contributions to critical literacy suggest that "there is not any use of language that is not related to reality" (p. 53). Furthermore, critical literacy is about "[how to] write and re-write reality, transforming reality through a conscious work" (p. 56). Thus, we understand critical literacy as a pre-requisite for social transformation. It embeds situated learning and interaction among individuals, words and contexts and a variety of specific literacies and skills to live in community. Furthermore, it leads to becoming aware of reality and playing an active role to bring about change.

Community literacies and pedagogies serve as a framework to enact critical literacy and language learning in the study. Though the basics of this pedagogical approach relate to Freire and Macedo (1987), Moll (1994) or

Toohey and Day (1999), this study is influenced by Sharkey (2002), Marshall and Toohey (2010) and Sharkey and Clavijo (2012) and their visions of community teaching and community-based pedagogies. Sharkey (2012) defines community-based pedagogies as:

> Curriculum and practices that reflect knowledge and appreciation of the communities in which schools are located and students and their families inhabit. It is an asset-based approach that does not ignore the realities of curriculum standards that teachers must address, but emphasizes local knowledge and resources as starting points for teaching and learning. (p. 11)

The definition above highlights the connection between contextualized knowledge of community and curricular practices for critical literacy. Nevertheless, the meaning of community is not explicitly given. Indeed, Smyth and Toohey (2009) acknowledge the complexity of community in relation to place by affirming that: "the concept of 'community' is complex and fluid" (p. 271). In the context of the study, we understand community beyond a geographical concept; it encompasses a social network formed by people who share interests and needs and who establish connections through the exchange of benefits (e.g., skills, services, and knowledge, among others) in a physical or digital space. The notion of community entails a dynamic process of identity construction and strengthening of social capital.

Multiliteracies Approach in the Digital Age
As the context of the study was an online EFL course, the critical reading of the community implied using multimodal literacies and digital literacy. The relation between technology and foreign language literacy has been evolving in the last decades. As a response to the proliferation of new multimodal texts in and out of cyberspaces, the concept of multiliteracies emerged to explain the changing rules of reading and writing according to the new type of texts that include other kinds of media such as image, voice and movement (Gee, 2009; Kress, 2003).

Due to the digital nature of the setting, an EFL online-based course, multimodal literacy practices occurred as mediated by digital literacies. With regard to the close relation between multimodal and digital literacy in the L2, Lotherington and Jenson (2011) assert that "multimodality does not necessarily utilize digital technologies, but it is clear that digital technologies intensify multimodal possibilities" (p. 227). Postings, videos, slideshows, Glogsters (i.e., digital posters) and voiced video comments were some of the multimodal and literacy practices students developed while working on the community projects. Figure 3.1 is a screenshot of a voiced thread used to make comments about a landmark in the community, a digital multimodal literacy tool that combines voice, video and text to share comments on a common image.

Figure 3.1. Voicethread about the community

Drawing on the aforementioned definitions, we implore Medina's (2013) elaboration of critical literacy as "a tool to interpret and re-create the social context through different modes such as languages, images, sounds or any other semiotic codes, and to raise awareness of power relations for individuals to become agents of change" (p. 12).

Methodological Framework
Context and Participants
The context of the study was an online-based EFL course in a public university that offers 90 undergraduate programs in different academic fields. The university has been recognized for its scientific and academic contributions

to the country. The campus hosts 38,000 students from different ethnic, cultural and socio-economic backgrounds and it is located in the heart of the capital city. The university offers a variety of academic, architectural, natural and cultural resources for students as well as for community members. The university has been the starting point for social movements within the city and the country.

The participants were students who enrolled in English level 3 in the virtual modality during the second semester of 2012 and the first semester of 2013. They were 10 male and 14 female junior and senior students in the undergraduate programs of Engineering, Medicine, Human Sciences, Agronomy, Sciences and Economics. Most of them came from a working class background and enrolled in the online EFL course due to time incompatibilities with their coursework, internships or full-time jobs.

The teacher was an alumnus of the same university that served as the research site, where she had been teaching for seven years at the time of data collection. She was in the position of teacher-researcher that enabled her to have an active membership, as she was responsible for the design of the online activities for the course. The study followed a participant observational approach as presented by Cohen, Manion and Morrison (2000). This approach allowed the main researcher to "develop a more intimate an informal relationship with those who are being observed and provide a superior grade of naturalness to the data gathering" (p. 188).

Research Design
Addressing community issues with EFL students in online contexts in order to research critical literacies from a qualitative perspective moved us to search for a research methodology that could capture the specific characteristics or behaviors from users within cultures and communities that students inhabit online. Online ethnography is one such methodology that offers research techniques to study the behaviors that online communities display. Thus, students' discussions online were recorded and analyzed in the light of Kozinets' (2010) research design, who wrote that "Online communities form or manifest cultures, the learned beliefs, values and customs that serve to order, guide and direct the behavior of a particular society or group" (p. 12). Netnography as a research approach is closer to traditional ethnographic standards of participant observation, prolonged engagement,

and deep immersion. In many of its renderings, netnography maintains the values of traditional ethnography through providing a Geertzian sense of "thick description" through the "immersion" of the researcher in the life of the online culture or community. Netnography is defined as "a qualitative research methodology that adapts ethnographic research techniques to study cultures and communities that are emerging through computer-mediated communications" (Kozinets, 2002, p. 62).

The computer-mediated communications used in this study helped us gain insights on the culture of the online community composed of the students of the virtual EFL course. We used the netnographic procedures of Kozinets (2002) to explore the following research question: How do students read the community critically in an online-based EFL course? These procedures consisted of: (1) making cultural entrée, (2) gathering and analyzing data, (3) ensuring trustworthy interpretation, (4) conducting ethical research and (5) providing opportunities for culture member feedback (p. 65).

We selected the data collection instruments responding to the netnographic research typology to evidence the literacy practices in which students engaged when sharing their critical insights in the EFL online course. The data set included transcripts of students' online interactions, visual and audiovisual online artifacts and a semi-structured questionnaire. Langer and Beckman (2005) assert that the best instruments to collect data for netnography are transcripts, which in this context are commonly defined as "a direct copy from the computer-mediated communications of online community members and observations of the community and its members, interactions and meanings" (p. 200). Postings were saved on the online platform as they are automatically archived and therefore easily accessible. Transcripts of the online discussions were stored in word processing and image file formats for content analysis.

Kozinets (2010) suggests collecting visual and audiovisual online artifacts for capturing online data. Non-textual, visual data were collected as "visual data often conveys information and emotional content and even audiovisual formats" (p. 35). As students produced visual displays, videos and audio artifact data were accessed mostly from the Internet using the university's on-line learning management system (i.e., Blackboard) or accessing other websites, such as Youtube or Voicethread. Photos and videos produced by students when sharing their insights of the community were analyzed in terms of content. Surveys are a common descriptive method in social sciences and specifically in the broader field of education. The questionnaire for this study included both open- and close-ended items. The goal of the open-ended items was to elicit information about students' perceptions and commentaries on the procedure and activities completed while addressing community issues in the EFL online course (See Appendix 3.1).

The data analysis followed grounded theory methods for qualitative data analysis as described by Corbin and Strauss (2014). The process of data analysis consisted of three phases: open coding, identification of patterns, and axial/theoretical coding. These techniques are used to construct theory inductively from the specific instances or fieldwork as proposed by this framework for analysis.

At the first stage, we read through the collected data and located frequent topics and themes. After reading the data several times, we identified codes and labeled the matching instances and statements using color coding. This helped us to shape the categories that directly addressed our research concern. The next step was making connections among the preliminary categories.. The initial codes were grouped into bigger themes and these were organized into bigger sets and smaller categories. In this phase, we considered the relationship between the preliminary categories that clustered together and the governing structure that included them. The third stage consisted of making connections with theory that reshaped the initial categories.

The section below presents and discusses the findings and shows graphic representations of the relations among categories and their thick descriptions based on data and theory.

Findings

We identified two key moments identified in the data analysis process. The first was the students' recognition of community assets as a way to become users of such resources (human, cultural, ecological, historical and linguistic) to learn. The second was their critical reading of the community to experience the university campus from a problem-solving perspective to seek solutions to problematic situations that affected them, including actions to improve their community. The university community appeared as a multimodal book that encouraged students to undergo quests, and it provided valuable critical literacy sources in the online course. The graph below displays the two main learning moments we identified: Recognizing the community assets and reading the community critically. The learning moments are displayed in Figure 3.2.

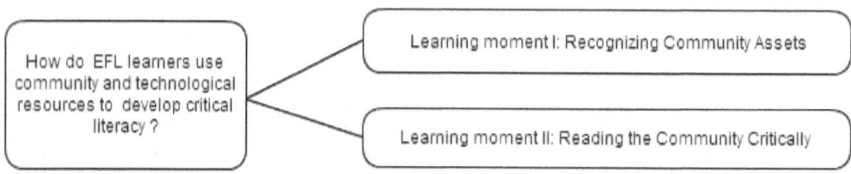

Figure 3.2. Learning Moments

First Learning Moment: Recognizing Community Assets
Recognizing community assets is the first learning moment towards critically reading the community. This was an eye-opening experience for many students who acknowledged valuable traditions, places, and people while developing their projects. This experience mirrors what Kretzmann and McKnight (1993) call community asset mapping, which is a process of documenting the tangible and intangible resources of a community by viewing the community as a place with strengths or assets that need to be preserved and enhanced, not deficits to be remedied. Recognizing valuable community sources helps learners to acquire the knowledge embedded in social, cultural and material contexts (Gee, 2000). In this particular case, community asset mapping allowed students to grasp several types of knowledge: linguistic, historical and disciplinary. Data from the students' postings and videos provided seven types of assets to the university community: human, cultural, historical, ideological, ecological, communitarian and linguistic. Below we provide examples of the most relevant assets for the development of a critical reading of the community.

Human assets. The first assets students recognized when working on the community projects had to do with the community inhabitants. Students' postings to the forum, videos and other online artifacts suggest the paramount importance of acknowledging people as valuable learning sources. The way and reasons why learners portrayed certain community inhabitants suggests issues of subjectivity, as well as social and academic capital. These issues are documented in the following excerpts from the online data and the students' survey.

Learners interviewed other community members. Many students interviewed university professors they admired while others selected university workers or classmates. The main features that prevailed in these characters were academic qualities and personal values. The following excerpts exemplify these characteristics. Some people were selected for their personal qualities, as shown in Figure 3.3, in which the students made a video on the life of a university employee who works for the animal medicine school.

Figure 3.3. Human Assets

The surveys also confirmed how students recognized human assets in the community as valuable. For example, Maira noted,

> This project allowed us to find out about the life-story that forms part of the university. We found out about the teachers that give us their best to improve the university, as well as the administrative staff whose smiles make us feel at home in the same way as the smiles of our fellow students.

The examples show that recognizing the community's human assets provided appreciation of the community's inhabitants, or what Kretzman and McKnight (1993) refer to as "building trust and 'social capital' through connections and linkages" (p. 7).

Cultural assets. Cultural assets were the second resource students identified when working on their community projects. Bourdieu (1986) asserts that cultural capital exists in material and non-material states. Students' online artifacts about cultural places and traditions in the community portray the cultural assets of the university community.

Another example (see Figure 3.4) is offered in Clara and Rafa's clip in which they portray a cultural tradition in the community, the university carnival. In their video, they tell their classmates about the history, organization and main components of this tradition (video available at: http://goo.gl/swKBes).

The university carnival is an event that is performed every year for the purpose of promoting an atmosphere of warmth and joy between different people within the university community. It is the right space to foster a spirit of integration for the benefit of community members. In the carnival, it is possible to see art exhibitions that describe the various cultures living in the university, where one can "learn more about these cultures and their customs through the representation of their dances, their songs, their stories and of their colorful parades" (Clara and Rafa).

Figure 3.4. Cultural Assets: The University Carnival

In the screen-shots, some images of the carnival performances are shown. In the excerpt, the students mention the community values that this event promotes every year such as integration, joy and multiculturalism, the last of which is of paramount importance in the university environment, since students come from diverse cultural backgrounds including African-Colombian, indigenous and rural communities. Music, arts, storytelling, traditional dances and parades represent all the regions of the country present in the university community.

Historical-ideological assets. Students not only researched information about human or cultural assets in the community, but they chose landmarks significant for their historical and ideological meaning. Historical and ideological assets are relevant in this community, since the university has been a breeding ground for social movements and historic figures that have influenced Colombia's national history. Take for example Alejandro's posting about a significant picture from the community.

> This image shows the faculty of law and political science this is the building where I study. By this faculty have studied great personalities of the country and countless people who are known for their fierce struggle against inequality in this country; so much history in these buildings make you think about you in the society.

In this posting, Alejandro pays close attention to the historical figures who studied there. For example, he mentions the case of political leaders who initiated social and historical movements in the country. The university community has both influenced and been influenced by the historical, political and ideological phenomena of the larger Colombian context.

With regard to the community's historical connotations, Lefebvre (1976) asserts, "Space has been shaped and molded from historical and natural elements, but this has been a political process. Space is political and ideological: "it is a product literally filled with ideologies" (as cited by Grunewald, 2003a, p. 31). In the space of the community, history, politics and ideologies have left indelible impressions on the minds of the community's inhabitants. These impressions are represented by quotations and art on the walls, as well as in landmarks and place names. Thus, the relation between communities and history, politics and ideologies constitutes a valuable resource for learners.

Linguistic assets. With graffiti, posters, cartoons, bulletin boards, flyers and notices, there is plenty to read in the university community. This set of linguistic tokens found on the community walls is defined by Shohamy as 'linguistic landscape'; the "linguistic objects that mark the public space" (as cited by Gorter, 2006, p. 14). In this way, some students were thrilled to develop their video projects based on this subject. The following students' artifacts (Figure 3.5) illustrate the community's linguistic landscape as seen by them.

In the storyboard, Rebel shows the university community's linguistic landscape. Although the community offers other types of linguistic objects, she focused on graffiti, which Shohamy and Gorter (2009) describe as a bottom-up (unofficial) form of expression, as opposed to top-down (official) alternatives. The university community as described by Rebel is a place where these two positions are in conflict. On the one hand, some authorities want the university to keep its walls blank. On the other hand, students like Rebel consider graffiti as a way to express discomfort, communicate messages and share their art. On this subject, Rebel prepared her final video project in which she showed some graffiti samples and interviewed four students to know their viewpoint regarding 'Blank walls, blank minds' (the clip is available at http://goo.gl/igJ6Sn). She asked the following questions: What is your opinion about the problems at the university and their connection to graffiti? What's your opinion about the graffiti you see?

As noted in the example above, linguistic landscape is a resource for critical literacy. In fact, similar projects using linguistic community landscape have been successful for literacy development. Sayer (2010) reports on a pedagogical intervention in which he and his students examined the linguistic landscape in Oaxaca, Mexico and identified the main uses of English in the community landscape. Another example is shown by Jiménez, Smith and Teague (2009), where the linguistic landscape samples from Mexican and Texan towns are the main resources for migrant students to develop community and transnational literacies.

The complex richness of the community is a valuable resource for critical literacy development. An asset-based approach is useful to take advantage of the embodied and non-material cultural, linguistic and social capital that students can earn if they open their eyes to the multimodal book of the community.

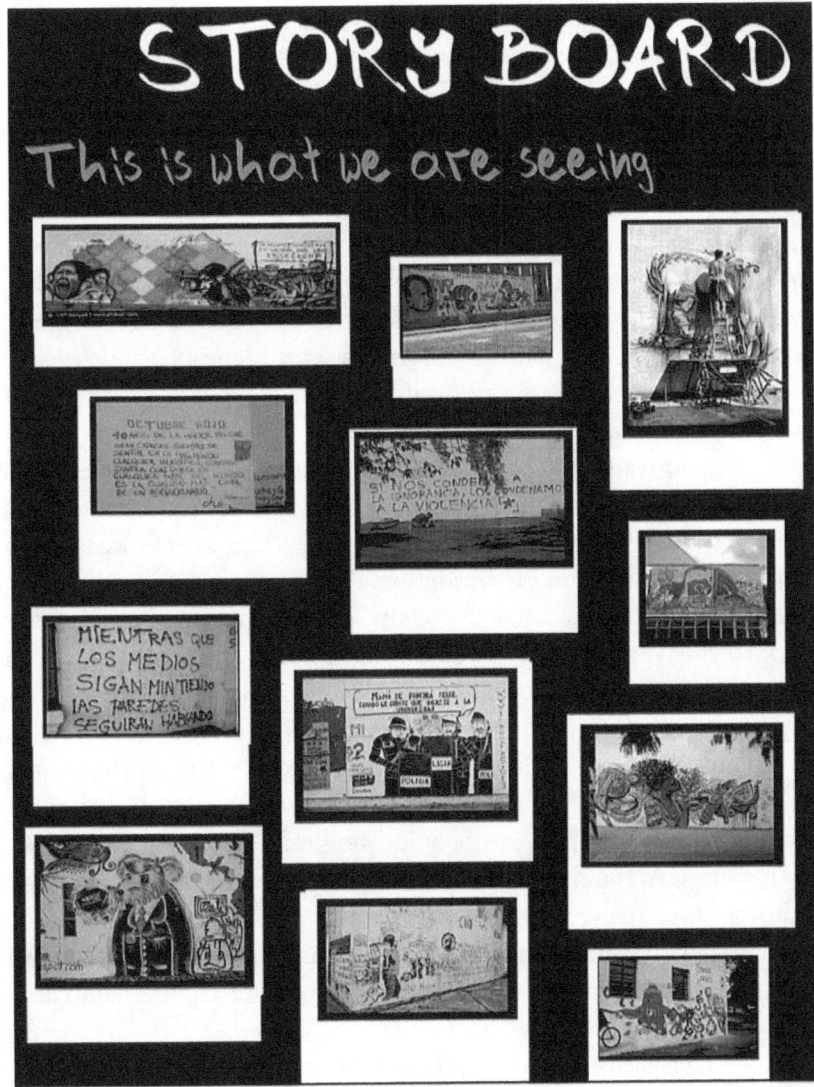

Figure 3.5. Rebel's Video Project Storyboard

Second Learning Moment: Reading the Community Critically
The second learning moment students went through when working on the online-based course was through a critical reading of their community. After

analyzing the community assets, students sought solutions to the problematic situations that affected them and proposed everyday actions to improve their community. The term critical in reading the community correlates to the component of critical framing proposed by the New London Group (1997) in the manifesto of the multiliteracies pedagogy. It involves students standing back from what they are studying and viewing it critically in relation to its context. Critical literacy emerged gradually after analyzing the community. Fairclough (1992) elaborates the concept of critical "as the ability to critique a system and its relations to other systems on the basis of the workings of power, politics, ideology, and values. In this sense, people become aware of, and are able to articulate, the cultural locatedness of practices" (as cited in New London Group, 1997, p. 84).

The critical reading of the community entailed two steps: looking into problematic issues and proposing simple everyday actions to transform their community. When working on their final projects, students went beyond the observation of community resources. Power issues, social struggles and budget problems affected the university community, and some students developed video projects to critique the struggles they face every day. On her final project, Gaby illustrated inequality struggles by historically relegated groups. Her video shows some graffiti associated with the indigenous and Afro-Colombian struggle for rights. The text reads "The unity that works is the one that joins us to the struggle." Gaby asks another student about this graffiti and the debate between people who prefer white walls to the ones who support it. At the end, she expresses her opinion; she agrees with graffiti but she rejects offensive messages. In this short part of the video, the student is concerned with issues of inequality; by selecting the graffiti associated with racial groups, she engages in a critical dialogue with another student and finally, she supports her viewpoint.

Another problem frequently mentioned on the discussion boards and video projects was the need for a university hospital for medical students to practice. Figure 3.6 shows evidence of critical reading of the linguistic landscape that revolves around this topic. Sonia commented that, "It makes me feel proud to belong to the medical school, no matter have not yet university hospital, yet we are still struggling. What do you think about this poster?"

In this posting, Sonia critically reads a poster that uses language in a creative way. Spanish words in the poster have omitted the letter H. The lack of this letter strikes the reader as the words appear incomplete and difficult to read. The message in the middle black chart reads "Even though H is mute, H is always going to be vital. We want our Hospital." Sonia's concise posting contains three main ideas: the pride of being a medical student at the university, the problems caused by the lack of a university hospital, and the struggle that "we" (i.e., the community) are faced with to resolve this issue.

Figure 3.6. Reading the Community Critically

As seen in the examples above, reading the community critically requires, as a first step, acknowledging issues of power and inequality. As Pennycook (1999) asserts, "nothing will change unless people know things need to ('if it ain't broken, don't fix it')" (p. 336). The students recognized inequalities and identified problems that affect the community. In the next step, students moved from recognizing problematic situations to proposing solutions to them.

Another meaning for critical, according to Giroux (1987), is transforming reality. Pennycook (1999) claims that: "critical approaches to TESOL have to do with a political understanding of the location of pedagogy and the development of a way of teaching aimed at transformation" (p. 338). Students were not only able to identify power relations and issues that affect the community negatively, but they questioned themselves on ways they can transform their reality. Take, for example, Francisco's posting:

Figure 3.7. A Picture of the Community: Caution, Reality Across

Francisco noted the following about this image:

> This image represents more than a door, an entry or an exit. I chose this place because is a division of the world, so it is known as "Caution, reality across" from inside of the campus. The reason is that the University is a space of criticism of the reality, the political power, government and capital and also for the construction of a new society. The most important is that after you study here your life, your feelings and your thoughts change. And only if you can understand happened, you can transform the reality. What do you think about the phrase Caution, reality across"?

In this posting, Francisco criticizes the separation between the educational system and society. Grunewald (2003b) citing Brand and Clinton (2002) mentions that schooling often distracts our attention from, and distorts our response to, the actual contexts of our own lives. They assert that people's everyday intimate experiences of literacy are in conversation with remote forces at play in the larger sociocultural context (p. 347). The student finishes his comment by recognizing that one must understand reality to begin changing feelings, thoughts and the larger context.

Another example of raising awareness to transform reality is given by Caro. On her final video project, she talks about contamination problems and she proposes solutions to them. She prepared a video show called Green News, in which she identified some environmental problems in the community. She raised awareness about water and electricity waste and she talked about the bad placement of garbage. After talking about these problems, the student proposed strategies to save energy and water and to deal with refuse. In the last half of the video, Caro gives simple recommendations to help solve environmental problems (the clip is available at http://goo.gl/LggIdd.) At the end of clip, she shows the recycling process; additionally, she explains how students can classify waste to facilitate the process.

The aforementioned examples show that after acknowledging the community assets, students moved to reading the community in a critical way. They were able to identify inequality and power relations issues to work towards a transformation, contamination problems in the city, the separation between the public educational system and the society. Once they had read the community as a book, students started re-writing their reality through the online discussions they held around the issues above mentioned.

Coda: Online Translanguaging
The multimodal literacy practices students developed when working on a critical reading of the community had some particular features with regards to L2 and L1 use due to the online nature of the course. Reading in Spanish and composing in English was a common literacy practice in the postings. To gather information about a community asset a student would read an online article in Spanish and then write a summary in English. In the following posting below, a student centered her attention on the meaning and used untraditional punctuation and spelling while other students used electronic translation tools. Another feature of the postings was translanguaging (the juxtaposition of L1 and L2 to convey meaning). Flores and Garcia (2013)

assert that "translanguaging as a pedagogy offers much promise to enable cultural constructions and transcend the nation state relationships of power" (p. 256). In spite of the mixture of L1 and L2 structures and nonnormative spelling, the message is intelligible, as Lina has shown below:

> Carnival University
> nacional history goes back to the year 1921, when you create the federation of students of the City, responding to similar latina university's trajectories, also founded traditions such as the anthem and the flag of the student, the national government suports this initiative decreeing the STUDENT'S DAY and carried out events by all the city with participation of the national army, senate, others schools and many people more from this date starts the carnival university to be staying until 1934 and he reappears in various moments in the history of the soul máter bibliography (Official website of the University in Spanish).

In terms of textual genres, students composed descriptions, narratives, comments, dialogues, even argumentative texts. On this subject and translanguaging, Cope and Kalantzis (2000) assert that "when learners juxtapose different languages, discourses, styles and approaches, they gain substantively metacognitive and metalinguistic abilities in their ability to reflect critically in complex systems and their interactions" (p. 8). Learning how to deal with different languages, modes, genres, sources and electronic tools constitutes an essential skill for additional language learners in digitally mediated environments.

Conclusions and Pedagogical Invitations

This study showed that critical literacy can be fostered through multiliteracies, digital literacies and community based pedagogies. We have further found that community-based pedagogies and multiliteracies are a suitable pedagogical approach for critical literacy development in digital environments. As Warschauer and Ware (2008) claim:

> Only a transformative pedagogical approach can unleash the potential of technology for literacy development—both for traditional and new literacies. Through such a transformative or critical approach, students make use of technology to analyze their own lives and social problems, develop and publish material that addresses social issues or positively promotes their identities, and collaborate with distant partners to [make] further exploration of social or identity issues. (p. 229)

Findings on how community based pedagogy and multimodalities shaped critical literacy practices involved two learning moments: recognizing the material and non-material assets of the community and critically reading the community. Aside from language learning, the students earned cultural, academic and social capital by experiencing the community and using its resources to learn. Furthermore, students became aware of situations and issues present in the university campus and were able to propose strategies to transform their shared reality. The findings point out the need to become aware of the social, situated, multimodal and transformative nature of literacy. The results also suggest that education in the digital age needs to be nurtured from communities.

We invite language teachers and learners to critique and break dichotomies such as school/community, teachers and students/community inhabitants, monolingual/multilingual texts, textual/multimodal practices, traditional/digital educational environments, and so forth. These and other dichotomies can be transgressed by juxtaposing multiple modes, genres and languages. Further work is needed to break dichotomies in terms of modality and culture as well as transmodaling, transculturing and transliteracing.

A final invitation is to open our minds to the use multiple languages and modes in non- linear ways in order to question reality and power relations, become aware and commit to self-transformation. Only then we will be able to initiate micro-transformations in the intricate fabric of power using literacy, community resources, multimodality and technology as tools.

References

Bourdieu, P. (1986). The forms of capital. In J. Richardson (Ed.), *Handbook of theory and research for the sociology of education* (pp. 241-258). New York: Greenwood.

Butler, J. (2002). What is critique? An essay on Foucault's virtue. In D. Ingram (Ed.), *The political: Readings in continental philosophy* (pp. 212-226). London: Blackwell.

Cohen, L., Manion, L., & Morrison, K. (2000). *Research methods in education* (5th ed.). London: Routledge Falmer.

Cope, B., & Kalantzis, M. (2000). Multiliteracies: The beginning of an idea. In B. Cope & M. Kalantzis (Eds.). *Multiliteracies: Literacy learning and the design of social futures* (pp. 3-8). NY: Routledge.

Corbin, J., & Strauss, A. (2014). *Basics of qualitative research: Techniques and procedures for developing grounded theory.* Thousand Oaks, CA: Sage Publications.

Freire, P., & Macedo, D. (1987). *Reading the world and the word.* London: Bergin & Garvey.

Flores, N., & Garcia, O. (2013). Linguistic third spaces in education: Teachers' translanguaging across the bilingual continuum. In D. Little, C. Leung & P. Van Avermaet (Eds.),

Managing diversity in education: Key issues and some responses (pp. 243-256). Clevedon, UK: Multilingual Matters.

Foucault, M. (1984). "What is Enlightenment?" In P. Rabinow (Ed.), *The Foucault reader* (pp. 32-50). New York: Pantheon Books.

Gee, J. P. (2000). The new literacy studies: From "socially situated" to the work of the social. In D. Barton, M. Hamilton & R. Ivanic (Eds.), *Situated literacies: Reading and writing in context* (pp. 7-15). New York: Routledge.

Gee, J. P. (2009). *A situated sociocultural approach to literacy and technology*. Retrieved from http://jamespaulgee.com/sites/default/files/pub/Approach%20to%20Literacy%20Paper.pdf

Giroux, H. (1987). Introduction. In P. Freire & D. Macedo (Eds.), *Literacy: Reading the world and reading the word* (pp. 1-28). London: Begin and Garvey.

Gorter, D. (Ed.). (2006). *Linguistic landscape: A new approach to multilingualism*. Bristol: Multilingual Matters.

Gramsci, A. (1988). *An Antonio Gramsci reader: Selected writings, 1916-1935*. D. Forgacs (Ed.). New York: Schocken Books.

Gruenewald, D. A. (2003a). Foundations of place: A multidisciplinary framework for place-conscious education. *American Educational Research Journal, 40*(3), 619-654.

Gruenewald, D. A. (2003b). The best of both worlds: A critical pedagogy of place. *Educational Researcher, 32*(4), 3-12.

Jiménez, R. T., Smith, P. H., & Teague, B. L. (2009). Transnational and community literacies for teachers. *Journal of Adolescent and Adult Literacy, 52*(9), 16-26.

Kozinets, R. V. (2002). The field behind the screen: Using the method of ethnography to research market-oriented virtual communities. *Journal of Marketing Research, 39*(1) 61-72.

Kozinets, R. V. (2010). *Netnography: Doing ethnographic research online*. Thousand Oaks, CA: Sage Publications.

Kress, G. (2003). *Literacy in the new media age*. New York: Routledge.

Kretzmann, J. P., & McKnight, J. L. (1993). *Building communities from the inside out: A path toward finding and mobilizing a community's assets*. Chicago: ACTA Publications. Retrieved from: http://www.abcdinstitute.org/publications/downloadable/

Langer, R., & Beckman, S. C. (2005). Sensitive research topics: Netnography revisited. *Qualitative Market Research: An International Journal, 8*(2), 189-203.

Lotherington, H. & Jenson, J. (2011). Teaching multimodal and digital literacy in L2 settings: New literacies, new basics, new pedagogies. *Annual Review of Applied Linguistics, 31*, 226-246.

Marshall, E., & Toohey, K. (2010). Representing family: Community funds of knowledge, bilingualism, and multimodality. *Harvard Educational Review, 80*(2), 221-241.

Medina, R. (2013). *Community based projects as literacy resources in an online EFL course*. (Unpublished Master's thesis). Universidad Distrital Francisco José de Caldas, Colombia.

Moll, L. (1994). Literacy research in community and classrooms: A sociocultural approach. In R. Ruddell, M. Ruddell & H. Singer (Eds.), *Theoretical models and processes of reading* (pp. 179-207). Newark, NJ: International Reading Association.

New London Group. (1997). A pedagogy of multiliteracies: Designing social futures. *Harvard Educational Review, 66*, 60-92.

Pennycook, A. (1999). Introduction: Critical approaches to TESOL. *TESOL Quarterly, 33*, 329-348.

Sayer, P. (2010). Using the linguistic landscape as a pedagogical resource. *ELT Journal, 64*(2), 143-154.

Sharkey, J. (2004). ESOL teachers knowledge of context as critical mediator in curriculum development. *TESOL Quarterly, 38*(2), 279-299.

Sharkey, J. (2012). Community-based pedagogies and literacies in language teacher education: Promising beginnings, intriguing challenges. *Íkala, 17*(1), 9-13.

Sharkey, J., & Clavijo, A. (2012). Promoting the value of local knowledge in ESL EFL teacher education through community-based field assignments. In B. Medrado & C. Reichmann (Eds.), *Projetos e praticas na formacao de professors de lingua inglesa* [Projects and practices in English language teacher development] (pp. 39-58). Brasil: Editora Universitaria UFPB.

Shohamy, E., & Gorter, D. (2009) Introduction. In E. Shohamy & D. Gorter (Eds.), *Linguistic landscape: Expanding the scenery* (pp. 1-10). New York: Routledge.

Smyth, S., & Toohey, K. (2009). Bringing home and community to school: Institutional constraints and pedagogical possibilities. In A. Kostogriz, J. Miller, & M. Gearon (Eds.), *Linguistically and culturally diverse classrooms: New dilemmas for teachers* (pp. 271-288). Bristol, UK: Multilingual Matters.

Strauss, A., & Corbin, J. (1990). *Basics of qualitative research: grounded theory procedures and techniques.* London: Sage.

Toohey, K., & Day, E. (1999). Language learning: The importance of access to community. *TESL Canada Journal, 17*(1), 40-52.

Warschauer, M., & Ware, M. (2008). Learning, change, and power: Competing discourses of technology and literacy. In J. Coiro, M., Knobel, C. Lankshear & D. J. Leu (Eds.) *Handbook of research on new literacies* (pp. 215-240). New York: Lawrence Erlbaum Associates.

Appendix 3.1
Semi-Structured Online Survey

Apreciados estudiantes, a continuación encontrarán unas preguntas sencillas para que reflexionen acerca la utilidad del proyecto que se realizó sobre la comunidad. También pueden agregar sus comentarios para mejorarlo. *(Dear students, you will find below a set of simple questions to reflect upon the usefulness of the project about the community. You can also add your comments to improve it).*

1. ¿Para qué sirvió la realización del proyecto sobre la Comunidad de la Universidad?* Escribe tanto como puedas relatando tus percepciones sobre los foros, los scripts y la realización del video. *(What was the usefulness of the Project about the University community?* Write as much as you can telling your perceptions of the discussion boards, script writing and video recording)*

2. ¿Cuáles actividades contribuyeron más al aprendizaje de la lengua? *(Which activities were the most helpful to learn English?)*

3. ¿Qué aprendiste durante la realización del proyecto acerca de la comunidad?* *(What did you learn while working on the project about the community?)*

4. Otros comentarios y recomendaciones* *(Do you have other comments or recommendations?)* Bottom of Form

CHAPTER 4

EXAMINING THE ROLE OF CRITICAL PEDAGOGY IN JAPANESE UNIVERSITY STUDENTS' DESIRE TO LEARN ENGLISH

Takayo Kawabe
Kobe College

Introduction

Investigating pedagogy in the critical view has not been largely conducted in the field of English as a foreign language (EFL) in Japan. This study explores EFL learners in Japan, and the relationship of their language use in the critical pedagogy classroom community and their desires to learn English. Critical Pedagogy is derived from the critical theory of the Frankfurt School, in which Paul Freire was one of the renowned critical educators. In *Pedagogy of the Oppressed*, Freire argues that education is traditionally framed as "an act of depositing, in which the students are the depositories and the teacher is the depositor" (1970, p. 58). Students are positioned as empty vessels to be filled by the teacher. In this framework, the teacher lectures, and the students "receive, memorize, and repeat" (p. 58). On the other hand, critical pedagogy focuses on the development of learners' critical consciousness that enables them to recognize connections between their individual problems, experiences and the social contexts. Raising critical consciousness is the necessary first step of the transformation of education in society. Freire also proposes a dialogical approach that advocates for teachers, students, administrators and other community members to become participants and co-learners in education. Based on Freire's approach of critical pedagogy, I will reflect on my implementation of his approach on my own class in a later section.

Since 2006, there have been 800 students in my university level English classes; however, only a few of these learners have visibly demonstrated a desire to learn English. In the beginning of the semester, the students have consistently shown a lack of effort for learning and a receptive attitude of just sitting, listening to the teacher, and easily falling asleep. This empowered me to teach them using a constant dialogue, a discussion about critical issues, as well as communicative and creative activities. This is a challenge in Japan, where "Not only have Japanese university students changed their attitude in learning, but also Japanese youth and children have changed. For 70% to 80% of the students have been in quite a serious crisis, in which they try to escape from learning" (Sato, 2000, p. 9). To counter this trend, the government has sought support from local self-governing bodies, schools and families, because teaching is not viewed merely as conveying academic knowledge. Moreover, the criteria, knowledge and abilities are not fixed concepts, but they are diverse concepts as individuals change according to the surrounding environment (Lave & Wenger, 1991). Therefore, without looking at the relationship between the individuals in the classroom as a society, the diverse views of what is considered learning, and society's changing values, we cannot grasp a real understanding of the learner's 'self' as a social 'self.'

The question of an inter-relationship between language use and the language learners' social identities has been extensively researched in the field of applied linguistics (Norton, 1995; Pavlenko, 2000, 2001, 2002, 2003, 2007, 2008). Considering motivation as the original focus for my pedagogical practice, I, as a researcher, was interested in the learners' social identity in order to better understand the factors at play in the learner's desire or lack of desire for English learning from the theoretically different framework of investment (Norton, 1995), which better accounts for the historical and macro-contextual factors that shape Japanese students' desires to learn English from a new perspective. It is, therefore, important to understand that "the investment that a given learner makes in learning an L2 can only be understood by consideration of [their] identities, [their] desires and [their] changing social world, as all three contribute to the structuring of different investments at different times and across contexts" (Ortega, 2013, p. 242). In this chapter, I contend the need for learner negotiations in order to gain newly constructed positions in learning English as a foreign language, where students experience "the right to speak" and "the right to be heard" being influenced by target language power and knowledge. In this flow, the present study uses narrative analysis as a methodological framework with a sociocultural approach to examine the change of individuals in society in the framework of critical pedagogy. In addition, I examine how EFL learners in my classroom construct their identities in their narratives utilizing the analytic device of social positioning theory (Bamberg, 2003; Davies & Harre, 1990) that is based on the notion that discourse is where speakers produce particular words in the pattern of word usages that demonstrate how they understand themselves and their relationship to their social surroundings.

Literature Review and the Purpose of Study

The focus of this study is critical pedagogy as my overarching framework and English language teaching. The goal of critical pedagogy is to critically examine the philosophy of teaching in aiming at bringing about change in the world, change in our students' point of view, change in identity, and change in the outcomes of education. Critical pedagogy takes the approach of teaching a learner by drawing on critical social theory that "seeks to understand and critique the historical and sociopolitical context of schooling and to develop pedagogical practices that aim not only to change the nature of schooling, but also the wider society" (Pennycook, 1990, p. 24). In addition, Giroux (1988) explores how power relations between individuals and communities affect the learners' life. His work is connected to individual experiences and social power in a theory of subjectivity (Norton, 1995). Weedon (1987) puts emphasis on the central role of language in her analysis of the relationship between the individual and the social: "Language is the place where actual and possible forms of social organization and their likely social and political consequences are defined and contested. Yet it is also the place where our sense of ourselves, our subjectivity, is constructed" (p. 21).

In this chapter, I also maintain the importance of viewing this study as a negotiation between the author participants and myself, in what Bakhtin (1984) refers to as authorship, in which human agency is possibly realized through a students' hope for the future. Bakhtin applied the Marxist dialectic to literary and rhetorical theory and criticism. He illustrated the tensions that exist in the deep structure of all human experience. Language interconnects dialogue with human identity. Dialogical process refers to the concept of dialogue and working together (Bakhtin, 1981). Building on Bakhtin's (1984) concept of authorship, I view participant narratives as dialogic constructions, as a form of authorship by EFL learners, in which the participants creatively appropriate linguistic resources and actively engage in voicing and positioning of others. Bakhtin's (1984) concept of answerability/addressivity refers to the need for dialogues between selves who act to answer one another's actions and others that conceptualizes language learners as authors of their 'selves.' Through jointly constructed discourse, individuals create, express, and position themselves in society, according to their own sociocultural histories, needs, and expectations. In addition, Lave and Wenger (1991) argue that "learning is an integral and inseparable part of social practice" (p. 31). Their notion, legitimate peripheral participation, implies that communities are composed of participants who differentially engage with the practice in learning so that research should focus on the social structures in particular communities and their positioning for learners (Norton, 1995).

In response to the educational philosophy, the purpose of this study is to teach English using critical pedagogy to my EFL students in Japan. However, looking back on my eight years of teaching experiences with over 5000 students, I have only met a small number of students who were taught English critically in their previous English classes. Initially the students always were frightened to address their ideas in English and showed a receptive attitude, just sitting and only listening to me, and not actively participating in my class. Their passive behavior was a good example of what has been called the *banking concept of education* (Freire, 1970). This has been the old-time popular concept in Japanese education. Freire explains the banking concept of education as the traditional student and teacher relationship where the teacher is the active agent or lecturer who knows everything, and where the teacher has authority, while the students are passive recipients of the deposited knowledge where they receive, memorize and repeat this knowledge rather than learning English as a communication tool. The banking concept of education symbolizes Japanese *tumekomi kyoiuiku* or *cramming education* (Sato, 2000). This negative influence still remains in English classrooms.

In my classes, however, I teach English language as a process of socialization and individual development with the hope of creating an occasion within my students of raising critical awareness in them that they might challenge and transform their identity in this contradictory and oppressive society. From my perspective, school should become a community which shares mutual understanding in learning, creating within each member a critical awareness to rise up to become a better being. In this context, in my view, teaching is not merely a tool for conveying academic knowledge and training language skills. Moreover, knowledge and ability are not fixed concepts, but rather are diverse concepts that change with individuals according to the surrounding environment. According to Lave and Wenger (1991), *legitimate peripheral participation* implies that communities are composed of participants who differentially engage with the practice in learning so that research should focus on the social structures in particular communities and their positioning for learners (Norton, 1995). In my teaching philosophy, I also see the classroom as a small society, in which my 'self' and students' 'selves' are related to one another in the classroom. Without looking at the relationship between the individuals in the classroom as a society, we cannot grasp a real understanding of teaching. In my view, then, teaching a new language is letting students actually use the language as a social being. Therefore, before I began teaching classes at "Act University" in 2006, I thought about how I could give as many opportunities to my students for meaningful language use in my classes.

For these reasons, not only do I speak English most of the time in my class, but I also always give my students English-speaking time as well. I used the text, *The 'I' in Identity* (Sato et al., 2005), in my class. The theme of the class was to think about the identity of multinational foreign students living in Japan. The most challenging aspect of teaching this class for me was to build a new student and teacher relationship based on open communication. At first the students were very quiet and did not want to speak up because they were so afraid of making mistakes. I lessened my authority and used their language to cross the boundary between us by avoiding the use of the honorific language of a traditional teacher. In other words, I used the casual language common among friends instead of using more rigid honorific language. I asked my students to write about themselves in their journals and to openly talk in their e-mails. Moreover, I told them that I am not a traditional teacher but a new type of teacher who is there to facilitate their development as a person and to enrich their ideas. I implemented a dialogical approach, which advocates for teachers and students to participate as co-learners in education. I encouraged them by sharing my old episode of how

I struggled to acquire English. The class became very active, as the students enjoyed sharing their critical ideas with their peers as well as in groups as they prepared for class presentations.

As I encouraged my students to write freely about themselves in their journals, our class talk became more open. The goal of the class was to conduct class presentations. The students chose their own topics based on some broad and general themes such as culture shock, discrimination, social injustice and identity. They gradually shared their own critical thoughts by thinking over and discussing the critical topics, and finally each came to seek his or her identity. As mentioned in the beginning of this section, although my students had never experienced a critical pedagogy class before, after a few weeks, they eventually became accustomed to my class and enjoyed sharing critical ideas with their peers and in groups and were able to successfully conduct the class presentation. The result was that students were actively communicating. The majority of my students liked my class and invested in my class activities. Students further developed themselves by doing presentations and sharing their critical ideas dialogically rather than simple receptive learning (i.e., the banking concept of education).

Method

This study investigates the role of Critical Pedagogy (Auerbach & Wallerstein, 1987; Freire, 1970; Giroux, 1988; Pennycook, 1990; Weedon, 1987) in Japanese university students' investment (Norton, 1995) in English learning. Drawing on positioning theory, the narrative data demonstrates how pedagogy influences learners' development, and the transformation of learners' social identity through community of practice (Bamberg, 2003; Davies and Harre, 1990; Lave and Wenger, 1991; Wortham, 2001). In other words, using narrative analysis as a methodological framework, I explain students' narratives in order to uncover different types of "positioning" that interviewees and the interviewer co-constructed. I analyzed the data collected through (1) active interviewing, (2) my field notes and reflective notes from observing a class and (3) my students' reaction reports and journals based on the conceptual framework of Bakhtin (1981, 1984), Norton (1995, 2001), Pavlenko (2007), and Lave and Wenger (1991). The study was conducted in Act University E class in 2006 from April to July in a teacher researcher's class with 33 students at the medium level. Five students majoring in economics volunteered for this study. The theme of the class was to think about the identity of international students from different countries living in Japan. The class was held twice a week for 90 minutes and for 48 class hours during the semester.

Each student's experience is an idiosyncratic event, which is related to larger social structures in the individual to the public (Richardson, 1997). With similar experiences and conditions in society that we undergo, we can legitimatize "discursive space for ourselves to explore ways of presenting our experiences as 'EFL learners' in Asian contexts" (Lin, Wang, Akamatsu & Riazi, 2005). Using narrative analysis as a methodological framework, as a collective story (Richardson, 1997), my students' narrative data present how the members of the community tend to view themselves in the world and interpret their English learning. In order to avoid misinterpretations, the students' English sentences are partially edited by the researcher. Also, students' names are pseudonyms in order to assure anonymity. Their meaning making by talking or writing creates the change to English learning in the world and the students' view in their community and society.

Findings: Narratives of Yoshi, Taichi, Nao and Kenji

In Act University E Class, narratives of Yoshi, Taichi, Nao, and Kenji demonstrate the following concepts in their use of the pattern of word: dialogical teaching, a membership as a legitimate participant, their desire to learn English, transformation of identity, new identity constitution that appears in authoring themselves, and investment in language learning. When I interviewed many students, they shared that due to their previous experience, they thought English was merely the repeated action of memorization and a very boring study time. They told me that they did not need English unless they were to become a teacher, an elite businessman or computer engineer. Therefore, teaching critical pedagogy to Yoshi, Taichi, Nao and Kenji was another challenge for me. As mentioned, I used the published textbook, *The 'I' in Identity: Talking with Foreign Students in Japan* (Sato et al., 2005). The theme of the class was to think about the identity of international students from different countries living in Japan. In this class, I encouraged active communication among students and me as a teacher. However, they were silent in the beginning because they were used to the receptive learning style in their previous classes. The biggest challenge for me was to build a new student-teacher relationship based on more open and natural communication.

I asked my students to write about their daily life in their English journals and encouraged them to talk to me. To begin with, I introduced myself to my students as follows:

> Hi, I'm Takayo Kawabe. It's so nice to see you. In this class, I will mainly speak English because then you can hear more English in your class, and also you can speak English. If you don't understand me, I can help you with Japanese translation, so don't worry too much. From the beginning of the class, I will always ask you to speak up in English. Well, you can speak about anything; for example, about what happened to you last week or your recent events. I know you are used to sitting and listening to what your teacher said in high school, right? However, what makes this class different is that, in this class, you are the major character! It's not me, okay?! If you are not sure how to express your thoughts or comments in English, I can help you. Just do not worry about making mistakes. We are non-native speakers of English, so we all make mistakes. We just need to learn from making mistakes as just like how we learned our first language.

This introduction helped to build a relationship between my students and me. However, it took a certain amount of time until my students started to speak up. They were afraid of making mistakes in front of others, because they had been taught that it was never good to make any mistakes. I understand this feeling, because students especially feel ashamed when they fail to live up to the expectations others have of them (Hiebert, 1985). Teachers struggle to induce students' agency while they feel guilty in tolerating the students' spoken English grammatical mistakes. This is often the reason why students avoid using English in class. My passion to teach English as communication and to examine how I could motivate my students by teaching English has continued until today. I claim that the ability to author words is essential for Bakhtin's (1984) subject agency, which is authorship, and in which human agency is possibly realized through each student's hope for future.

Looking back on my own experience, I am certain that exchanging dialogue, discussing critical topics and communicative language use are a significant key point in my teaching. Sometimes, when only one or two students spoke up while most of the students were quiet, I felt disempowered and was tempted to reverse my teaching style. However, I hoped to see what I could do and how my pedagogy influenced the learner's development with the transformation of learner's social identity through a community of practice. I patiently encouraged students to speak up through pair work and group discussion. Because it was easy for them to fall into the pitfall of speaking Japanese, I walked around the class with a smile as I encouraged my students to speak up, giving them hints as to how they can express their ideas in English. Eventually, I saw a change in my class.

For instance, the next narrative is the reflection of a Japanese male student, Yoshi, who is an earnest student. He was not confident at the beginning of the semester, so was worried about his learning. However, he worked seriously in class and finally at the end of the semester, he gave a good presentation. He wrote in his learning journal:

> Your class is different from other classes because we frequently speak English and present our ideas. It is only this class doing these things. I came to think that I want to participate spontaneously in this class. Although I am scared to make mistakes in English even now, I began to feel like "Let's use it!" a little by little. I think it is good if I come to like English gradually.

Yoshi's words confirmed to me that my class was on the right track. As he mentioned, in many other classes, students do not spend much time in speaking and presenting their ideas in English. However, as I taught them more, they changed. I taught them to exchange dialogue in English in the peer and group discussion. The common narrative among them was that they felt my class was different from other classes because they actually had to speak English as they discussed critical topics and presented their ideas.

The next excerpt is a reflection about our class by Taichi, a Japanese male student in the same class with Yoshi, who also shared that my class had a different atmosphere. In this excerpt, Taichi shows the narrative of absolute English knowledge. He wrote in his learning journal that

> I have felt a different atmosphere in this class compared to my junior and high school English classes. I attended most of the lessons in this class unless I had an unavoidable excuse. This class is a participatory class, so if I do not try to learn by myself, I feel like I am wasting time. Honestly, I sometimes get tired, but the class is actually good for me, so I intend to learn English for my future. I will keep working.

As Taichi learned in my class, his experience of learning English was different from the one in junior high and high school. His words proved that my aim of teaching English as a real communicative tool was a good and rewarding learning experience for him because, as he shared in his narrative, "I attended most of the lessons in this class unless I had unavoidable excuse. This class is a participatory class" refers to his investment (Norton, 1995) in my class as a participant. When the participant becomes a legitimate participant, sometimes a new image of positive self emerges, as Lave asserts (2009). My pedagogical practices influenced my students' constructed positioning in relation to their self-construction as members of a new community, their desire to learn English, and the language socialization opportunities within the EFL classroom context, which are indicative of Taichi's transformation of identity. Depicting the mind and self in the context of learning is best described in the participants' identity constitution and authorship (Bakhtin, 1984) in their narratives about my class. Nao's narrative in his reflective journal also illustrates how this constitution and authorship took place:

> Thanks to this class; I acquired English. In this class, we presented our opinions with other classmates. In the process, we began to think about our own ideas rather than following what our teacher said. I think that this is the way that we establish identity. According to a dictionary, one of the two definitions of identity is that the demonstration of being whom or what a person is. When we demonstrate our opinion, we want to act new and different things from our traditional Japanese custom because we think in English. This represents our change in identity, and because of this class, I started to form identity in my mind.

Nao's narrative is very interesting because using English changed his identity. In my school days, I also had a similar experience and have noticed that I form a new identity when I speak and think in English with my native English-speaking friends. When I speak in Japanese, I am more introverted and hesitate to assert my opinion; however, on the other hand, when I speak in English, I author myself actively using the language. Thus, identity constitution appears as authorship (Bakhtin, 1984).

The common comment in my students' narratives was that they felt my class was different from other classes because they author themselves using English. They also said how critical topics helped them to present their ideas. Furthermore, in Yoshi's case, the underlined words "have to," "participate in this class spontaneously," and "I began to feel like 'Let's do it!'" indicate his strong desire to learn English. In this way, pedagogical practices influence my students' constructed positioning in relation to their self-construction as a member of a new community. Through these particular words, the speakers demonstrate how they understand themselves and their relationship to their social surroundings.

The next narrative written by Kenji reflects how my teaching critical pedagogy influenced his self-awareness of identity. His identity was transformed from an "uncommunicative self" who was unable to speak English in school, to a "communicative self" who was now open to foreign culture. On the first day of the semester in April, 2006, when everyone in our class wrote their introduction in a short essay, Kenji wrote:

> I have never seen a person who came to be able to speak English only by studying in school, so I do not think I really need English. I think it is enough to have basic knowledge for every day practice. The subject that I want to take in university is the subject of using a computer, because I feel the class is short. The knowledge that I want to acquire by studying is the knowledge that adults should have.

The word "adults" is the evaluation of adults as others and where he positions his social identity as that of "children." Therefore, at the university, he wants to acquire the knowledge that adults should naturally possess. In the beginning of my class, his self-awareness of identity appeared in his perception of himself not as an "adult." He positioned himself as a child who did not have knowledge. However, as I taught Kenji critical thinking and discussion skills in English, he drastically changed. In his latter essay, he wrote that some people who studied English helped themselves to re-confirm their identity as Japanese. Moreover, he wrote that one of his reasons for studying English was that he could re-examine Japanese culture after learning about a foreign culture:

> Why do we come to learn English in our compulsory class? Many may say that we do not have specific reasons. I think that the people who like to work using English skills should study abroad. <u>Most people who study English in Japan do not seem to understand why they study English. If I give a reason, it may be to confirm their identity as Japanese.</u> I have no intention to use English in my career, but <u>one of my reasons to study English is that I can re-examine Japanese culture by learning about a foreign culture</u> …. Some people may think that if we study English very well, we may lose Japanese identity. However, knowing English is different from merging our culture into the culture of English speakers.

> Therefore, I think we do not need to be worried about whether or not Japanese culture will be assimilated into English culture.

Kenji emphasized that he can forge a new identity maintaining his own Japanese identity and Japanese culture without being assimilated into western culture. For him, knowing English vocabulary and grammar did not necessarily mean that one would adapt his concept into their ideology of English speakers. My intention was not to change or affect his opinion and identity. As a facilitator, I posted the source for critical thinking and just encouraged Kenji to ponder how his social identity related to language and culture. It is amazing to see my students' identity transformation in this way. Even if they do not like studying English as a school subject, as they author their social selves, they come to like English because they will be able to critically express their ideas. In Kenji's group members' presentation handout, they said that they needed to go beyond the boundaries of their own culture and religion in order to understand African American's culture and religion and not to discriminate against them:

> Today what we talk is about discrimination in sports. Discrimination happens in all kinds of fields, for example, occupations, gender roles, and religions. We examined discrimination of people by skin colors. What do you think about discrimination in this area? I don't understand. Such discrimination is said to be of people of a different color. I feel very sad. I don't understand discrimination. We need to respect others. In order to be respected by others, we should try our best to understand their traditional culture. We should also understand their religion. This is the way to solve the problem of discrimination. It should be forbidden.

Teaching critical pedagogy helped Kenji and his group to reconfirm ethnic affiliation and local contextualization. Many other students in my class also said that critical pedagogy can help them to like learning English. Of course, it is not applied to everybody because many also say that English is of no use to them because it is a sort of a language most commonly used in the West, and they do not need the English language as long as they live in Japan. However, teaching how to author their "selves" by critical pedagogy appears to help some students to see the world critically where they gain new identity through meaningful dialogue among students and teachers.

In Yoshi, Taichi, Nao, and Kenji's narratives, these participants used the pattern of word that demonstrated several concepts: dialogical teaching, a membership as a legitimate participant, their desire to learn English, transformation of identity, new identity constitution appears in authoring themselves, and investment in language learning.

Reflections and Discussion

As I reflect on the students' narratives, I realize that when my students come to be able to express themselves in English, which is a difficult foreign language, and have received recognition for their efforts, they feel a sense of belonging in my class community, and they develop a deeper desire to learn English. It also facilitates the expansion of their language identity. Their narratives show that although the students for the first time experienced a critical pedagogy class with me, they gradually enjoyed sharing critical ideas with peers and in groups, successfully conducted the class presentation, and finally were able to seek their own identity. Through active communication, students enjoyed my class, and invested in my class activities. Active language use is a significant key point of my teaching methodology and also for changing one's identity. As previously mentioned, identity constitution appears as authorship (Bakhtin, 1984). In this way, pedagogical practices influenced my students' situated self-construction as a member of a new community of global citizens. Teaching critical pedagogy seems to help some students to see the world critically and open their eyes to gain new critical knowledge through meaningful dialogue in English with other students and teachers.

Even if English is a foreign language, the participants in my class used and acquired English as a communicative tool to be able to author themselves. This occurred because teaching language is not merely teaching knowledge of the language; it also means internalization, which means "to know how to apply the skill." For example, I explain this by using a metaphor; "teaching children how to use a pencil." Initially, a parent or a teacher instructs them how to use it because in the beginning, children do not know how to use a pencil. Children copy their parent or teacher in order to master the skill through repetitive practices and writing activities. After they know its use, they gradually appropriate how to use a pencil. They can draw pictures, draw manga, write novels, or write essays. They do not merely continue copying the instruction of their parents and teachers. Just as children learn how to use a pencil, I can first teach English as a basic communicative tool. Then I help them to use language skills to author themselves in my critical pedagogy class. This means that each student can apply their language skills to express themselves. Therefore, exchanging dialogue for using English as a language appropriation is the philosophy of my critical pedagogy class. As a result, they receive recognition and feel a sense of security in the space where they can belong to. This appeared in students' positive positioning, a new emerged identity, and a desire to learn English.

Conclusion

In this chapter, I have explained how critical pedagogical practices can influence my students' desire to learn English and to develop their identity based on various students' narratives. I have focused particularly on excerpts relating to how critical pedagogy influences the students' constructed positioning in relation to their agency in learning English and language socialization opportunities within the EFL classroom context. As they become a member of the community they empower their "selves" and come to like English through having a desire to learn the language; consequently, as the agent of empowerment, they participate in learning English in the class. Regarding a dialogical approach and enhancing students' desire to learn English as language socialization, the findings from this study should be a significant contribution to the ESL/EFL curriculum.

Having taught 15 semester classes in a Japanese university, I confirmed that critical pedagogy class is powerful for facilitating agency and emancipating students from the invisible bondage coming from excising social power as Japanese EFL students in the classroom context. Enhancing students' new identity constitution is one of the key factors for using English as a positive tool to empower their agency and release from their negative selves in language use as indicated by common responses in my students' narratives. However, there is no ultimate goal in critical pedagogy class as Auerbach (2000) asserts that teachers and students "are always in the process of becoming" (p. 161). The goal of transformative education (Freire, 1970) is the development of the student as a whole person in a society concerned with real-world social political issues that are meaningful to the students. Transformative education also requires dialogue between teacher and student. This has been my special concern as an educator. I have to keep considering critical pedagogy with praxis (Freire, 1970), which engages in a cycle of theory, application, evaluation, reflection and then back again to the theory. Social change is the outcome of praxis. Therefore, my purpose in this study was to evaluate my own use of critical pedagogy in the classroom as a part of praxis. Investigating the role of critical pedagogy in Japanese university students' desire in English language learning may cast a new light on this matter.

References

Auerbach, E., & Wallerstein, N. (1987). *ESL for action: Problem posing at work*. Reading, MA: Addison-Wesley.

Auerbach, E. (2000). Creating participatory learning communities: Paradoxes and possibilities. In J. K. Hall & W. G. Eggington (Eds.), *The sociopolitics of English language teaching* (pp. 143-164). Clevedon, UK: Multilingual Matters.

Bakhtin, M. (1981). Discourse in the novel. In M. Holquist (Ed.), *The dialogic imagination: Four essays by M. Bakhtin* (trans. C. Emerson and M. Holquist, pp. 259-422). Austin, TX: University of Texas Press.

Bakhtin, M. (1984). *Problems of Dostoevsky's poetics* (trans. C. Emerson). Minnesota: University of Minnesota Press.

Bamberg, M. (2003). Positioning with Davie Hogan: Stories, tellings, and identities. In C. Daiute & C. Lightfoot (Eds.), *Narrative analysis: Studying the development of individuals in society* (pp. 135-157). London: Sage.

Davies, B., & Harré, R. (1990). Positioning theory: The discursive construction of selves. *Journal of Theory and Social Behavior, 20*, 43-63.

Freire, P. (1970). *Pedagogy of the oppressed*. New York, NY: Herder and Herder.

Giroux, H. (1988). Teacher education as cultural politics. In H. Giroux (Ed.), *Schooling and the struggle for public life* (pp. 188-202). Minneapolis: University of Minnesota Press.

Hiebert, P. G. (1985). *Anthropological insights for missionaries*. Grand Rapids, MI: Baker Book House.

Lave, J. (2009). *Community of practice* [lecture notes]. Presentation at Kansai University, Osaka, Japan.

Lave, J., & Wenger, E. (1991). *Situated learning: Legitimate peripheral participation*. Cambridge: Cambridge University Press.

Lin, A., Wang, W., Akamatsu, N., & Riazi, M. (2005). Transnational TESOL professionals and teaching English for globalized communication (TEGCOM). In A. S. Canagarajah (Ed.), *Reclaiming the local in language policy and practice* (pp. 197-222). Mahwah, NJ: Routledge.

Norton, B. (1995). Social identity, investment, and language learning. *TESOL Quarterly, 29*(1), 9-31.

Norton, B. (2001). Non-participation, imagined communities, and the language classroom. In M. Breen (Ed.), *Learner contributions to language learning: New directions in research* (pp. 159-171). Harlow, England: Pearson Education.

Ortega, L. (2013). *Understanding second language acquisition*. New York: Routledge.

Pavlenko, A. (2000) Access to linguistic resources: Key variable in second language learning. *Estudios de Sociolinguistica, 1*(2), 85-105.

Pavlenko, A. (2001). "How am I to become a woman in an American vein?": Transformations of gender performance in second language learning. In A. Pavlenko, A. Blackledge, I. Piller, & M. Teutsch-Dwyer (Eds.), *Multilingualism, second language learning and gender* (pp. 134-174). Berlin: Mouton de Gruyter.

Pavlenko, A. (2002). Poststructuralist approaches to the study of social factors in second language learning and use. In V. Cook (Ed.) *Portraits of the L2 user* (pp. 277-302). Clevedon, UK: Multilingual Matters.

Pavlenko, A. (2003). "I feel clumsy speaking Russian": L2 influence on L1 in narratives of Russian L2 users of English. In V. Cook (Ed.), *Effects of the second language on the first* (pp. 32-61). Clevedon, UK: Multilingual Matters.

Pavlenko, A. (2007). Autobiographic narratives as data in applied linguistics. *Applied Linguistics, 28*, 163-188.

Pavlenko, A. (2008). Structural and conceptual equivalence in acquisition and use of emotion words in a second language. *Mental Lexicon, 3*(1), 91-120.

Pennycook, A. (1990). Critical pedagogy and second language eduation. *System, 18*(3), 303-314.

Richardson, V. (1997). Constructivist teaching and teacher education: Theory and practice. In V. Richardson (Ed.), *Constructivist teacher education: Building new understandings* (pp. 3-14). Washington, DC: Falmer Press.

Sato, R., Groff, D., Asai, A., Ishii, M., Nakamura, J., & Matsuda, M. (2005). *The "I" in identity: Talking with foreign students in Japan.* Tokyo: Nanun-do.

Sato, M. (2000). *Manabikaratousousurukodomotachi* [Children escape from learning]. Tokyo: Iwanami Syoten.

Weedon, C. (1987). *Feminist practice and poststructuralist theory* (2nd ed.). London: Blackwell.

Wortham, S. (2001). *Narratives in action.* New York: Teachers College Press.

CHAPTER 5

CHALLENGES AND TRANSFORMATIONS:
Using Narratives to Forefront Writing Pedagogy

Nancy Wasser
New Mexico State University

This paper examines challenges and transformations preservice elementary school teachers and I experienced while participating in a Teacher Action Research (TAR) project as part of an elementary (K through eighth grade) Language Arts Writing Methods university course I taught. I looked for factors in the course content that helped or hindered preservice teacher participants to engage in collaborative research forefronting narrative writing as primary writing pedagogy with which to teach poetry, narrative (genre), essay, and expository writing. I also searched the data for places of transformation, places where participants' teacher discourse about teaching children to write changed or evidenced a transformation-in-process through their participation in the project.

The theme of our classroom research was using *personal narrative through a social justice lens as literacy pedagogy in elementary classrooms*. Saavedra (2011) states that, "[a]llowing students to voice their stories is much more than just permitting them to speak of relevant experiences…[W]e can decenter our adult conceptions of language/literacy, and create *nuevas posibilidades* for teaching and learning" (p. 265). My thought was to explore with preservice teachers, through personal narrative writing, the pedagogical question of "whose knowledge counts" (Bernal, 2002; González, Moll, & Amanti, 2009; Yosso, 2005). I wanted to determine what factors in using narrative as primary writing pedagogy challenged preservice teacher participation.

Most of the students in the teacher education program at this university came from the southwest desert region, specifically the states of New Mexico and Texas and the country of Mexico, "The Borderland" between the United States and Mexico. Issues of social justice related to teaching language arts arise daily as students leave the university and venture forth into area public schools. Gee (1996) states that,

> The most striking continuity in the history of literacy is the way in which literacy has been used, in age after age, to solidify the social hierarchy, empower elites, and ensure that people lower on the hierarchy accept the values, norms, and beliefs of the elites, even when it is not in their self-interest to do so. (p. 36)

I posit that the solidification of "the social hierarchy" of which Gee (1996) speaks is particularly true in many of the area schools participants attended as children and now visit as practice teachers. For example, the district has a policy that provides "Advanced Education Services" (2013) for 'gifted' students. According to the district's website, in school year 2011-2012 it was predicted that 6.4% of the student population would be considered 'gifted.'

Parenthetically, it is important to point out that the district policy explains that they believe they are not catering to a wealthy elite class by providing this program. The justification for a gifted program is that the wealthy among the population will provide special academic enrichment for their children; however, it is the poor who are not able to do this unless the public schools provide the opportunity (District's gifted task force, 2011).

The district's Advanced Education Services (AES) philosophy is as follows:

> AES facilitate the process skills of critical thinking, creative thinking, achievement, self-efficacy, and social/emotional needs to engage gifted learners in lifelong learning skills. Gifted students *require differentiated curriculum of depth and complexity*, appropriate instruction, materials and planned interaction in a combination of settings with intellectual peers. AES recognizes the importance of the social and emotional needs of gifted students and the impact that these needs have upon their academic and life goals. [italics mine]

This paper does not intend to minimize the importance of the above stated approach to meeting the academic, social and emotional needs of gifted students. It is my contention, however, that all students should have the "differentiated curriculum of depth and complexity" which appears to be the exclusive provenance of the 'gifted' students at this time.

For example, according to the Center for Education Policy Research (2012), in the county in which the school district is located, 38 to 45 percent of students attending colleges within the state in 2009 needed remedial course work. How is the district addressing this situation of four students out of ten requiring academic remediation in order to be successful in college? One way is reliance on standardized tests.

Although the district's mission is, in part, to "provide a student-centered learning environment that cultivates character, fosters academic excellence, and embraces diversity," their specific goal is for students to reach 85 percent proficiency on the state assessments by May, 2016:

> In order for us to gauge our effectiveness in meeting the district's mission, we rely on multiple data sets that allow us to triangulate information and give us a full picture of whether we are indeed meeting the diverse needs of all learners. While formal assessments are only one piece of the puzzle, they give us information that helps determine whether we are making progress in improving academic outcomes.

The reading assessment criteria, for example, uses "six measures to function as indicator of phonemic awareness, alphabetic principles, accuracy and fluency with connected text, reading comprehension, and vocabulary."

Clearly there is a line being drawn between students who are designated as gifted and the rest of the school population. The reading assessment criteria demonstrate a different set of criteria from that of the gifted students. While admitting that assessments are only one diagnostic tool, there is no specification stated in the reading criteria for the majority student population that "critical thinking, creative thinking, achievement, self-efficacy, and social/emotional needs" are a consideration for engagement in learning.

Embracing diversity is contained in this district's vision statement; however, good intentions often manifest as celebrations of ceremonial customs such as *El Día de los Muertos* or *Cinco de Mayo*. While these celebrations may bring much-needed variety to the prescriptive standardized instructional day, I submit they are insufficient to represent multiple cultures in general and the Latino-American Southwest culture in particular. Furthermore, these "boxed-lunch" efforts at multiculturalism may actually exploit the very cultures they seek to serve. Expressed in the discourse of social justice, pedagogy that ostensibly promotes multiculturalism while advancing a packaged version of the discourse of middle-class, white America as the "commonsense" curriculum (Apple & Buras, 2006; Delgado Bernal, 2002; Edelsky, 1996; Gandara & Hopkins, 2010; Gee, 2001, 2003; Kumashiro, 2008), actually suppresses deep knowledge about the cultures-of-origin of many students in the U.S., particularly in the Borderland region.

Apple (2004) maintains that "schools assist in the creation of hegemony through the 'socialization' of students" (p. 97), thus participating in a model of authority that legitimates an "ideological world view" (p. 79) that promotes both economic and political hegemony. Dewey, writing in 1936, spoke against this tendency in American schools. In his Laboratory school he "specifically denied that there was any desire to 'adjust' individuals to social institutions, if by adjustment is meant preparation to fit into present social arrangements and conditions" (as cited in Kliebard, 2004, p. 70). Henry (1963) asserted that "[s]chool is an institution for drilling children in cultural orientation" (p. 283). Pinar (2012) stated that "for the foreseeable future, most teachers will be trained as 'social engineers,' directed to 'manage' learning that is modeled loosely after corporate work-stations, focused on test preparation" (p. 37). It is well documented that schools have served and continue to function to acculturate, socialize, politicize, and norm students to a prevailing hegemonic economic model and cultural ideology through its curriculum. (For an earnest discussion of this argument see Apple, 2004; Kliebard, 2004; Pinar, 2012, among others).

Preservice teacher participants in this study were steeped (however unwittingly) in the pedagogy of the social canon of the dominant culture of white America, or as Giroux (2004) explains it, "modernity's universal project of citizenship, *its narrow understanding of domination*, its obsession with order, and its refusal to expand both the meaning of the political and the sites in which political struggles and possibilities might occur" (italics mine, p. 32). Their focus on test preparation as status quo was expressed to me by questions such as: *How do [we] prove that students have been learning if there are no easy reading test scores for people to see? In focusing on the writing progress students make from draft to draft (Christensen, 2009), how do we account for grade books & report cards?* These questions are analyzed below; however, they are indicative of the state of disequilibrium of some of the students as they entered into our research project. They displayed varying degrees of skepticism or openness to this "new" way of looking at literacy in general and writing in particular as personal funds of knowledge waiting to be expressed as deep pedagogy, as will be shown.

Methodology
Research Objectives, Questions, and Theme

My research objectives for this study were: (1) for preservice teachers to investigate employing narrative as writing pedagogy by using personal/cultural/linguistic funds of knowledge in their third- through eighth-grade Language Arts practica classrooms, and (2) to determine whether or not this pedagogy would encourage a social justice perspective on teaching language arts.

Thus, my research questions were: By using personal narrative as writing pedagogy, would preservice teachers embrace the question of "Whose knowledge counts?" (Delgado Bernal, 2002; González, Moll, & Amanti, 2009; Yosso, 2005). Would this pedagogy encourage a social justice perspective from which to teach writing as literacy pedagogy?

The research theme for the course was using personal narrative through a social justice lens as writing pedagogy in elementary language arts classrooms. To this end, participants, both collaboratively and individually, constructed lesson plans based on the theme, and then wrote reflections on their processes of construction, on the experience of teaching the lesson, or on any other facet of their teaching and learning experience, particularly as it related to the theme.

Research Framework

I used Teacher Action Research (TAR) as the research framework. Teacher Action Research is evolutionary ongoing research in a classroom setting. It is self-reflective inquiry, often with a social justice focus, designed to improve classroom practice (Carr & Kemmis, 1986; Pine, 2009). This improvement can be for both teachers and students due to its nature as participatory and collaborative. It is a process of meaning-making through a cycle of reflection, planning, action and revision. Noteworthy to the process is that the research questions may change as participants move through the cyclical process. According to Pine (2009), TAR is recursive because practitioner/researchers "circle back to address and *modify* research questions based on reflection for, reflection in, and reflection on action" (p. 30, italics added). Another characteristic of TAR, according to Elliot (1991) is that, "in action research theories are not validated independently and then applied to practice. They are validated through practice" (p. 69).

To the extent possible in a classroom setting, TAR seeks to promote participatory democracy. Constraints and limitations exist; therefore, in this project, in order to retain the participatory nature of the research model as much as possible, I attempted to model ways preservice teachers could include public school curriculum requirements, such as state standards and benchmarks, in their lesson plans, while staying within the larger framework of our writing pedagogy. The TAR process may facilitate transformation at any one of the following points of entry as demonstrated by Figure 5.1.

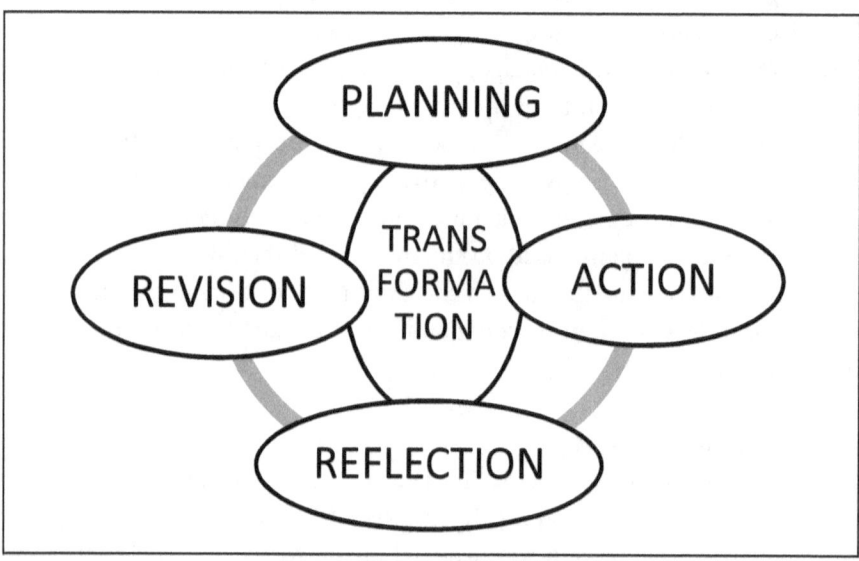

Figure 5.1. The Cyclical Nature of Teacher Action Research may promote transformation at any point in the ongoing process, particularly upon reflection of the action taken. Thus, the research question(s) may change as participant's move through the evolutionary cycle.

Participants and Research Setting
The participants in the project were fourteen Elementary (K-8) Education majors, twelve of whom were college seniors and two who were graduate students, in an Elementary Language Arts/Writing Methods class for preservice teachers. The project took place in spring semester 2014. Six of the students identified as Latino/Hispanic, four as Caucasian, two as African American, and two identified as being of mixed heritage. The research setting was a Southwestern United States university serving a large Latino/Hispanic population.

In addition to the university classroom, preservice teachers observed and practiced teaching at a local public school. Thus, by extension, the school became part of the setting not only for participants' practice of the pedagogy, but also as a database, which they brought back to our classroom. This kindergarten through eighth grade school was a charter school with a racial/ethnic composition of 62.4% Caucasian students, 30.6% Hispanic/Latino, 3.8% Asian, and 2.5% African American. The school was atypical for the community in terms of racial and ethnic composition and also due to its status as primarily a school for children considered "gifted." As well, the total school population was small compared to most of the community public schools—only 157 students as of the 2012 school census. The school had a Standards Based Assessment (SBA) rating of 18th out of 377 elementary schools in the state as of 2013 (SchoolDigger.com). The school is a project-based instructional program, and, according to one of the teachers, is a school for students "who don't fit into the public school environment" (personal interview by a study participant, 2014). Thus the setting for these practice teachers was atypical for them as well. It was a first experience for most of them to work in a school designed for gifted students.

Methods of Data Collection and Analysis
The data for this study was drawn from a number of classroom sources. Specifically, data sources included my reflective journals and notes taken during class. Likewise students' reflective journals, personal accounts of their experiences in the practicum, were a large research data source. To the extent possible, students wrote their reflections after teaching one of the four writing genres as required by the course syllabus, specifically poetry, narrative, essay, and expository writing.

The participants' four lesson plans, written over the course of the semester, became another data source, along with my own weekly lesson plans. As well, our primary textbook, Linda Christensen's *Teaching for Joy and Justice* (2009), is devoted to a writing methodology that encourages teachers to construct a writing curriculum relevant to students' own experiences and one that explores ways of promoting social justice through writing and sharing one's writing. In addition to the lesson plans, participants wrote their own sample narratives for each of the four writing genres we studied. These samples were later used as models with students in participants' practicum classrooms.

Each student kept Reading Logs based on concepts and skills presented in the Christensen textbook, and these were another data source. The Logs provided a place where students could write questions to me that arose for them during the reading. I compiled these questions and they became material for in-class discussions, shared writing, and research data. On alternative weeks students wrote narrative summaries of their readings that also became research data. In addition, students engaged in freewriting in class on various topics concerning their personal experiences with writing.

Another data source was an online question and answer (Q&A) discussion group. These discussions were based on focus questions I posed as scaffolding for reading taken from the other required text, *Teachers as Cultural Workers* (Freire, 2005).

Two evaluations of the course were given at the end of the semester. One was in the form of written reflections about the use of narrative as pedagogy in the language arts classroom. The other was a Q&A evaluation treating the course in a more general manner. These also became a rich source of data. Finally, email communications were a source that provided me with insight into individuals' concerns about the course as well as providing research data.

Data analysis. I used Critical Discourse Analysis (CDA) for the purpose of data analysis, specifically some of the CDA *tools* described by Gee (2011). CDA is a form of analysis of social practices (Gee, 2011, p. 28) that examines the "token-meaning" (p. 24), the meaning assigned by the social group, of the utterance (words and phrases) typically used by a given group of people, in the case of this study, preservice teacher participants. Gee (2011) called this the "situated meaning task" (p. 24) (i.e., the meaning is located in the culture and social setting from which it derives).

Specifically, the tools I employed from Gee's (2011) toolbox were *The Figured World's Tool* and *The Big "D" Discourse Tool*. One of the appeals to me of Gee's (2011) discourse analysis methodology is that he centered the theoretical tools "in different theories about how language ties to the world and to culture" (p. 150). This was suitable for the diverse cultures participants represented and also taught.

The Figured Worlds Tool draws from psychological anthropology. It treats "narratives and images that different social and cultural groups of people use to makes sense of the world" (Gee, 2011, p. 150). It explores what is "normal and natural" to the group, allowing for a way of acting and being in the world that assumes certain ideas/perceptions to be true, thus saving the individual the need to examine every thought and idea before expressing it (p. 150).

Big "D" Discourse borrows concepts from cultural anthropology, cultural psychology, sociolinguistics, and philosophy (Gee, 2011, p. 150). Due to its broad reach, it is one of the major tools I used for data analysis. This tool analyzes language from the perspective of social identity and the ways that participants in a given social identity group perceive and relate to the world of objects "including our own bodies, tools and technologies in concert with other people" (Gee, 2011, p. 151). In other words, this tool takes into account how we act/speak/write as members of certain social and cultural groups.

Factors that Challenged Preservice Teachers' Participation
Open-ended Planning

One factor that impeded collaborative planning of curriculum was a strong push-back on the part of participants in terms of evolutionary, open-ended planning of themes for writing activities (what the lesson plan might look like) and timeframes for submission of work. They were uncomfortable working within a general structure where guidelines were provided but specifics were left to students' creative construction. Although all due dates were collaboratively agreed upon, and students' other course work and life schedules were included in those decisions, they were much more comfortable with a course schedule set by me that stated firm due dates and explicit requirements for lesson plans, including a formatted template within which to "write" their plan. This was the case even with participants' reflective journals. Although I gave guidelines in the form of a rubric (e.g., what went well, what did not go well, what would you do differently next time, etc.), students wanted a template of questions to which they would then write short paragraph answers. This was the Discourse they were used to in their teacher education classes, and deviating from it caused some disquiet and disequilibrium.

Pushback Against Writing as Primary Literacy Pedagogy
At the beginning of the course, participants expressed doubt about employing writing, especially narrative, as a way to approach writing literacy pedagogy for elementary and middle school students. Fears surfaced through their own narratives to me, to each other, and in class discussions. The questions participants raised were legitimate in terms of the prevailing U.S. public school Discourse in which they were embedded. Questions and comments reflected the emphasis on standardization of curriculum and testing as the primary assessment tool to determine student learning. As well, fears of their own evaluations as practice teachers, and later as classroom teachers, loomed large. These fears were and are legitimate in terms of the current "commonsense" that teaching and learning should be standards based and test driven (Apple, 2001, 2006; Apple & Franklin, 2004; Au, 2010; Kohn, 2000; Kumashiro, 2008; Meier, Kohn, Darling-Hammond, Sizer, & Wood, 2004; Ravitch, 2010; Sleeter, 2005). Examples of their questions and concerns are summarized and quoted as follows:

- Does narrative writing to connect to students' lives and to write from an authentic and personal knowledge base "really prepare students for what they are going to be testing on?"
- "How do [we] prove that students have been learning if there are no easy reading test scores for people to see?"
- In focusing on the writing progress students make from draft to draft (Christensen, 2009), how do we account for "grade books and report cards?"

The "Discourse" (Gee, 2011) (i.e., the position of the social group) is evident in the above comments. In the case of the first two questions, no suggestion of a subtext questioning the fact of testing as the ultimate and possibly only assessment criterion exists. The agreed upon Discourse was that, of course testing is the primary assessment tool. Their questions to me and to peers were, therefore, embedded within that unexamined discourse.

The "figured world" of participants as teachers at the beginning of the course, with one or two exceptions, was that testing was a big part of the world of K-8 literacy education. The corollary to their unexamined and unwittingly agreed-upon discourse was, if teachers have no reading test scores for parents and school personnel to see and interpret, how can we prove (i.e., defend) that learning has taken place? Embedded in this question was a profound subtext of reading as primary literacy pedagogy, and, implied, writing as secondary in importance to reading.

The last question asked how teachers could demonstrate that students were being evaluated if they were not giving grades for every draft and all writing assignments. This question was a reaction to our text and to class discussions that suggested working with students through peer and teacher guided revision processes until they achieved a final acceptable (to student as well as to teacher) product. Again, the embedded assumption was that every paper needs to be graded and this was the way to show student progress. Their figured world of teaching writing did not include how students might feel if and when their writing drafts received poor grades, or how poor grades might affect students' perceptions of themselves as competent writers, or what the effect of poor grades might have on their engagement with writing or their identities as writers.

This "training" willed out despite the stories preservice teachers wrote about their own early school experiences with writing. The following examples serve to illustrate the point.

> I see the kitchen table. I am 6 or 7 years old…I have my hand writting [sic] practice sheets in front of me. One thick solid line with a dotted line below followed by a thick solid line below… with an example of the letter I was supposed to copy over and over. "My hand writting [sic] is so ugly," I would murmur to myself…These practice sheets would never go away everyday it seemed I was doing them all the way through third grade. And what was the point. I always got "C's" in hand writting [sic].

Another student also experienced her first identity as a writer with handwriting: "We were given worksheets with a few different letters on them and just had to write the letter over and over again."

Still another felt a vacuum where her writer's identity should have been:

I am in my 6th grade class sitting at my desk with a paper in front of me and a pencil in my hand. My teacher just finished telling us about an assignment and that is writing a poem. She didn't specifically say what she wanted us to write our poem on, which made it that much harder...I just sat at my desk staring at a blank sheet of paper with nothing to write.

However, as the semester progressed, the discourse (unexamined positionality) began to change. The following reflective narratives were written after preservice teachers spent some time in their practicum classrooms, had delved into the reading of our text, had entered into discussions about purposeful writing from authentic experience, and had experienced writing personal narratives themselves.

- First and foremost we as teachers have to stop putting a grade on writing, especially at a young age when writing is very new. I know when I was growing up my writing assignments always came back with red marks all over and I didn't want to write anymore. Students are still like that.
- Students do better when they care about what they are learning and doing, [as] opposed to shoving standardized data down their throats...Before a teacher can start helping to correct grammar and punctuation, the student must first be encouraged by telling them what they did right, [as] opposed to what they did wrong.
- I thought it was interesting to read about how poetry class can slowly teach grammar. It seems as though you don't always need to learn the rules first but you can learn them as you go.
- When a student's paper is filled with errors, only point out the positive things to show the student he or she is doing something right...In class [we learned] how to look for patterns of error[s] (Christensen, 2009, p. 269-270) and this seemed really helpful because we get to see what the student struggles with and we can slowly work on that with that child.

López-Bonilla (2011) "contend[s] that, as an analytical tool, figured worlds can be viewed as an interface between discourse and Discourse" (p. 47). From the above samples a clear pattern of change in participants' discourse (unexamined assumptions about teaching writing) emerged. The figured worlds of these future teachers were undergoing a transformation. In the first example the participant reached back in her own memory to a time in her figured school world when she was learning to write and the discouraging feeling she had when papers were returned "with red marks all over" them.

She claimed that, "I didn't want to write anymore." Here her discourse begins to shift to a new Discourse. Her teacher talk forecasts a glimmering of transformation in perception of her figured world of children learning to write in the telling phrase, "Students are still like that." Childhood memories of learning to write, re-experienced through writing, enabled her to relate those early experiences to her present day teaching and learning situation, helping to change her Discourse.

In the case of the second narrative the writer's discourse concerned teaching grammar and punctuation, which she now placed as secondary to facilitating children to care about what they were learning. What she termed "standardized data being shoved down their throats," exemplified her figured-world-in-transition after spending time in the course. Her Discourse contended that what was primary was for teachers to encourage students by "telling them what they did right as opposed to what they did wrong." "What they did right" was the new Discourse rising from the ashes of the old discourse of correcting "what they did wrong." She did not dismiss teaching and learning academic writing (i.e., grammar and punctuation). She did, however, think through her position as to when and how it should be taught.

The final two discourses also considered approaches to teaching the structure, grammar, and mechanics of language as part of the writing process. The phrase, "it seems as though," by the third commentator, signaled a transformation of his figured world of writing pedagogy in process. This participant was pondering a new idea. His historical figured world, signaled by the phrase, "you don't always need to learn the rules first," implied that he was taught grammar as a skill-based activity. Furthermore, those grammar skills were probably taught in isolation from the actual writing process, based on a "rule" that, once learned, would produce the skill, hence, "good" writing. After our first unit on poetry, his viewing lens for teaching grammar started to change. He was seeing and experiencing an alternative strategy that would still teach "the rules," but would allow them to be taught as the context for those rules where context arose from students' own poetry texts. "You can learn [the rules] as you go." However, the phrase *"it seems as though"* implies that, at this point, he was not completely convinced. He was willing to suspend judgment as he examined and practiced this new way of teaching grammar. Perhaps then his figured world about how teachers teach English grammar would change to be enfolded in a larger Discourse of writing pedagogy.

Similarly, the last narrative expressed the participant's willingness to teach grammar and mechanics of writing by accentuating the positive (i.e., correct) examples from the child's own writing. He considers the possibility of using student writing samples to extract patterns of errors for each child in order to work individually with him or her. His statement that "it seemed really helpful" revealed that he was considering the value of assessing a child against his or her own progress. This new figured world may be a transformational bridge for him into a thoughtful freshly examined Discourse about teaching writing as pedagogy.

Pushing Back Against Issues of Language and Power
López-Bonilla (2011) discussed differences between narrative *analysis* used "to explore the relationship between form and function...[and] narratives as a way of knowing" (p. 49). As discussed above, I encountered resistance to using narratives as primary writing pedagogy with which to teach writing. To preservice teachers, this was a new way to "explore the relationship between the form" (i.e., narrative-as-writing-pedagogy) and its "function" as a methodology with which to teach the mechanical skills of writing.

In contrast, pushback against the use of narrative as pedagogy with which to explore issues of language and power was expressed by preservice participants mainly in the context of students' losing their primary language upon entering public school and being forced to speak, read, and write in English. (Depending on the age of the children when their parents arrived as immigrants, this meant learning to read and write in English as they continued to speak their first language at home, or, as many experienced, learning to read and write in English in addition to their first language.) This pushback is not surprising in terms of the linguistic background of many of the students. However, it was interesting to note that participants' Discourse (Gee, 2005) about teaching writing *skills* included the conviction that writing should be taught from part to whole (i.e., as a skill-based activity). Conversely, when confronted with notions of language as power, this part, at least, of their Discourse shifted from teaching writing atomistically to teaching "narrative as a way of knowing" (López-Bonilla, 2011, p. 49) or, put another way, holistically.

The situated meaning for some participants of this study became a transitional zone where using personal narratives as cultural "funds of knowledge" (González, Moll, & Amanti, 2009) was not only writing pedagogy, but potentially an act of social justice. Narrative writing became for some a social justice Discourse that honored their cultural and linguistic identities as will be shown in the following.

Conversely, learning to write first in a second language, which removed participants and their students from their cultural roots and identity, was viewed as an act of injustice. Although this particular school's mission statement included a commitment to a dual language program, preservice teachers' comments perhaps reflected their own early schooling experiences:

- Mainstreaming is the tool schools use to "wash out and destroy" languages other than English.
- "Bilingual programs aim to wipe out the speaker's native language" by employing subtractive language models.

Indeed, the university does not have a formal policy about the importance of teaching the home (first or primary) language as an equal player with English language instruction. It merely states that, "A key dimension of the program includes the advancement of issues related to equity and social justice by encouraging participants to serve as advocates for bilingual children, their families and communities." While this is laudable in terms of sociocultural and identity support, it does not empower teachers to leverage the two languages as equally worthy.

Gee (1996) made a distinction between primary and secondary Discourses. He stated that "Primary Discourses are those to which people are apprenticed early in life during their primary socialization as members of particular families within their sociocultural settings. [They] constitute our first social identity..." (p. 137). When we enter school and other institutions, we "are apprenticed as part of [our] socializations...outside early home and peer-group socialization" (Gee, 1996, p. 137). Gee refers to these apprenticeships as secondary Discourses (p. 137).

Similarly to the lack of specificity in university policy, the public school district's vision statement affirmed students' right to be literate in more than one language in school. To wit: "To work collaboratively with schools and the community to help students achieve academic success, become bi-literate, productive, and competitive members of our global society."

However, their mission statement has quite a different and powerful subtext of which some preservice teachers were aware. Its goals are as follows:

> To enhance and foster best instructional practices that will prepare and support all students to achieve academic success while acquiring a second language by:
> - Supporting the implementation of proven research-based practices that result in increased language proficiency for culturally and linguistically diverse students;
> - Supporting the implementation of proven research-based practices that result in increased academic proficiency as outlined in the Common Core State Standards;
> - Providing and supporting purposeful and meaningful professional development; and
> - Providing essential support to migrant students and families

Although the vision (ideological basis) was to support Biliteracy, the mission (actual practice) is to support children as they learn English. Referencing Gee's (1996) differentiation between primary and secondary Discourses, we see that what the mission statement advocates is to support the learning and development of a child's secondary Discourse (i.e., English).

The first participant comment above concerns the practice of mainstreaming students whose first language is not English. The writer claims that this practice is intentionally designed to "wash out and destroy" other languages. Schools, she implies, want to eradicate their students' primary Discourse, i.e. the language they acquired that defines and explains them as individuals and as members of certain cultural and linguistic groups, and replace it with the secondary Discourse of schools, which is the language of power. Examining this writer's claim in light of the mission statement and scrutinizing it under a Critical Discourse Analysis (CDA) lens, we see the possible truth of this writer's perceptions.

She writes, "Mainstreaming is the tool schools use to 'washout and destroy' languages other than English. Luke (2000) defines discourse as "Systematic clusters of themes, statements, ideas, and ideologies [that] come into play in the text" (p. 456). Clusters of themes that arise in the mission statement of the District are: "research-based practices that result in increased language proficiency… [and] increased academic proficiency." This is to happen as "students… achieve academic success while acquiring a second language." This "second language" is English. While not overtly stated that the students' first language will be destroyed, the writer was, herself, a victim of that process. Nowhere in the mission statement is there a reference to supporting and implementing the first language.

The second commentary goes even further by claiming that the aim of *bilingual* education programs is *"to wipe out the speaker's native language."* Period. This writer boldly claims that bilingual programs were and are not intended to preserve the first language and teach the secondary one, but rather are programs intentionally designed to use a child's primary language as a way to scaffold English, the important secondary Discourse (the language of power). Furthermore she believes that representatives of school policies are aware that their motives are to replace all other languages with English, not only insofar as school is concerned, but with the goal to *wipe out* students' first language and sociocultural identity (i.e., the primary Discourse, altogether).

López-Bonilla (2011) states that, "[A]s a tool of inquiry, figured worlds can help us to understand the interface between discourse (language in use) and Discourse (a socially enacted identity)" (p. 50). This is an important albeit nuanced distinction due to the position of secondary Discourses as commonsense "discourses," particularly for teachers, because these discourses belong to their "figured worlds" of being a teacher. Thus, teachers of the secondary Discourse of schools are often unaware of the fact that they are apprenticing students to a new Discourse heretofore unknown to many, including those from English-speaking backgrounds whose primary Discourse is less formal than "school English," as well as speakers of other languages. What I discovered in the data was that some participants entered a transitional zone that made a bridge between their commonsense figured world of teaching writing to a new Discourse in which they sought to balance their previous commonsense discourse with the new secondary Discourse. Some examples follow:

- Teachers are made out to be "bad people" because they have been a party to language discrimination. This is wrong thinking because at present teachers embrace diversity.
- "As a teacher, how much do I give my students the love of their language, but yet I know and they know that outside the classroom the pressure builds to 'change' to succeed. How do I avoid giving them a false sense of hope?"

The comment that, "Teachers are made out to be "bad people because they have been a party to language discrimination" represents a different point-of-view from those participants who claimed that the practices of mainstreaming or bilingual education were/are deliberate strategies designed to eradicate any language but English. This writer decries the idea of blaming teachers for the egregious act of "language discrimination," stating that teachers are not "bad people" and that "this is wrong thinking because at present teachers embrace diversity." She implies that in the past teachers may not have embraced diversity therefore the criticism may have been justified. Implicitly however, she believes that her figured world is one in which, in the present time, teachers possess a conscious awareness of diversity and, by implication, a positionality of honoring students' primary languages. Her subtext can be interpreted as, "I am a teacher who embraces diversity; therefore, I will teach the language of schools (children's secondary Discourse) consciously." She does not say how she intends to do this, and here we arrive at the core issue facing many bilingual educators in the U.S. today. A student majoring in Bilingual Education learns about various ideological and delivery models, historical and legal policies regarding bilingual education, and even, at the undergraduate level, methods for teaching and scaffolding dual language instruction. However, what is not taught, perhaps because it is not understood, is how to honor equally primary and secondary Discourses and how to reflect that honor in active instruction. This is an important area for future examination.

The next writer inquired how she could avoid "giving her students a false sense of hope" by honoring their primary Discourse and encouraging it in the classroom in order to "give them the love of their language." Her present figured world, her transitional world, is one in which holding on to your native language is a "false hope." Thoughtful despair lay just beneath the surface of her plea. She declared that "I know and they know that outside the classroom the pressure builds to 'change' [in order] to succeed." Her critical thought here rises above the commonplace acceptance that, of course, children need to learn to speak English, or what Fairclough (2010) refers to as "the legitimizing common sense which sustains relations of domination" (p. 265). She is caught in a dilemma.

Fairclough (2010) explains that "The political concept of 'hegemony' can usefully be used in analyzing orders of discourse…[that]a particular social structuring of semiotic difference may become hegemonic, ... but hegemony will always be contested to a greater or lesser extent, in hegemonic struggle" (p. 265). This was the internal hegemonic struggle this participant faced.

Essentially she was saying that if she honored children's first language and employed it as an equal Discourse with English she would probably be doing her students a disfavor. She would be knowingly holding them back from future success which requires students to be well-versed in what she knows to be the language of power. She is aware that achievement in society is brokered by the way the hegemonic structure defines the Discourse of language and power, to wit, English. Thus, her moral dilemma. Perhaps the most powerful situated meaning of all was contained in the following comment: "Through the loss of [one's] language, culture is also lost, values and beliefs are gone, and morals desert the mind."

This writer was fully aware of the importance of primary Discourse to sociocultural and personal identity. She believed the loss of it would cause the loss of not only one's culture, but indeed the entire structure of values and beliefs embedded in that culture. Moreover, this would cause an individual's moral code to "desert the mind." Fairclough (2010) in his book *Critical Discourse Analysis* discusses "the merits of 'locating' ideology in language structures or language events and conclude[s] it is present in both" (p. 56). Similarly, this participant was firmly established in her opinion (ideology) that *values* not only *reside* in primary language [structures], but indeed *compose* the figured world of its participants. Thus its retention as primary Discourse is imperative. From my perspective, *Discourse* includes all the embedded values, ideologies, and commonsense notions that a culture embraces—shared sociolinguistic beliefs. A *language* is merely that which one speaks to negotiate the dailiness of life.

The idea that one's moral code could disappear as a result of losing the primary language was one heretofore unexamined by me. It profoundly enhanced my own Discourse on bilingual education. Although a firm believer in retaining one's first language *and* learning the second, my figured world of bilingualism had never included the notion that replacing children's primary Discourse could foster desertion of their moral code for living. Thus, the intent to supersede the primary Discourse of childhood and culture with the secondary Discourse of schools is tantamount to what this astute preservice teacher stated as: causation of an individual's moral code to "desert the mind." I posit that this insight may have profound implications for the importance of retaining one's primary Discourse as infrastructure for negotiating the moral and ethical pathways of life. This may be an area ripe for further research. As will be shown, this participant lost her primary Discourse as a child, but due to her dedication to her culture, returned to it in adulthood.

Transformative Actions to Address Issues of Language and Power
Later narratives, as participants spent more time with course readings, writings, and discussions and more time in practice classrooms, revealed some profound changes in their Discourse about language and power and how that is best divested in classrooms. Data demonstrates deep thought about those figured worlds and changes they would make in order to teach from a place of linguistic integrity. Following are some of their ideas.

- "Dig deeper." Be a proactive teacher by promoting linguistic diversity in the classroom.
- Go beyond using materials reflecting diversity to understand effects of language discrimination on our students
- Research students' languages and facilitate students' researching their own languages to gain deeper understanding of their culture and history
- Teach students to analyze how language functions in society and in families
- Affirm diversity but teach social and linguistic norms—establish harmony between them
- Important for students to know what can be done to restore languages
- "Have students research and study authors in their own languages" as well as in English
- "I relearned Spanish"

There is no doubt that participants' figured world of language and power has undergone transformation. Those who already viewed language Discourse as a language of power *over* certain groups gained strength in their commitment to promote language diversity and equality and evolved strategies they could employ as future teachers. They were aided by the Christensen (2009) text and by narratives written from childhood memories of learning to write. Equally, class discussions and writing about these memories served as catalysts that helped shift their situated learning about writing pedagogy from discourse to Discourse.

Many participants were able to move beyond a skill-based notion of what it means to teach writing to consider actions creating a new canon. This is evidenced by the following injunctions: "Dig deeper;" Be... proactive; Promote linguistic diversity; Go beyond...; Research; Teach...how language functions... treating narrative "as a way of knowing" (López-Bonilla, 2011).

Another perspective was represented by the participant who advised to "affirm diversity, but teach social and linguistic norms [and] establish harmony between them." This participant moved from a position of insecurity about how to honor diversity and still teach the dominant Discourse to a place of decision to teach the language of power while respecting the linguistic diversity among the students.

Other participants decided to advance the research of languages represented in their classes or study authors in students' native languages implying that linguistic diversity would be not only allowed in their classrooms, but cultivated. The participant who wrote that "I relearned Spanish" was she who contended that, "Through the loss of [one's own] language, culture is also lost, values and beliefs are gone, and morals desert the mind."

Fairclough (2010) stated that "ideology is located...both in structures which constitute the outcome of past events and the conditions for current events, and in events themselves as they reproduce and transform their conditioning structures" (p. 58). By relearning Spanish, this participant writer "transform[ed] [her] conditioning structures" into a resurrected primary Discourse. She may use this resurrected Discourse to transform the situated meaning of what passes for "commonsense" discourse about teaching and learning the language of power in her future teaching settings.

Conclusion

The data show that participants embraced narrative writing as pedagogy that may encourage a linguistic social justice perspective. As the study concluded, I perceived that many stood on a transitional bridge looking back on their indoctrination into writing as pedagogy to serve the Discourse of power and looking forward to evolving a new secondary Discourse concerned with incorporating diverse funds of knowledge into new writing pedagogy. This "new" Discourse will probably retain some structures of the old skill-based canon while broadening to include language diversity and ideas of promoting social justice through writing the stories of our lives. Importantly, the data affirm that people learn by undergoing a period of "cognitive dissonance" (Festinger, 1957), or a period of uncomfortability, where we stand on a transitional bridge between the figured worlds of unexamined discourse and thoughtful Discourse. Teachers' imperative is to scaffold and support this period of cognitive dissonance. This is difficult in today's standardized curriculum and skill-based-testing environment; therefore, it is incumbent upon teachers to support each other in this endeavor and for the university to support preservice teachers in their practice classrooms as they embark on a shared mission of teaching students to think critically. In this manner we may cross the bridge of cognitive dissonance into a teaching and learning environment of social consonance.

References

Apple, M. W. (1986). *Teachers and texts: A political economy of class and gender relations in education.* New York: Routledge & Kegan Paul.

Apple, M. W., & Buras, K. L. (Eds.). (2006) *The subaltern speak: Curriculum, power, and educational struggles.* New York: Routledge.

Apple, M. W. (2004). *Ideology and curriculum* (3rd ed.). New York: Routledge Farmer.

Au, W. (2010). The idiocy of policy: The anti-democratic curriculum of high-stakes testing. *Critical Education,* 1(1), 1-15. Retrieved from http://ices.library.ubc.ca/index.php/criticaled/article/view/182239/182300

Carr, W., & Kemmis, S. (1986). *Becoming critical: Education, knowledge and action research.* Barcombe, UK: The Falmer Press.

Center for Education Policy Research. (2012). [*Title removed to protect the identity of the participants and research site*].

Christensen, L. (2009). *Teaching for joy and justice: Re-imagining the language arts classroom.* Milwaukee, WI: Rethinking Schools.

Delgado Bernal, D. (2002) Critical race theory LatCrit theory and critical raced-gendered epistemologies: Recognizing students of color as holders and creators of knowledge. *Qualitative Inquiry,* 8(1), 105-126.

Edelsky, C. (1996). *With literacy and justice for all: Rethinking the social in language and education* (2nd ed.). Bristol, PA: Taylor & Francis.

Elliot, J. (1991). *Action research for educational change.* New York: State University of New York.

Fairclough, N. (2010). *Critical discourse analysis: The critical study of language* (2nd ed.). New York: Pearson.

Festinger, L. (1957). *A theory of cognitive dissonance.* Evanston, IL: Row Peterson.

Freire, P. (2005). *Teachers as cultural workers.* Boulder, CO: Westview.

Gandara, P., & Hopkins, M. (2010). *Forbidden languages: English learners and restrictive language policies.* New York: Teachers College Press.

Gee, J. P. (1996). *Social linguistics and literacies: Ideology in discourses.* New York: The Falmer Press.

Gee, J. P. (2001). What is literacy? In P. Shannon (Ed.), *Becoming political, too: New readings and writings on the politics of literacy education* (pp. 1-8). Portsmouth, NH: Heinemann.

Gee, J. P. (2003). New people in new worlds: Networks, the new capitalism and schools. In B. Cope & M. Kalantis, (Eds.), *Multiliteracies: Literacy learning and the designs of social futures* (pp. 43-68). New York: Routledge.

Gee, J. P. (2011). *How to do discourse analysis: A toolkit.* New York: Routledge.

Giroux, H. (2004). Critical pedagogy and the Postmodern/Modern divide: Towards a pedagogy of democratization. *Teacher Education Quarterly, 31*(1), 31-47.

González, N., Moll, L. C., & Amanti, C. (2009). *Funds of knowledge: Theorizing practices in households, communities, and classrooms.* New York: Routledge.

Henry, J. (1963). *Culture against man.* New York: Random House.

Kliebard, H. M. (2004). *The struggle for the American curriculum: 1893-1958* (3rd ed.). New York: Routledge Falmer.

Kohn, A. (2000). *The case against standardized testing: Raising the scores, ruining the schools.* Portsmouth, NH: Heinemann.

Kumashiro, K. K. (2008). *The seduction of common sense: How the right has framed the debate on America's schools.* New York: Teachers College Press.

López-Bonilla, G. (2011). Narratives of exclusion and the construction of the self. In R. Rogers (Ed.), *Critical discourse analysis in education* (2nd ed., pp. 46-67). New York: Routledge.

Luke, A. (2000). Critical literacy in Australia: A matter of context and standpoint. *Journal of Adolescent and Adult Literacy, 43*(5), 448-461.

Meier, D., Kohn, A., Darling-Hammond, L., Sizer, T. R., & Wood, G. (2004). *Many children left behind: How the No Child Left Behind Act is damaging our children and our schools.* Boston: Beacon.

Pine, G. J. (2009). *Teacher action research: Building knowledge democracies.* Thousand Oaks, CA: Sage.

Pinar, W. F. (2012). *What is curriculum theory?* (2nd ed.). New York: Routledge.

Ravitch, D. (2010). *The death and life of the great American school system: How testing and choice are undermining education.* New York: Basic Books.

Saavedra, C. M. (2011). Language and literacy in the Borderlands: Acting upon the world through testimonios. *Language Arts, 88*(4), 261-269.

Sleeter, C. E. (2005). *Un-standardizing curriculum.* New York: Teachers College Press.

Yosso, T. J. (2005). Whose culture has capital? A critical race theory discussion of community cultural wealth. *Race Ethnicity and Education, 8*(1), 69-91.

CHAPTER 6

EVALUATIVE EXPRESSIONS IN PERSUASIVE ESSAYS BY L2 LEARNERS OF JAPANESE

Kazumi Matsumoto
Ball State University

Introduction

Language is used to accomplish various purposes in a wide range of social contexts. One of the most common purposes of language use is to persuade others in a variety of social settings, such as advertising, politics, debate, and so on. For the academic context, students are likely to work on persuasive writing to convince the reader of a stated opinion or belief. In order to successfully complete persuasive writing, writers need to not just describe facts, but also express their own opinions, feelings, attitudes, and perceptions while keeping in mind readers' expectations. Hyland (2010) noted that such interactivity of the language is expressed using linguistic resources, such as evaluation (Hunston & Thompson, 2000), appraisal (Martin & Rose, 2007; Martin & White, 2005), and stance (Biber & Finegan, 1989; Hyland, 2010). Previous studies suggest that control of evaluative resources as interpersonal language is essential in constructing a critical voice and building persuasion in essays (Liu, 2013), but this topic has been largely ignored in foreign language writing. Therefore, the present study examines how FL writers use evaluative resources to express themselves in their persuasive essays compared to native speakers, and how FL writers' language proficiency affects their usage of resources.

Evaluative Expressions
Appraisal Framework in English

Evaluative expressions are important tools for writers in negotiating with readers, because such projects reveal the writer's feeling or stance (Hyland, 2005), and the ability to control the expressions seems to be correlated with literacy skills (Abasi, 2014). The Appraisal Framework proposed by Martin and White (2005) covers a variety of works on evaluation in other research and includes a broad range of categories for evaluative resources (Hyland, 2005). Thus, the present study utilizes this framework to examine such expressions.

The framework indicates how linguistic resources represent the way in which speakers and writers share their emotions, values, and judgments with listeners and readers. The theory consists of three major categories: *Engagement*, *Attitude*, and *Graduation* (see Martin & White, 2005, p. 38, for a figure that illustrates this framework).

Engagement concerns how speakers or writers make a connection with their audience by means of showing their negotiable or nonnegotiable viewpoints. This can be achieved by using *monoglossic* or *heteroglossic* positioning (Marin & White, 2005). The monoglossic viewpoint does not show alternative views of the current assertion, whereas the heteroglossic viewpoint indicates alternative viewpoints available, rather than giving a decisive opinion. An example of the former is, *The government strategy for recession in Japan is not effective*, while examples of the latter are, *I think that the government strategy for recession in Japan is not effective* or *There can be no denying the government strategy for recession in Japan is not effective.*

Attitude refers to a way of feeling and is represented by three subcategories: *affect*, *judgment*, and *appreciation*. Affect describes positive and negative feelings or emotions associated with reacting to behavior, texts, or phenomena such as happiness or sadness; such emotions can be expressed directly or implicitly. For example, *My parents gave me a ticket to Japan for my birthday present. So I am very* **happy**. The bolded word, *happy*, is an example of a positive affect. In another example, *Since I did not do any interesting stuff, I was* **bored**. *Bored* is an example of negative affect. Judgment, on the other hand, is concerned with evaluating people and their behaviors in terms of normality, capability, tenacity, veracity, and propriety, and it contains both positive and negative evaluations (Martin & Rose, 2007; Martin & White,

2005). For example, *I trust him because he is always **honest** with me. But I do not trust his brother because he is a **deceitful** person.* The bolded *honest* is an example of positive judgment, while the word *deceitful* is an example of negative judgment (c.f. Martin & White, 2005). The last element of attitude is appreciation, which indicates aesthetics, the speaker's or writer's evaluation of things, especially that which he or she makes or performs (Martin & Rose, 2007; Martin & White, 2005).

The last component of the Appraisal Framework is Graduation. The Graduation system concerns the intensification of a speaker's or writer's appraisals and dialogic positioning. The properties based on the attitudinal system, including affect, judgment, and appreciation, are gradable; they can be realized by a greater or lesser degree of positiveness or negativeness. Moreover, the properties found in the Engagement system can be scaled by the speaker's or writer's intensity, with up-scaling and down-scaling, or the degree of sharpening and softening values. This grading can be done by either *force* or *focus*. Force concerns the degree of *intensification* of quality as well as process, and *quantification* of numbers, mass/presence (e.g., as small, thin and bright) and proximity (e.g., near, recent, distant)/distribution (e.g., short-term, wide-spread). An example to illustrate this point, *The service in this restaurant is **slightly** better than in the other.* The word *slightly* indicates the degree of service quality. Another subsystem of Graduation, focus, concerns whether non-attitudinal items have sharp or soft values, such as *a true friend* versus *a kind of friend*. Graduation entities can control the degree of positive or negative evaluation in a text, leading to effective writing (Martin & White, 2005).

The Japanese System of Attitude Based on the Appraisal Framework

Since the Appraisal Framework was created for the English language, there is the risk that this model will not perfectly fit another language such as Japanese. Sano (2011) claimed that there are three main issues in using attitude in the Appraisal Framework to analyze the Japanese language. The first issue is that the English Attitude system cannot capture the precise relationship between two synonyms in terms of semantics. For instance, both *mezurashii* (unusual) and *itan* (unorthodox) express rareness as evaluation, but *mezurashii* can be used for both people and things; *itan* can only be used for people. Since the English system of Attitude has two separate categories for evaluation toward people (judgment) and toward things we make, performances we give and the value we place on things (appreciation) (Martin & White, 2005), the English system of Attitude cannot capture the similarities in terms of the meaning between these words (Sano, 2011). Another problem raised by Sano is that Japanese evaluative expressions sometimes cannot clearly be separated from judgment (evaluating behavior) to appreciation (evaluating things). This is because the Japanese language uses ideograms, which represent a concept, an idea, or an object without necessarily becoming a word (Yamaguchi, 2007), and many ideograms attach to other ideograms to become words evaluating either behavior or things (Sano, 2011). For instance, the character 要 'yoo' (necessary/important) can become the following words by adding another ideogram: 要人 'yoo jin' (important person), categorized as judgment, and 要所 'yoo sho' (important place), categorized as appreciation (Sano, 2011). The last issue in the English Attitude is that each English evaluative expression fits into a single sub-category, whereas Japanese words can sometimes be classified into multiple sub-categories; 勇猛 'yuu moo' (brave and strong), for example, can be classified as both *tenacity* (how dependable) and *capacity* (how capable), sub-categories of judgment (ibid.). In order to overcome the issues mentioned above, Sano reconstructed attitude in the Appraisal Framework for the Japanese language, shown in Figure 6.1. A description of the system follows.

As in the English system of attitude, evaluative expressions in the Japanese system of attitude refer to one's personal feelings and reactions, evaluation of behavior, and evaluation of things (c.f. Martin & White, 2005). All of the terms fall into one of two groups: either positive or negative, or *Internalized* or *Externalized*. Internalized refers to the *appraiser*'s (a person who evaluates) feelings and acts (e.g., 悲しい 'kanashii' [sad]; 泣く 'naku' [to cry]; 楽しむ 'tanoshimu' [to enjoy]), and is roughly matched with affect and partially with *reaction*, which is a sub-category of appreciation in the English system of Attitude. Externalized refers to characteristics of *Appraised* (the target that is evaluated) (Sano, 2011). Internalized has two sub-categories: *passive* and *active*. Passive refers to evaluative expressions which describe the Appraiser's emotional reaction and roughly matches the categories, such as *happiness*, *security*, and *fear* in affect in the English Attitude system (e.g., その手紙を読んだら、嬉しくなった。'sono tegami wo yondara, ureshiku natta' [When I read the letter, I became happy.]).

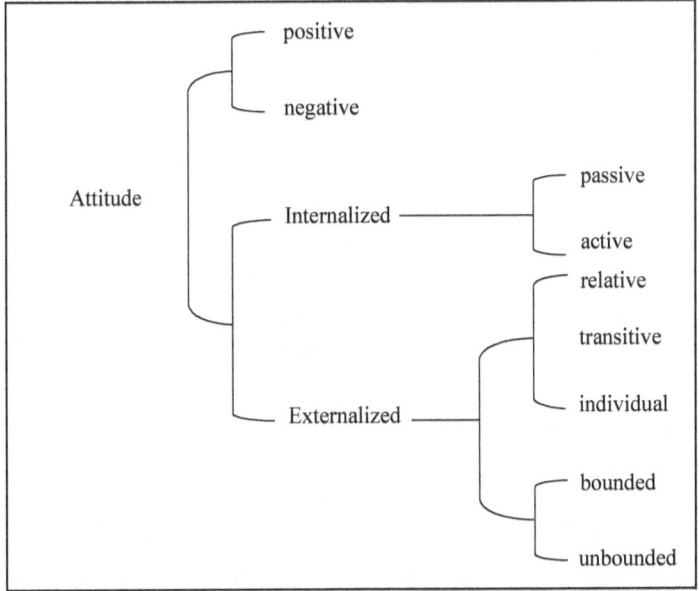

Figure 6.1. Japanese system of Attitude (Sano, 2011, p.17)

The second sub-category of Internalized is Active, which roughly matches with the categories *satisfaction* and *desire* in the English Attitude system. An example of this sub-category is 私が恨んでいる男はここにいる。'watasi ga urandeiru otokowa kokoni iru' (A guy who I hate is here).

Externalized falls into both categories: *boundness* and *group-oriented-ness*. Boundness includes expressions related to people, people's activities and the value of things, and has two sub-categories: *bounded* and *unbounded*. Bounded includes expressions to evaluate only human subjects, behavior, or products of human activities and is approximately the same as judgment with a part of appreciation in the English Attitude system. For instance, 落ち着きがない 'ochitsukiga nai' (antsy) can be used only for the subject of human activity or human behavior. Another feature, unbounded, on the other hand, describes evaluations of things that humans make or perform, or value placed on things (e.g., 公平だ 'koiheida' [fair]). This feature is more or less appreciation with partial judgment from the English Attitude system. Another group in Externalized is group-oriented-ness, which represents evaluation based on group value, comparison with others, or stand-alone value. Group-oriented-ness includes three sub-systems: *relative, transitive,* and *individual*. Relative refers to the evaluation of the target based on a comparison with others and shows the uniqueness of the target that is evaluated (e.g., 他の作品と比べると独特だ 'hokano sakuhinto kuraeruto dokutokuda' [It is unique in comparison to other works]). Transitive describes the influence of the target that is evaluated. An example of transitive is 髪形を変えたら魅力的になった。'kamigata wo kaetara miryokuteki ni natta' (Her new hairstyle makes her attractive.). The last sub-category is individual, which refers to stand-alone evaluation without any consideration of other related factors or any comparison with others (e.g., 彼は聡明だ。'kare wa soumei da.' [He is intelligent]) (See Center for Corpus Development, National Institute for Japanese Language and Linguistics, 2012 and Sano, 2011 for further details).

Since attitude is the most studied subsystem within the Appraisal Framework (Liu, 2013) and given that Sano (2011) has offered a Japanese version of the model, the present study examined thirty persuasive texts produced by low-intermediate learners of Japanese, high-intermediate learners of Japanese and native speakers of Japanese to investigate how evaluative expressions were used in persuasive essays to express the writer's position, attitude, or feeling, and to communicate with the audience using the Japanese Attitude system.

Attitude in L2 Essays

In recent years, interpersonal communication has received more attention in the L2 writing field because proper use of interpersonal language contributes to the success of written texts in the L2 (Abasi, 2014; Lee, 2008; Liu, 2013). Previous research has examined how evaluative expressions as interpersonal language were used in L2 texts using the Appraisal theory (Martin & White, 2005), which is the most systematic and comprehensive system to use in analyzing interpersonal language since this covers broader categories compared with other research (Hyland, 2005). As previously noted, Attitude is one of the three components of the Appraisal Framework.

Abasi (2014) examined evaluative expressions in film critiques written in Persian as a foreign language to see how successful writers used expressions. The study analyzed 50 written samples in Persian produced by advanced learners of Persian over a 15-week period. The study found that texts with few or no evaluative expressions seemed to give an impression to teachers that students were disengaged from the task. In addition, certain evaluative language correlated positively and negatively with students' essay grades. Specifically, expansive Engagement expressions such as, *It is believed that....* which explicitly express alternative positions in texts, along with appreciation, contributed to higher grades, while affect expressions indicating emotion or personal feelings tended to more frequently appear in essays with low scores than the ones with high scores. Moreover, the instructors preferred an objective tone in the students' film critiques using appreciation (evaluation of the movie) (e.g., *This is one of the worst films I have ever seen...* [p. 238]) and judgment (evaluation of a person or a person's behavior) (e.g., *I think Kiarostami focuses on a specific audience too much...* [p. 238]), rather than using affect (personal feelings) (e.g., *I didn't like this film* [p. 237]). It seemed that proper use of appreciation and judgment expressions were the key to encoding their viewpoint from a personal to an impersonal manner. In addition, the study suggested that variety of evaluative choices contributed not only to recognize the writer's voice, but also to perceive that the student disengaged with the task. More interestingly, the assessment of the film critiques placed great more value on the intended meanings in the texts with evaluative expressions, rather than grammatical accuracy.

In another study, Xinghua and Thompson (2009) examined argumentative essays in Chinese and English produced by one Chinese student to compare attitude expressions in Chinese and English essays using Appraisal Theory (Martin & White, 2005). The study revealed that, unlike Abasi's study (2014), the writer successfully used ample affect resources to interact with other attitudinal expressions, such as judgment, to express a strong sense of persuasion, by presenting both emotional and moral support for the thesis. According to White (2012), writers can express attitudinal meanings in an explicit and an implicit manner, and writers can evoke one of the attitudinal meanings by using another attitudinal resource. The writer in this study successfully used a strategy, which was to evoke judgment or appreciation, by using affect to achieve persuasiveness in an English essay. Another important finding is that the writer used a variety of resources in the English essay, whereas in the Chinese essay, only specific categories of resources were used. The writer used only a few affect resources in the

Chinese essay and more appreciation resources than judgment in the Chinese essay, while there were more judgment resources than appreciation in the English essay. The author suggested that this was due to a reflection of traditional Chinese rhetorical perspective; Chinese argumentation should be less personal, and the appreciation resource, valuation, is a typical main resource in Chinese writing. The results of the two studies regarding Chinese and Persian essays indicate that evaluative expressions are affected by cultural standard rhetorical perspectives, such as socio-cultural value.

Liu (2013) examined argumentative essays produced by 30 third-year English majors at a Chinese university to see how they supported their opinions in their essays. The results showed that among theree attitude subsystems, the essays included more appreciation and judgment than affective expressions; this pattern was recognized as characteristic of the argumentative genre (Lee, 2006; Liu & Thompson, 2009). The tone of the essay was more appreciative than offering personal and ethical judgment (Hood, 2004). In addition, judgment resources often appeared in nominalized form, which makes an essay more impersonal and formal. For example, ...*the compound achievements (judgment: capacity) from all those fields stimulates the speed of civilization....* (p. 47). This study also found that the high-score essays included affect resources, whereas the lower graded ones had no affect items. The higher graded essays successfully projected a clear writer's stance by using authorial (first person) affect through behavior surges or raising feelings. For instance, ...*we are deeply impressed (affect: satisfaction) by the interaction cooperation and humanitarian aids which play vital roles in those events...*(p. 45). Affect resource that shows personal emotion is necessary to express the writer's perspective.

Lee (2008) also found significant characteristics of attitudinal resources used in persuasive essays through examining high- and low-score essays produced by 12 L2 learners of English. The study found that the successful writers were able to use a variety as well as a high number of attitudinal resources in their arguments. Successful writers made full use of judgment invoking through exploiting other attitudinal resources, such as affect or appreciation. Moreover, similar to the finding in Liu's (2013) study, the attitudinal resources were highly nominalized in the high-score essays. The following is the example in Lee (2008, p. 48):

This work ethic has been a major contributing factor in the rebuilding (judgment: capacity) of Japan after the widespread destruction and devastation (affect: unhappy) caused by the humiliating (affect: unhappy) defeat (judgment: capacity) in the Second World War (judgment: propriety/affect: security) (Invoked attitude; judgment: propriety/appreciation: valuation).

The nominalization of affect resources makes the agency of the sensor of the emotion vague, depersonalizes the essays and displays formality.

All in all, based on previous studies, attitude resources reflected quality in the writing. The high-score essays included more variety as well as more attitudinal resources than the counterparts. In addition, successful essays used resources in both an explicit and an implicit manner. In particular, the strategy evoking one of the attitude resources through exploiting other attitudinal resources is a salient feature of successful essays. In addition, the higher-graded ones depersonalized the essay by using formal words such as nominalization, as well as affect invoking judgment, even though they used affect resources, which showed subjective feelings.

To date, there have been no studies that have examined evaluative expressions in Japanese persuasive essays, so it is not known how L2 learners of Japanese utilize attitudinal resources to communicate with readers. In order to understand how L2 writers manage interpersonal communication in Japanese persuasive essays and to apply this to the pedagogy of L2 writing, the present study investigated: (1) what kind of characteristics of attitudinal resources there are in L2 persuasive essays, and (2) how use of evaluative expressions differs across language proficiency levels.

Methodology

Participants

The present study includes two types of participants. The first group is learners enrolled in the fifth, sixth and seventh semesters of Japanese courses at a large Midwestern university (N=20) and they were chosen from 66 students enrolled in the Japanese courses. Only native speakers of English were selected to avoid an influence from their L1. This is because previous studies suggested that there was L1 transfer in L2 writing (e.g., Kobayashi, 1984; Kubota, 1998; Zainuddin & Moore, 2003). The writing assignments were required in the Japanese courses and the process approach to writing instruction was used. The essays were graded using modified ACTFL written proficiency scales (see Appendix 6.1) and divided into two groups: (a) 10 low-intermediate learners and (b) 10 high-intermediate learners. The other group, serving as the control group, was ten native speakers of Japanese; they were included in the present study in order to compare learners of Japanese with native speakers of Japanese. The criteria of native speaker participants in this study were (1) the subjects were over 18 years old, (2) they were college students, graduate students, recent college graduates, or of a similar age; they had a minimum requirement of high school graduation in Japan, (3) their majors and minors were not related to languages such as Japanese or other languages, (4) they had no experience with intensive English composition classes; general English courses with a writing component at Japanese universities were allowed, and (5) they had no experience with study abroad or long stays abroad.

Task

The subjects were asked to write persuasive essays in Japanese as one of the assignments in the courses and the essays were written outside of class. The persuasive topic was *A Social Issue* such as air pollution, human abuse, the educational system, national insurance and so on, and the first draft was used for the analysis.

Grading Criteria and Inter-Rater Reliability

The present study used a modified version of the ACTFL written proficiency scale (see Appendix 6.1) in evaluating the essays. Each text was rated by two raters so as to minimize rater subjectivity: the researcher in the present study and a Japanese instructor. Both raters have acquired an official ACTFL OPI tester certificate and know ACTFL proficiency scales fairly well. The inter-rater reliability between the researcher and the instructor was .88 for the persuasive texts and the rating of the essay was reliable, indicating that the proficiency groups were valid.

Measures

The present study examines evaluative expressions using the Japanese Attitude system (Sano, 2011) based on the Appraisal Framework proposed by Martin and White (2005) as quantitative and qualitative analyses. The Appraisal Framework consists of three categories: (a) Attitude, (b)

Graduation, and (c) Engagement; however, since only Attitude has a Japanese version, the present study examines only attitude resources to see how the writers show their attitudes in the text. In addition, in order to examine what type of Attitude resources are used by low-intermediate, high-, and native Japanese writers, the present study also investigates a variety of expressions in the essays produced by the three groups as well as the lexical frequency level in the essays based on the frequency rate in the written corpus. The less frequent vocabulary is considered rare and more complex than the ones that frequently appear in the written text.

Results
Characteristics of Attitudinal Resources in L2 Persuasive Essays

In order to see the variety as well as the degree of lexical complexity of the resources, the present study calculates the variety of expressions (Type/Token), as well as the average frequently appearing rate of evaluative expressions based on the data of the frequency rate of these words in the Balanced Corpus of Contemporary Written Japanese (Center for Corpus Development, 2012).

The results show that all the groups expressed their feelings or attitudes by mainly using negative connotation words with Externalized expressions, including both judgment and appreciation, rather than Internalized resources (affect) due to the topic of the essays, that is, social issues.

Table 6.1

Average ATTITUDE resources of persuasive essays in Japanese across three levels

	Positive	Negative	Internalized (Affect)	Externalized bounded (Judgment)		Externalized unbounded (Appreciation)	
				Explicit	Implicit	Explicit	Implicit
Low-Intermediate	10.4	22.5	1.7	12.9	1.8	17.7	3.0
High-Intermediate	14.9	22.2	5.2	6.8	4.1	14.3	6.8
Native Speakers	12.8	26.4	6.1	8.3	5.8	13.0	7.2

More superficially, Externalized (appreciation) resources were predominantly used and Internalized resources are the least used in the essays. These results indicate that the persuasive essays in the L2 are more or less descriptive.

Differences in Evaluative Expressions Across Proficiency Levels

This section focuses on differences in evaluative resources across the three proficiency levels. The results suggest that the participants with higher proficiency use a higher number, as well as greater variety, of the evaluative resources (see Figure 6.2).

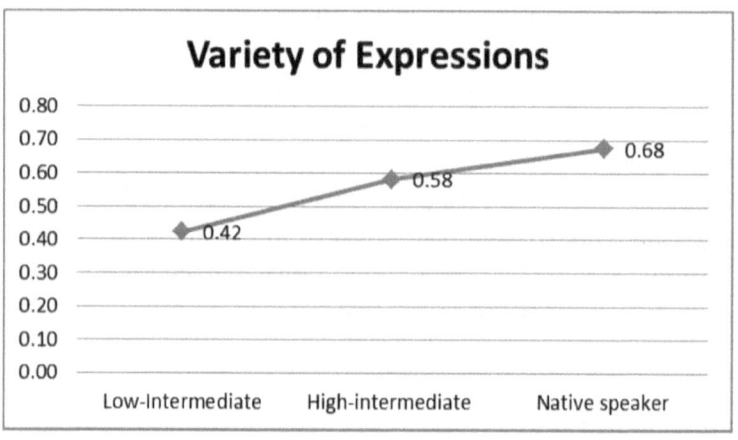

Figure 6.2. Average Diversity of Evaluative Expressions Across Three Proficiency Levels

More interestingly, the participants with higher proficiency, the high-intermediate as well as the native speakers of Japanese, utilize more words expressing emotion. However, the writers who use more affect resources are able to express their stance or that of someone else clearly than the ones who do not use much. The following examples illustrate a variety of uses of Affect resources:

Example 1. Low-Intermediate
不法入国者[- externalized; bounded]は違法[- externalized; uncounded]で
いるので、就労ビザがありません。そして、不法入国人[- externalized;
bounded]は学生のアルバイトが<u>したい</u>[- internalized; active]です。
Illegal aliens do not have working visa because they are illegally in the country.
They **want to have** a part-time job which college students usually do.

Example 2. High-Intermediate
税金が高く[- externalized; unbounded]なったら、払っている人たちが<u>文
句</u>
[-internalized; active]を言います。
If taxes are raised, people paying the tax will **complain** about it.

Example 3. High-Intermediate
部落民[- externalized; bounded]は差別されなかった[- externalized;
bounded]というわけではありません。残念[- internalized; passive]なこと
に、人の考え方が変わりませんでした。[t: - externalized; bounded]
It is not saying that outcast people were not discriminated against.
Unfortunately, the way people think has not changed.

Example 4. Native Speakers
それが人間にとって、食べたり、使ったり、有益な[+ externalized;
unbounded]生き物ならば、いなくなっては<u>困る</u>[- internalized; passive]理
由も分かります。
If the animal is beneficial for humans to eat or use, we understand the reason
why we feel **uneasy** when the creature becomes extinct.

As previous studies have found, successful writers in the present study evoke judgment or appreciation by using affective resources, whereas the low-intermediate learners use only a few affects. The followings are examples of how internalized resources evoke externalized connotation:

Example 5. High-Intermediate
熱帯雨林の破壊[- externalized; bounded] が止まらなかったら、生物
を永遠に失う[- internalized; active]かもしれません。[t – externalized;
uncounded]
* [t] indicates indirect expressions.
If we do not stop forest destruction, we may **lose** living creatures forever.

Example 6. Native speakers
犯罪者[- externalized; bounded]でもない人の追跡を行うなんて恐ろしい[- internalized; passive]ことだなと思いました。[t –externnlized; bounded]
* [t] indicates indirect expressions.
I think that tracking a person who is not criminal is **awful**.

Example 7. Native speakers
これまで通り、当局が好ましくない[- internalized; passive]と考える外国サイトを遮断しているのです。[t – externalized; bounded]
* [t] indicates indirect expressions.
As in the past, Authorities block foreign websites they **do not approve**.

Also they expressed judgment or appreciation by employing Engagement resources. The high-intermediate and the native speaker groups express their personal stance indirectly, whereas the low-intermediate group tends merely to describe the facts. The following are examples to illustrate how participants used engagement resources to evoke externalized connotation:

Example 8: High-Intermediate
An Engagement resource [べきだと思います; should] evokes Externalized connotation.
これらの美しい[+ externalized; unbounded]熱帯雨林を破壊すること を止めるべきだ[と思います。[t – externalized; bounded]
* [t] indicates indirect expressions.
I believe that we **should** stop destroying the beautiful rainforest.

Example 9: High-Intermediate
An Engagement resource [わけにはいけないと主張しています; propose] evokes Externalized connotation.
若い[+ externalized; bounded]女性をセックスシンボルとして表している漫画やゲームを売らせるわけにはいけないと主張しています。[t – externalized; bounded]
* [t] indicates indirect expressions.
She proposes that we **should not** sell comic books or games that depict females as sex symbol.

Example 10. High-Intermediate
An Engagement resource [べきです; should] evokes Externalized connotation.

人々と社会は汚染[- externalized; unbounded]をし過ぎ、二酸化炭素をたくさんだしています。（ちきゅうの）温度がもっと上がらないように、皆はもう少し気をつけるべきです。[t: - externalized; bounded]
* [t] indicates indirect expressions.
People and society pollute the planet too much and create much CO2. Everyone **should be careful** not to raise the temperature of our planet.

Example 11. Native speaker
An Engagement resource [なければならないと思います; must] evokes Externalized connotation.
私たちは児童虐待[- externalized; bounded]について知ることからはじめなければならないと思います。[t: externalized; bounded]
* [t] indicates indirect expressions.
We **must** start increasing awareness of child abuse.

The present study also examines the frequency rate of the evaluative resources based on the Japanese written corpus. The results reveal that the high-score essay groups use less frequently appearing words in their persuasive essays (see Figure 6.3).

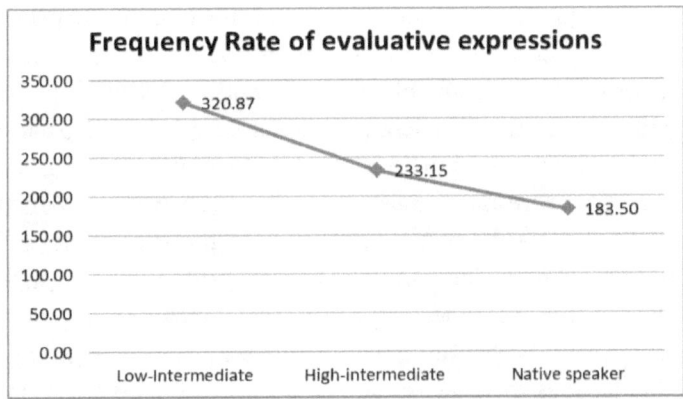

Figure 6.3. Average Frequency Rate of Evaluative Expressions Across Three Proficiency Levels

Based on the ANOVA analysis, there are significant differences between the low-intermediate group and the native speaker group (p < .05). The less frequency words are typically more complex words and they are often nominalized nouns. Similar to nominalization in English, the Japanese language uses nominalization, which often consists of two compound Chinese characters. For example, the word 'difficult' can be written 難しい 'muzukashii' and 困難 'konnan' in Japanese. The latter is typically recognized as more complex and formal than the former one; therefore, it appears less frequently in the written corpus. The high-score essays tend to contain more complex and formal words than the low-score essays.

Discussion

Previous studies suggested that appreciation and judgment resources were more often used than affect resources as characteristics of the argumentative genre (Lee, 2006; Liu & Thompson, 2009). Liu (2013) found that English persuasive essays contained mainly appreciation resources, whereas Liu and Thompson's study (2009) found that more judgment items appeared than appreciation in English persuasive essays. Moreover, the previous studies suggested that types of evaluative expressions in persuasive essays were affected by socio-cultural perspectives. Liu and Thompson (2009) revealed that Chinese persuasive essays used more appreciation than judgment, while English essays used more judgment than appreciation resources. This is a reflection of the traditional Chinese rhetoric; less disclosure of personal emotion and avoidance of direct ethical judgment occurs in Chinese traditional essays. Since Japanese shares some cultural aspects with Chinese, and many Japanese cultural aspects were adopted from China, results for Japanese essays can be similar to those of Chinese essays. The results of the present study, however, indicate that the Japanese persuasive essays are similar to those written in English, which is supported by Liu (2013). Japanese persuasive essays include more appreciation (unbounded) resources than judgment across all proficiency groups, which indicated that Japanese persuasive essays mainly focused on evaluation of the significance of things or events, and English and Japanese persuasive essays use a similar amount and type of resources.

Lee (2008) found that high-score essays included a greater number as well as variety of evaluative resources. The present study also suggests that native speakers of Japanese as well as high-intermediate learners use a greater variety and greater number of evaluative resources than the low-intermediate group. The text analyses imply that the low-intermediate group has a shortage of resources. The English argumentative essay consists of three stages: (1) thesis statement, (2) arguments, and (3) textual closure (White, 1998). The low-intermediate group repeats similar sentence structures with the same vocabulary over and over in the first three stages, resulting in fewer diverse expressions used in their essays than in the other groups. One of the essays contains similar sentences structures with the same vocabulary approximately five times in the essay. It seems that the topic the writer tried to express is a significant social issue, but since she or he is not able to describe the details of the issue, she or he ends up repeating the same sentences to try to prove that the issue is significant.

Another finding is regarding lexical complexity. Previous studies found that nominalized words often appeared in argumentative essays, and this nominalization made the essays more formal (Lee, 2008; Liu, 2013). The present study found that the low-intermediate group used more frequently appearing expressions, whereas native speakers used less frequently appearing expressions in their persuasive essays. Less frequent words in this case typically are words that combined two ideograms (Chinese characters). These words are more complex and formal and are often used in formal articles. However, the low-intermediate group may focus more on constructing comprehensible sentences with their language knowledge rather than being cautious of what vocabulary they should use or how their text sounds.

The most important result that the present study suggests is the usage of affectual resources. Previous studies found that successful writers used a strategy that invokes one of the three attitudinal resources by exploiting different types of resources; for example, judgment can be evoked by using affect resources (Lee, 2008; Liu, 2013). The present study supports these previous studies. Both the high-intermediate group and native speakers of Japanese use Internalized (affect) or Engagement resources to successfully evoke judgment or appreciation, whereas the low-intermediate group explicitly uses evaluative expressions. Most of the low-intermediate students' essays do not include affectual resources to interconnect with other evaluative expressions. Affect describes personal feelings that contradict the characteristics of persuasive essays, but proper usage of affectual resources can help to communicate a strong personal stance in a persuasive essay (Lee, 2008). The low-intermediate group is not able to use the strategy to express their stance properly because of a shortage of Japanese language resources and language skills, so they end up only describing the social issue in the essay.

Conclusion

The results of the present study clearly reveal the characteristics of persuasive essays in Japanese as well as differences in evaluative expressions across the three language proficiency levels. Japanese persuasive essays predominantly use unbounded (appreciation) resources to describe social issues. However, due to limited resources, the low-score essays have fewer, as well as less variety, of evaluative resources. The essays produced by successful writers contain more complex and more formal lexical items than the ones by their counterparts. In addition, invoking attitudinal strategy is a key to producing a persuasive essay with a strong personal perspective. These findings are very similar to those found in English persuasive essays, which indicates that rhetoric in Japanese and English persuasive essays may not be very different.

Despite the results of the present study with respect to socio-cultural aspects show that there are not many differences between Japanese and English, it is undeniable that languages are affected by social and cultural aspects because language and society have a deeply rooted relationship and always influence one another. Since the previous study clearly showed the influence of the cultural aspect in essays and the present study examines only one category of the Appraisal Framework (Martin & White, 2005), more analyses of influence of social and cultural aspects should be done to understand how FL writers clearly present their stance, opinions or feelings in a variety of social contexts.

References

Abasi, A. (2014). Evaluative choices and rhetorical impact: American learners of Persian as a foreign language writing to appraise. *International Journal of Applied Linguistics, 24*(2), 224-249.

Biber, D., & Finegan, E. (1989). Styles of stance in English: Lexical and grammatical marking of eveidentiality and affect. *Text, 9*(1), 93-124.

Center for Corpus Development. (2012). *Japanese dictionary of appraisal-attitude-(JAppraisal Dictionary)*. Tokyo: National Institute for Japanese Language and Linguistics.

Hood, S. (2004). Managing attitude in undergraduate academic writing: A focus on the introductions to research reports. In L. Ravelli & E. R. (Eds.), *Analyzing academic writing: Contextualised frameworks* (pp. 22-44). London: Continuum.

Hyland, K. (2005). Stance and engagement: A model of interaction in academic discourse. *Discourse Studies, 7*(2), 173-192.

Hyland, K. (2010). Researching writing. In B. Paltridge & A. Phakiti (Eds). *Continuum companion to second language research methods* (pp. 191-204). London: Continuum.

Hunton, S., & Thompson, G. (2000). *Evaluation in text: Authorial stance and the construction of discourse*. Oxford: Oxford University Press.

Kobayashi, H. (1984). Rhetorical patterns in English and Japanese. *TESOL Quarterly, 18*, 737-738.

Kubota, R. (1998). An investiation of L1-L2 transfer in writing among Japanese university students: Implications for contrastive rhetoric. *Journal of Second Language Writing, 7*, 69-100.

Lee, S. (2006). *The use of interpersonal resources in argumentative/persuasive essays by East-Asian ESL and Australian tertiary students.* Unpublished PhD thesis, University of Sydney, Australia.

Lee, S. (2008). Attitude in undergraduate persuasive essays. *Prospect, 23*, 43-58.

Liu, X. (2013). Evaluation in Chinese university EFL students' English argumentative writing: An appraisal study. *Electronic Journal of Foreign Language Teaching, 10*(1), 40-53.

Liu, X., & Thompson, P. (2009). Attitude in students' argumentative writing: A contrastive perspective. In L. J. O' Brien & D. S. Giannoni (Eds.), *Language studies working papers* (Vol. 1; pp. 3-15). Reading: University of Reading.

Martin, J. R., & Rose, D. (2007). *Working with discourse: Meaning beyond the clause.* London: Continuum.

Martin, J. R., & White, P. R. (2005). *The language of evaluation: Appraisal in English*. New York: Palgrave Macmillan.

Sano, M. (2011). *Reconstructing English system of attitude for the application to Japanese: An exploration for the construction of Japanese dictionary of appraisal.* Paper presented at the 38th International Systemic Functional Congress, Portugal, July. Retrieved from http://researchmap.jp/mu50eix2d-14097/#_14097

Silva, T., & Brice, C. (2004). Research in teaching writing, *ARAL*, 70-106.

White, J. (1998). Getting the learners' attention: A typographical input enhancement study. In C. Doughty, & J. Williams (Eds.), *Focus on form in classroom second language acquisition* (pp. 85-113). Cambridge: Cambridge University Press.

White, P. R. R. (2012). The language assitutde, arguability and interpersonal positionin. *The Appraisal Website: Homepage.* Retrieved from http://www.grammatics.com/appraisal/index.html

Xinghua, L., & Thompson, P. (2009). Attitude in students' argumentative writing: A contrastive perspective. *Language Studies Working Papers, 1*, 3-15.

Yamaguchi T. (2007). *Japanese linguistics: An introduction*. London: Continuum.

Zainuddin, H., & Moore, R. A. (2003). Audience awareness in L1 and L2 composing of bilinguial writers. *TESL-EJ, 7*, 1-18.

Appendix 6.1
Holistic Writing Scale

Writing Holistic Score based on ACTFL Guidelines

1 point
- Writers have no practical communicative skills.
- Writers can copy and produce isolated and basic strokes in the language.
- If writers have adequate time and familiar cues, they can reproduce a very limited number of isolated words or familiar phrases.

2 points
- Writers supply minimal information, but the task is not accomplished due too little information.
- Writers are able to copy or transcribe familiar words or phrases.
- Writers are able to reproduce a modest number of isolated words and phrases which they have learned in context.
- Vocabulary and phrases are extremely limited.
- Writers show a high degree of accuracy when writing on well-practiced, familiar topics using limited formulaic language.
- With less familiar topics, accuracy dramatically decreases.
- Errors in spelling or in the representation of symbols may be frequent.
- There is little evidence of functional writing skills.
- Writing may be difficult to understand even by those accustomed to reading the text of non-native speakers.

3 points
- Writer's performance is partially satisfied with limited information.
- Writers can express themselves within the context in which the language was learned, relying on learned vocabulary and phrases.
- Writers can recombine learned vocabulary and structures to create simple sentences on very familiar topics.
- Writing consists mostly of short and sometimes incomplete sentences in the present tense.
- But the language the writer produces may only partially communicate what is intended.

- Their vocabulary and syntax are still limited.
- Since their vocabulary is very limited, they may often borrow vocabulary from their first language or other languages that they have learned.
- Writers at this level are often comprehensible to native speakers used to the writing of non-native speakers, but gaps in comprehension may occur.

4 points
- The performance completes the task with minimally adequate information.
- Most sentences are combining and recombining learned vocabulary and structures.
- Writing productions are short with basic subject –object –verb word order.
- Writing productions are written mostly in present time with occasional and often incorrect use of past or future time.
- Some cohesive devices are used. The devices are limited to the most frequently used ones such as *soshite* or *sorekara* and the usage is sometimes inappropriate.
- Writing tends to be simple sentences often with repetitive structures.
- There may be basic errors in grammar, word choice, punctuation, spelling, and in the formation and use of non-alphabetic symbols.
- Their vocabulary is still limited and may borrow vocabulary from their first language or other languages that they have learned.
- Their writing is understood by native speakers used to the writing of non-native speakers, although additional effort may require.

5 points
- Writers manage to complete the task with adequate information.
- Writers are able to write short, simple communications, compositions, descriptions, and requests for information that are based on topics related to common events or personal experiences.
- Writers control syntax in non-complex sentences and in basic verb forms.
- Writers are able to express personal meaning by combining and recombining learned materials.
- Those writings are mainly sentence length and some strings of

sentences appear by using simple cohesive devices as well as complex structures such as *ga, node* or *tara.*
- Writing consists of discrete sentences loosely tied together.
- Most writing is framed in present tense with inconsistent references to other time frames.
- Writers can be understood readily by native speakers used to the writing of non-native speakers.

6 points
- Writers are able to complete their task relatively well with quite adequate information, but errors may still be evident.
- Writers narrate and describe in major time frames (present, past, and future) using connected discourse of paragraph length with some consistency with some inaccuracies and inconsistencies.
- Tense and aspect are not consistently accurate.
- Writers connect sentences into paragraphs using a limited number of cohesive devices that tend to be repeated.
- Writing includes numerous and perhaps significant errors.
- Writers are able to use a relatively wide variety of vocabulary; however, a few words may be still evident from their first language influence.
- Writers can be understood by native speakers used to the writing of non-native speakers, but gaps in comprehension may occur.

7 points
- Writers perform adequately with detailed information.
- Writers shows ability to narrate and describe in major time frames with some control of aspects.
- Writers are able to combine and link sentences into paragraph length and structure.
- Writers can incorporate a limited number of cohesive devises, leading to much redundancy and awkward repetition.
- Writers can control simple target language sentence structures and partially control complex structures.
- Their writing consists of a wide variety of lexical items.
- Writers can be understood by native speakers who are not used to writing produced by non-native speakers, but some additional effort may be required in reading the text.

8 points
- Writers are able to handle a task with more than adequate information.
- Writers can narrate and describe with detail in all major time frames.
- Writing performance includes various vocabulary words which express thoughts clearly by rephrasing and elaboration.
- Writing also contains some variety of cohesive devices in texts of several paragraph in length.
- Frequently appearing syntactic structures appear with good accuracy, but errors may appear in complex sentences and punctuation, spelling, formation of non-alphabetic symbols.
- Writing incorporates organizational features both of the target language and the first language.
- Writing is understood readily by native speakers not used to the writing produced by non-native speakers.

9 points
- Writers can produce language on a variety of topics with significant precision and detailed information.
- Writers are able to deal with most social and informal situations with appropriate conventions.
- Writers can describe and narrate in all major time frames with good control of aspects.
- Writers demonstrate some ability to develop some arguments and construct hypothesis.
- Writers may have difficulty in dealing with a range of topics in abstract, global, or impersonal areas.
- Writers use a wide range of vocabulary and have good control of a full range of structures, but sometimes errors appear.
- Native speakers are sometimes distracted from messages because of inadequacy in texts in terms of grammar, syntax, vocabulary, and so on.
- Writers are not consistently flexible in changing their style corresponding to different tasks and readers.

10 points
- Native-like writing; only extremely minimal errors present
- Such errors, if they exist, do not interfere with comprehension and they rarely distract native readers,

LANGUAGE, POLICY, AND SOCIETY

CHAPTER 7

LINGUISTIC IMPLICATIONS THAT AID OR UNDERMINE NATIONAL UNIFICATION:
In France and the Former Yugoslavia

Anton Vegel
Kent State University

France is a well-established nation-state frequently referenced in language policy research (Gillo, 1989; Hélot & Young, 2006; Martel, 2008; Raijman, Davidov, Scmidt, & Hochman, 2008). Yugoslavia, on the other hand, is not nearly as infamous for its ambiguous linguistic policy as it is for its elaborate historical dilemmas (Hélot, 2003, p. 255; Watchtel, 1998, p. 10). A prototype of contemporary French language ideology began to emerge as early as the seventeenth century, as patois became a public debate among the high-status public (Grillo, 1989, p. 24). Many of the problems within France particularly comprised the southern region and the Occitan regional languages or the northern standards, *"Langue d'Oïl,"* as opposed to the southern regional dialects, *"Langue d'Óc"* (Ager, 1999, p. 15). In congruence, the former Yugoslavia inhabited many national questions, including linguistic unification, despite its pre-established constituent regions (Rogel, 1994, p. 13; Wachtel, 1998, p. 28). Furthermore, the constituent state of Slovenia was in a particularly singular position throughout the emergence of Yugoslav national image due to its highly developed literacy initiatives, linguistic exclusivism, and educational autonomy, providing, eventually, a quick secession (Čopič & Tomc, 2000, p. 48; Dolenc, 2006, pp. 481-483). These two regions or state constituents were the subjects of many similar national questions, and although they are in many ways contextually different, their internal movements of isolation and autonomy, and external pressures of marginalization and stratification provide a useful base for comparison.

To approach these goals, a brief literary review in an attempt to frame the terminology and contextual aspects used throughout the study is initially presented. The usage of the terms "nation-state" and "ideology" (and various facets) are established for comparisons within the work of various fields such as sociolinguistics, sociology, social psychology, anthropology, political science, and philosophy. To support this approach, Kymlicka and Grin (2003) suggest that the study of intervention of language within a state requires an "interdisciplinary approach, yet integrated perspective" due to the unstated aims of nationalist ideologies in "overt and covert policy goals," which demand a broad yet detailed focus (p. 25). In further support, Edwards (1996) suggests a framework that emphasizes a need for embedding language in context and in cross-disciplinary study due to the complexity of understanding social life and the obvious role that deep meaning can provide for contextual comparisons (p. 34). Edwards further describes this framework within the notion of "a changing world," which includes the realities of language contact, policy and planning, sociolinguistic mobility, the struggles of majority and minority languages, and negotiated identities of which "none can be adequately understood in temporal, geographical or disciplinary isolation" (p. 36). This approach then begs that we take a broad view in understanding the relationships between language policies, national linguistic realities, ideologies, and the historical and contemporary motivations of policy-makers and public opinion.

Nation-State

"Nation-state" is a ubiquitous term compounded to define, not only the unity of a nation and a state, but also the implications that both include (Breuilly, 2001, p. 791). Although the specific parameters that define a nation and a state and the examples of nation-state are not always clearly apparent, visible, or marked, they are necessary dimensions for labeling particular groups (Edwards, 2003, p. 563). In an attempt to make the usage of these terms clearer, support for a general sense of nation-state will be provided through a comparison of general and specialized definitions and literary support.

"Nation" may be used, according to Lakoff (2001) as a term used to *describe* the public or "civic body" within a state as a political expression (p. 101).

Suny provides two additional usages specific to early modern Europe which "maintain a territorialized sense" and *indicate* the people of a state or: (a) ethnicity, shared culture, and language, and (b) people living under a sovereign state (Suny, 2001, p. 338). Accordingly, people who are part of a nation share culture, language, or history and constitute what is inherently needed for political expression. In other words, the realizations of these cultural or ethnic units constitute the world's multiple significations of nation-ness and nationalism or cultural artifacts and myths (Wachtel, 1998, p. 4).

As Grillo (1989) cites Ernest Renan in his 1882 nationalist address "*Qu'est-ce qú une nation*," this notion of cultural artifact emphasizes that what makes a nation is people "having done great things in the past" creating a "nation as association" or "nation as community" (Grillo, 1989, p. 22). In Rene's view, the population does not choose national identity, and in nationalist theory, people must be taught the very idea of nationalism (Wachtel, 1998, p. 3). Wachtel cites that we can find evidence of "creators" of nations. For example, Paul Brass (1991) expresses nationalism as being the creation of elites, who make decisions and reinforce what defines a nation, which then "trickles down" to the population (Brass, 1991, p. 16; Wachtel, 1998, p. 3). Benedict Anderson (1983) also claims that the elites who construct a nation must be aware of the fact that their "eternal" nation is bound by cultural systems that are used as "frames of reference" and make nations seem "plausible" (Anderson, 1983, pp. 9-13; Wachtel, 1998, p. 3). Therefore, it seems as though a nation is a cultural artifact and a myth based on past unity or confederation (not just sensed) that gives natural justification to historical intentions, and makes "contingency appear eternal" (Wachtel, 1998, p. 3). Woolard and Schieffelin (1994) also maintain the point that a "naturalizing move" is vital for the ideological process of nationalism, nationality, and nation-ness to remain, in ideology, "universally and/or timelessly true," re-emphasizing that the ideology of nation and its eternal sense is not only created it is also taught (p. 58).

In consideration of these creations, we can further delineate that because nations are often made up of constituents that have experienced some form of unity or confederation in the past, nations will always have some kind of historically based contingent aim (Edwards, 2003, pp. 562-563). Watchtel (1998) additionally describes the nation as a created union in that even if such a union may appear heterogeneous to an observer, there is some choice involved in prescribing to national consciousness, which is similar to Freud's principle of narcissism, and which is further reflected in Raijman et al. (2008) as constituting elements of chauvinism and patriotism (Watchtel, 1998, p. 2). Furthermore, even if a heterogeneous image of nation somehow seems to be a reflection of reality, there is always some homogeneous device present within a nation. In line with Renan's *"Qu'est-ce qú une nation"* address, Kymlica and Grin (2003) claim that "nationalist ideology defines a 'normal' state as a state with one official language-'one state, one nation, one language'" (p. 21). Kymlica and Grin's definition then demands a deconstruction of "state."

"State" may be used to refer to the defined border that is maintained through sovereignty and the degree to which the national consciousness exists within the population of a geological region (Kaiser, 2001, p. 322; Sugar, 2001, p. 285). Due to the sovereignty that is contingent within a state, majority-based action of state power must often be tolerated by minorities. This tolerance as a condition of majority sovereignty can include influences on educational institutions and cultural associations (Kymlica & Grin, 2003, p. 21). This condition of sovereignty also refers to a sense that minorities are in some way tolerated within a nation or a state. Furthermore, Radan's (2004), description of nation, which includes both an inseparable sense of nation and state, similarly to Rene, emphasizes that "in the romantic theory of self-determination the nation is briefly defined as a group linked by a common history and culture bound to national ideology that the nation should be autonomous, united and distinct in its recognized homeland" (2004, p. 12).

This amplifies that a sense of "nation-state" refers to a notion of "common destiny," but, in addition, it also marks the congruence between nation, state, and the particular interests of the dominant national ideology in state functions (Kaiser, 2001, p. 315; Yuval-Davis, 2001, p. 297). Radan (2004) suggests in a more conceptual sense that "a state based upon a nationalist ideology is thus a nation-state. Such a state will in most cases also contain a segment of the population who are not members of the nation in question" (p. 12). Differences between Rada (2004), Yuval-Davis (2001), and Kaiser (2001) suggest a gap between strictly defining the ideological base of the state versus the framework in which a state is dominated. As expressed by Edwards (2003), although "nation" is lexically defined and clear criteria are present to identify it, the parameters that stipulate our identifying culture and ethnicity (and elements of sovereignty) are far more complex (p. 563). Therefore, the use of nation-state will be used to refer to an observed orientation that includes notions of constructedness, sovereignty, and autonomy, and the presence of homogeneous devices, contingent aim, and a sovereign state based within a national ideology.

Language Ideology

Silverstein (1979), in "Language Structure and Linguistic Ideology," makes it a point to clarify that linguistic ideologies (or ideologies about language) are judgments based on "rationalization of justification" through the perception of "language structure and use" (p. 193). These perceptions, as he cites Benjamin Lee Whorf and Franz Boas, are the result of cultural or linguistic observations filtered through a "range of personal experience" emphasizing the categorical rationalization of language. He later cites Boas (1911) in terms of objectification in language as being contingent on worldview, habitual thought patterns, or the natural logic of the speaker (pp. 197, 201). Throughout his paper he presents and demonstrates a connection between metapragmatics and ethno-metapragmatics and concludes that a mere description of grammatical structures is incredibly insufficient for understanding the micro-scale of linguistic research (pp. 208, 233). Recognizing not only philosophy of language ideology but also the social dynamics in which ideologies exist, Silverstein points to "linguistic relativity."

Basil Berstein's work on language and communication codes led to his constructions of theory on thought and social structure. Despite being controversial, he was able to show disparity in labor, the family, and the school (Sadovnik, 2001, p. 2). Similarly, Grillo (1989) cites Berstein's term "speech economy," which people are ranked, are not equally competent in, or have equal access to, emphasizing the educational contributions to social stratification. Further, this "speech economy" is made up of modes (or codes) that link ideologies and economic structures (pp. 184-185). Berstein's work makes a point of illuminating the relationships between language and social structure and the difficulty in transcending linguistically ordained structures and stratification.

Further criticality in language ideology is often concerned with the legitimation of social domination (particularly fields such as critical discourse analysis). Such a position often illuminates marked language policy issues and linguistically based social maintenance (Woolard & Schieffelin, 1994, pp. 56-57). Because of the connections between language, social perception, and policy, language ideology can be an essential point in identifying reasons for the creation and maintenance of educational and linguistic policy. Studies in language ideology can potentially show considerations of power and implications of literacy strategies (particularly different in regions of south France and the former Yugoslavian states) and how links of cultural categories are formed (similar to Grillo's perspective of "speech economy") by either laypeople or by national elites, highlighting that often "public problems hinge on language ideology" (pp. 66, 72).

In further verification of the effects of language ideology, Edwards' article "Refining Our Understanding of Language Attitudes" (1999) surveys research techniques of both a qualitative and quantitative nature. Edwards first cites Lambert's "matched-guise" technique, in which, in qualitative design, a subject guesses two or more speech varieties while generalizing attitudes about the speaker (Edwards, 1999, p. 103; Lambert, 1960, pp. 44-45). Edwards further surveys evidence of social perceptions and language attitudes as predictable through linguistic triggering of "received pronunciation." This attends to the historical shift of the notion of linguistic supremacy and deficiency, which linguists have deflated and, in turn, shown that there is a difference between inherent value and imposed norms (Edwards, 1999, pp. 102-104). These "received pronunciations" or linguistic triggers might be again related to Freud's principle of narcissism, or in Bourdieu's voice "fetishism" (Bourdieu, 1991, p. 52; Watchtel, 1998, p. 2). As for quantitative research on understanding social perceptions through language perception, Strand (1999) provides a study focused on the perception of the boundaries between the fricatives /s/ and /ʃ/ (as well as the gradient between the two fricatives) and how these perceptions change with expectations of a male or female speaker. Citing May's (1979) previous study, in differentiating the boundaries between these two fricatives, the individuals' guessed boundaries changed due to their expectation of either a male or female speaker. Strand took the study further with what she coined the "Face Gender Effect." Strand found that when presented with an image of a face, the individual differentiated the boundary between the /s/ and /ʃ/ based on the perception of whether the face was male or female (1999, p. 91). As Strand explains the results, "social expectations might have an influence on such low-level basic processes as phonological categorization" adding to our understanding of cognitive processing and language perception (1999, p. 93). The overall correlation and purpose for citing this study is to convey empirical support for the belief that perception of language changes systematically and that these perceptions delineate social consciousness (Edwards, 1999, p. 103; Strand, 1999, p. 93). What then are the powers of these perceptions on ideology?

Ideological Emergence and National Questions
France

Abbé Grégoire (1750-1831), a well-cited priest and revolutionary, contributed to the development of a compulsory system of public primary education and the universalization of the French language (Grillo, 1989, p. 24). In 1794, Grégoire tackled the mounting patois contentions with a questionnaire prompting for the opinion of the professional-status public. In detailing the ideas behind the linguistic initiatives, "enlightenment" was used as a maxim for intellectual, moral, and political improvement (of which could apparently be met with the emergence of a monolithic society) (p. 32). Gégoire's influence is cited in Brunot (1967), which emphasizes the recognition and support of French because of its clarity of reason and application of principles, which were, at the time, perceived to be true manifestations of liberty (p. 33). Moreover, in 1794, Grégoire presented his report, "The Grégoire Report," at a national convention emphasizing "the need and means to eradicate the patois and to universalize the use of the French language," and therefore, heightening the sense that, within the early modern period, stigma against the patois was beginning to mount and support for unification was clearly becoming an objective (pp. 23-24). These notions of "purity" express the ideological standardization in France within its early modern period and further attend to the linguistic formations of "definite ideas about what is 'correct' in language use and the belief that all people should use language in the same 'correct' way" (Jones, 2011, p. 505).

Bernstein's "speech economy" and "sociolinguistic code theory" had been motivated by the need to understand the reasons for stratification between language speakers (Grillo, 1989, p. 181). Particularly, this need was apparent due to his findings regarding social stratification in education between working class children and middle class children. The deficit that he describes is not one of a linguistic sense (in terms of linguistic deficiency), but instead one relating to "dominant code" and "contexts of production" that are consequently instrumental to categorizations of class, systems, and success (Grillo, 1989, p. 181; Sadovnik, 2001, pp. 2-3). Bernstein's divergent points provide some ideological support for the direction of the heightened linguistic cultivation in France, *la langue cultivée*, which had been a contingent goal since the seventeenth century, and which regulation through language reform had aided well (p. 190). In affirming the hegemonic tasks of linguistic cultivation, Grillo cites Brunot (1930) on the Académie Française in stating that these regulations were providing the language with "exact rules, rendering it pure, eloquent and capable of dealing with arts and science," again stressing a hierarchical order based on competence and "linguistic policy, whose goal [was] to spread French, and only French" (Grillo, 1989, pp. 134, 180, 190; Martel, 2008, p. 199).

Yugoslavia
The former Yugoslavia's constituent regions, modular borders, linguistic questions, changing political structures, and national ambitions create a broad field of research that is far greater than any one study can respectfully address. Therefore, to best frame a comparison between France and the former Yugoslavia's regional constituents, educational policies, and linguistic implications, the emergence of the Yugoslavian national idea and the particular implications of the constituent state Slovenia will be detailed first.

By the end of the eighteenth century, the former South Slavic groups began to emerge in tripartite cultural structures. Three faiths, three separate societies under separate governmental systems, and variously refined cultural practices began to flourish within the once unified groups. These initial changes show somewhat of a marked beginning in ideas "awakening" from the ideological influences of early Germanization on southern regions (Rogel, 1994, p. 3; Wachtel, 1998, p. 13). In 1830, the idea of Yugoslavia began to emerge from intellectuals in reaction to many of these influences, pointing to unification as an appropriate response, motivated by shared ethnic backgrounds, cultural traditions, and linguistic features; the risks of being divided from neighbors due to a lack of united ideology; and as a means of providing territorial and ideological group defense against Austro-Hungry (Wachtel, 1998, p. 13). These seemingly meticulous acts of caution within the pre-Yugoslavian polities (in response to dominant powers) are brought to point by Marko Hren in an interview in Ljubljana by Jill Benderly (1990), as he describes that "from this part of the planet it is easy to overcome the attachment to any state or devotion to any artificial form of identity [and furthermore, that] the only natural policy for living peacefully is nourishing good links, understanding and cooperation" (Benderly & Kraft, 1994, p. xii). Hren seems to describe a perspective in which national cultivation is based on necessity due to the particular geopolitical contexts, illuminating some deeper ideological justification for the region's unification process.

Linguistic questions began to emerge soon after Yugoslavian ideas first began to develop. In 1850, a linguistic initiative emerged between Croatia and Serbia through the creation and adoption of a synthetic language, Serbo-Croatian, in an effort to reduce deficient literary idioms while providing a communicative device to the "united" population. At least seven major Croatian, Serbian, and Slovenian writers, philologists, and linguists presented the initiative at a conference in 1850 (Rogel, 1994, p. 13; Wachtel, 1998, p. 28). However, most Slovenians resisted artificial cultural merging of any kind as they did not feel that a political union was contingent on linguistic or cultural homogeneity, similar to Watchtel's (1998) perspective, stating that some kind of homogeneous device is always present within national consciousness although this device may not necessarily be universally synonymous or defined (p. 2).

Slovenians' rejection of linguistic and cultural unity within Yugoslavia, even in its emergent stages, may have been the result of their linguistic and cultural accomplishments up until that point. Slovenians had been developing independent national ideas during the nineteenth century, despite being divided into multiple regions, potentially further contributing to their inclinations towards autonomy (Rogel, 1994, p. 3). Before 1850 and the Serbo-Croatian linguistic question, Slovenians had made considerable linguistic developments. Jernej Kopitar, a Slovene linguist, helped established Slovenian as discrete within the South Slavic languages through his "monumental work on grammar." Anton Slomšek further propelled Slovenian by introducing the language into local schools and administrations, and Janez Bleiweis initiated newspaper publications for farmers and craftsmen in 1843 (p. 7). These services would prove to be the foundation of the following centuries' Slovenians.

In 1848, the idea of a united Slovenia was becoming ever more necessary for the stateless and geographically surrounded Slovenians (Italians, Austrian

Germans, and Hungarians) as the Austrian Empire, which failed to recover its economic infrastructure as a result of the Spring of Nations, emerged as a German national state. The linguistic objective for unifying the divided Slovenians into "one administrative unit" was, consequently, in part due to the demand that the Slovenian language be maintained as the language of the schools and administrations over German (pp. 3, 8). Despite an overwhelming support for Slovenian unification among intellectuals, gains made by the Slovenians in areas of linguistic isolation within local administrations, a movement towards manhood suffrage, and the domination of Ljubljana between 1860 and 1890, the mounting influence of Germanization on the still fragile and dismembered territories resulted in a modest submissive turn in the Slovenian ideology. Edwards describes these national pressures as being responded to by groups more spontaneously or cautiously than others and that these responses are related to the groups' willingness to accept isolation, as he states that the cost of isolation is beyond what most groups have been historically "willing to pay" (Edwards, 1996, p. 30). Slovenians were not an exception to these geopolitical pressures. However, instead of rigorously pursuing unification in isolation, which would have likely led to linguistic weakening or at least cultural suppression, and of which, as Marko Hren explained, would have been a contradictory reaction to their geopolitical ideology, Slovenians reluctantly accepted the necessary resolution to their biggest problems (Vodopec, 1994, p. 32).

The Yugoslavian ideology began to gain political strength in 1914 as a larger unification tool to respond to the influence of Hungarian power and Germanization (Rogel, 1994, pp. 12-13). In part due to Serbia's success in World War I, it was able to impose "centralist rule and ... hegemony on the new state [of Yugoslavia]." Consequently, Slovenians still supported and preferred independent unification for themselves through autonomy (Rogel, 1994, p. 16). At least from a linguistic perspective, the Slovenians with their accomplishments in a unified literacy (before the formation of the Yugoslavian state) were able to maintain autonomy in Belgrade because Slovenian had not been established in many of the southern regions, providing linguistic exclusivism that helped Slovenians avoid what Woolard and Schieffelin detail as "considerations of power [that have the potential to] significantly affect literacy strategies" (Rogel, 1994, p. 17; Woolard & Schieffelin, 1994, p. 66). Without this optimum reality Slovenian language and culture may not have survived in the same wholeness as it had managed to within Yugoslavia, providing a marginal avoidance from many of the sociopolitical outcomes that often inevitably lead to "political and cultural negotiations and change" (Edwards, 1996, p. 32). As a perspective of the Slovenian's linguistic accomplishments up to the twentieth century, literacy rates in Slovenian regions reached 80-90% as a result of the mid-nineteenth century linguistic and ideological unification initiatives, including accessible published reading materials that contributed to their political voice and national consciousness (Rogel, 1994, p. 11).

Outcomes and Evidence of Aiding or Undermining
France: Educational Implications

In his book "Language and Symbolic Power," (1991) Pierre Bourdieu states that "in the process which leads to the construction, legitimation and imposition of an official language, the educational system plays a decisive role" (p. 48). France's universalism through educational initiatives helped facilitate the revision and reform of French society that ultimately valued a unified ethnic community. Within a cultural framework based on monolithic national objectives, the eradication of divergent educational initiatives was an essential factor in realizing a contingent aim for France (Fenet, 2004, p. 39). These motions can be seen as acts of "linguistic isolationism" whereas the most "authentic" language is suspended from other influences, resulting in a "well-defined, static, and relatively homogeneous social grouping" that only "authentic speakers" have access to (Bucholtz, 2003, p. 404). This objective methodology emphasizes stratification in literacy initiatives and ultimately social perceptions. In a modern French context this gap is still widening, but the biggest questions, directed towards national identity in the eighteenth century, regarded the polarity between northern and southern regions, positing questions of integration, separation, or tolerance (Martel, 2008, p. 186). The southern regional questions presented a few significant conditions to the French unification process. These questions were, in Bucholtz's terms, related to "essentialism" and the connection between perception and power. Essentialism further addresses tools created for "redressing" power imbalances against "illegitimate," "trivial," or stigmatized groups (p. 401). Particularly, the southern Occitan region in France is referenced as one of two language labels, *"Langue d'Óc"* (language of the Occitan region or

Occitanians with a negative connotation referring to language deficiency) and "*Langue d'Oïl*" (northern dialects including standard French) (Ager, 1999, p. 15; Bourdieu, 1991, p. 46).

As Martel (2008) further details, the linguistic singularity of the southern regions laid a roadblock in the path of the national myth of a "pure" French history (p. 210). The ideological nation building of the eighteenth and nineteenth centuries demanded a "reassuring story" of unification that could not include Occitan exceptionalism or proliferation and instead pressured to reject anything limiting or jeopardizing French unity (p. 216). However, if the history books were written in favor of the Occitan regions' social, cultural, and linguistic initiatives, it might not have seemed unreasonable. The southern region could have emerged as a separate nation "with a separate language and conscience" although this may have been an unlikely scenario despite the fact that there were movements attempting to facilitate such separatist or at the very least counter-marginal outcomes (p. 210). Such a historical shift was avoided, as Martel (2008) describes the Occitan region in "The Troubadours and the French State:"

> They lacked the institutions that could match the weight and influence of national French culture and national ideology [and] socially speaking, the protagonists of the Occitan renaissance [were] mainly middle-class men: marginal to the cultural elite in terms of class as well as geography [and] possessed neither the cultural capital nor the actual wealth and social weight to enable them to establish an alternative society milieu. (p. 217)

The implications of these situations fall well into place with nation building goals. An argument in favor of the developments of homogeneous nation-states might well be that homogeneous nations are often more economically developed, educationally well advanced, and generally more ideologically and politically stable although in so many cases anticipations and desires for these goals easily lead to guidance through stricter authoritarian measures (Fishman, 2007, p. 152). Furthermore, Ager (1999) describes a genuinely present fear, which is likely promoting French policy (a fear that is not exclusive to France), of "social fragmentation," and even the "destruction of universalism or of [the] myth of ethnic Frenchness" (Fishman, 2007, p. 85; Raijman et al., 2008, p. 201). Hélot (2003) further maintains, in close parallel to Ager, that supporting diversity in policy reflects an aim for society that supports diversity and as a result may mislead national contingent aim (p. 274). As Raijman et al. (2008) further describe, these reactions to perceived threats and insecurities towards diversity due to national attachments "operate as a catalyst for the emergence of ethnic exclusionism" (Raijman et al., 2008, p. 200). Finally, Kymlica & Grin (2003) bridge a gap between national initiatives and educational outcomes, providing an explanation for France's lack of support of regional languages, which has marginalized regional efforts to succeed by forcing national unification and centralization. Kymlica and Grin further explain that "groups are (more or less) tolerated if they 'stay in their place'-that is, if they confine their claims to elementary schools, cultural associations and churches, but do not make any claims to share public space or state power" (p. 21).

Yugoslavia: Educational Implications
Similar to France, Yugoslavia had strong national unification goals towards centralization. Although these goals were based on the regionally shared myths and cultural artifacts from the eighteenth and nineteenth centuries, they were not nearly as clear or apparent as those in France. Despite this, Yugoslavia promoted its national contingent aim throughout the state. Pursuing this goal, a general sense of authoritarian power emerged throughout the 1970s particularly targeted at cultural dissonance (Čopič & Tomc, 2000, p. 43). In both cases, at least in terms of linguistic pressures, a generally "repressive" tolerance was pursued as the regions were stigmatized and marginalized (p. 42). Dissimilar is the fact that Slovenia was not only linguistically more developed through language use within educational institutions (than Yugoslavia) it also had a more developed linguistic infrastructure within administrative units (Dolenc, 2006, p. 486). Čopič and Tomc (2000) posit key requisites for cultural development in Slovenian. Initiatives can "encourage cultural development nationally"

1. by protecting cultural heritage as the foundation of national identity;
2. by developing a national, cultural infrastructure and information exchange;
3. by supporting current artistic creativity, especially in areas that are less well-developed culturally; and
4. by supporting cultural industries (e.g., publishing, film, and music; Čopič & Tomc, 2000, p. 48)

Dolenc (2006) provides statistical evidence that, particularly during the first Yugoslavia, Slovenians had been able to prepare themselves well for national development before Yugoslavian unification and, despite the Yugoslavian unification, were able to maintain their Slovenian identity through cultural infrastructure and industry, information exchange by means of accessible publications and control of the publishing administrations, and literacy rates based on singular language promotion through control of educational institutions in primary education and higher education (pp. 474-486). Dolenc further provides a comparison of literacy rates and primary school attendance throughout the Yugoslavian states. The Drava Banate, Ljubljana or Slovenian, literacy rates were 39% above the Yugoslavian average in 1931 (Drava: 94.4%, Yugoslavia: 55.4%) including Zagreb and Belgrade (Dolenc, 2006, p. 470; Wachtel, 1998, p. 135). The Drava region also proved dominant over the Yugoslavian educational average, in the "number of students per 1,000 inhabitants" (Drava: 141, Yugoslavia: 97) (Dolenc, 2006, p. 473). Furthermore, the number of periodical publications in 1936 (Drava: 174, Yugoslavia: 77), the number of publications juxtaposed to the number of periodical publications per million inhabitants (Drava: 90/170, Yugoslavia: 60/80), and finally, satisfying Čopič and Tomc's key requisites for cultural development and maintenance, the average number of cinemas per million inhabitants (Drava: 45, Yugoslavia: 23) are consistently found to be significantly higher in Drava (Ljubljana) regions than the Yugoslavian averages (Čopič & Tomc, 2000, p. 48; Dolenc, 2006, pp. 481-483). Although Slovenian regions might seem to have been superior on paper, they remained stratified and in many ways subordinate to Yugoslavia. Vodopivec cites Sundhausen (1982) in identifying the stereotype of the time: "The Serbs rule, the Croats debate, and the Slovenes work" (Vodopec, 1994, p. 31). Sundhausen gives some insight to the stratification within Yugoslavia at the time. Despite Slovenians' literacy rates, organized education, and developed cultural industries, they were well marginalized and, for nearly a century, remained nationally subordinate to Yugoslavia through artificial ideologies of "brotherhood and unity," "socialism," "titoism," etc. (Wachtel, 1998, pp. 2, 15, 231).

Ultimately, Yugoslavia eventually broke, and as Wachtel points out, in the 1990s, Yugoslavia was in a "perfect condition for breakup." This condition might be considered to be the results of the then dying political system and tired economic foundation although the Yugoslavian elites were still radically pushing for positive outcomes by pursuing nationalist policy and rejecting compromise to unification goals. Furthermore, Slovenia was abled to secede far easier than the other state constituents, delineating a clear picture of the Slovenians' unification accomplishments despite their stratification (Wachtel, 1998, p. 230). As the Slovenian party was consistently refused during the Fourteenth Party Congress in Belgrade, the members ultimately decided to walk out concluding their subordinate position to Yugoslavia and seceding soon after (Benderly & Kraft, 1994, pp. xi-xii). Unfortunately, other states were unable to secede as swiftly as Slovenia i.e. the Serb-Croat conflict and the brutal wars in Bosnia and Herzegovina validating the powers of nationalist ideologies (Wachtel, 1998, p. 231).

Conclusion

The goal of this study was to illuminate linguistic realities of subordinate regions and marginalized languages. In the Western eye, nation-state realization has demanded a homogeneous device to reach the beneficial status of nationalization (Anderson, 1983, p. 14). French national image emerged with strong linguistic ideological underpinnings (*la langue cultivée*) towards sovereign, autonomous, and homogeneous goals, and furthermore, emphasized the use of "pure" language (under maxim-based principles) and competence-based language policy (Grillo, 1989, pp. 33, 134; Martel, 2008, p. 188). From the onset of this ideological emergence, regional constituents of France were unable to develop the linguistic and cultural isolation and autonomy that could have provided a centralized authority for their individual goals (Martel, 2008, p. 217). These implications include control of educational systems, organization of literacy initiatives, and momentum towards secure cultural establishments or sociocultural outlets. In contrast, at the dawn of the Yugoslav question, and despite not being geopolitically unified, Slovenians had already begun to develop a national contingent aim through insulated education, literacy initiatives, and cultural establishments. In particular, Slovenians reached literacy rates beyond those of other Yugoslavian constituent states as well as remaining linguistically isolated from dominant hegemony (Dolenc, 2006, p. 470). These accomplishments both aided Slovenians' unification pursuits and ultimately undermined the unification and marginalization efforts of Yugoslavian elites (Benderly & Kraft, 1994, pp. xi-xii; Dolenc, 2006, p. 486).

References

Ager, D. (1999). *Identity, insecurity and image*. Philadelphia: Multilingual Matters Ltd.

Anderson, B. (1991). *Imagined communities reflections on the origin and spread of nationalism*. (revised & extended ed.). New York: Verso.

Benderly, J., & Kraft, E. (1994). Editor's introduction. In J. Benderly & E. Kraft (Eds.), *Independent Slovenia: Origins, movements, prospects* (pp. ix-xxii). New York: St. Martin's Press.

Boas, F. (1911). *Handbook of American Indian languages*. Washington, DC: Government Printing Office.

Bourdieu, P. (1991). *Language and symbolic power*. J. P. Thompson (Ed.). (G. Raymond & M. Adamson, Trans.). Cambridge, UK: Polity Press.

Bucholtz, M. (2003). Sociolinguistic nostalgia and the authentication of identity. *Journal of Sociolinguistics*, 7(3), 399-416.

Brass, P. (1991). *Ethnicity and nationalism theory and comparison*. Newbury Park, CA: Sage Publications Inc.

Breuilly, J. (2001) The state. In A. Motyl (Ed.), *Encyclopedia of nationalism* (pp. 769-792). London: Academic Press.

Brunot, F. (1967). *Histoire de la langue française des origines à nos jours: La révolution et l'empire* [History of the French language from the beginning to present day: The revolution and the empire]. Paris: Armand Colin.

Brunot, F. (1930). *Histoire de la langue française des origines à nos jours: Tome 1* [History of the French language from the beginning to present day, Vol. 1]. Paris: Colin.

Čopič, V., & Tomc, G. (2000). Threat or opportunity? Slovenian cultural policy in transition. *Journal of Arts Management, Law & Society*, 30(1), 42-52.

Dolenc, E. (2006). Comparative analysis of cultural development statistics: The case of the first Yugoslavia. *East European Quarterly*, 39(4), 465-489. Retrieved from https://www.questia.com/library/p4124/east-european-quarterly

Edwards, J. (1996). Language and society in a changing world. In T. Hickey & J. Williams (Eds.), *Langauge, Education & Society in a Changing World*, 1, 29-37. Bristol, PA: Multilingual Matters Ltd.

Edwards, J. (1999). Refining our understanding of language attitudes. *Journal of Language and Social Psychology*, 18(1), 101-110.

Edwards, J. (2003). Contextualizing language rights. *Journal of Human Rights*, 2(4), 551-571.

Fenet, A. (2004). Difference rights and language in France. In T. Judt & D. Lacorne (Eds.), *Language, nation, and state: Identity politics in a multilingual age* (pp. 19-62). New York: Palgrave Macmillan.

Grillo, R. D. (1989). *Dominant languages: Language and hierarchy in Britain and France*. NewYork: Cambridge University Press.

Hélot, C. (2003). Language policy and the ideology of bilingual education in France. *Language Policy*, 2(3), 255-277.

Jones, M. C. (2011). État présent: Diatopic variation and the study of regional French. *French Studies*, 65(4), 505-514.

Kaiser, J. (2001). Geography. In A. Motyl (Ed.), *Encyclopedia of nationalism: Fundamental themes* (Vol. 1, pp. 315-334). New York: Academic Press.

Kymlica, W., & Grin, F. (2003). Assessing the politics of diversity in transition countries. In F. Daftary & F. Grin (Eds.), *Nation-building, ethnicity and language politics in transition countries* (Vol. 1, pp. 5-27). Budapest: Local government and public service reform initiative.

Lambert, W., Hodgson, R., Gardner, R., & Fillenbaum, S. (1960). Evaluational reactions to spoken langauges. *Journal of Abnormal Social Psychology, 60*(1), 44-51.

Lankoff, S. (2001). Democracy. In A. Motyl (Ed.), *Encyclopedia of nationalism: Fundamental themes* (Vol. 1, pp. 101-120). New York: Academic Press.

Martel, P. (2008). The troubadours and the French state. *European Studies: A Journal of European Culture, History & Politics, 26*(1), 185-219. Retrieved from http://www.ingentaconnect.com/content/rodopi

May, J. (1976). Vocal tract normalization for /s/ and /s/. *Journal of the Acoustical Society of America, 48*, 67-73.

Radan, P. (2004). *The break-up of Yugoslavia and international law*. New York: Routledge.

Raijman, R., Davidov, E., Scmidt, P., & Hochman, O. (2008). What does a nation owe non-citizens? National attachments, perception of threat and attitudes towards granting citizenship rights in a comparative perspective. *International Journal of Comparative Sociology, 49*(2-3), 195-220.

Rogel, C. (1994). In the beginning: the Slovenes from seventh century to 1945. In J. Benderly & E. Kraft (Eds.), *Independent slovenia: Origins, movements, prospects* (pp. 3-21). New York: St. Martin's Press.

Sadovnik, A. R. (2001). Basil Bernstein (1924-2000). *Prospects: The Quarterly Review of Comparative Education, 31*(4), 678-703. Retrieved from http://www.springer.com/education & language/journal/11125

Sliverstein, M. (1979). *Langauge structure and linguistic ideology*. In P. R. Clyne, W. F. Hanks, & C. L. Hofbauer (Eds.), *The elements: A parasession on linguistic units and levels* (pp. 193-245). Chicago: Chicago Linguistic Society.

Smith, A. (2001) State and nation. In A. S. Leoussi (Ed.), *Encyclopaedia of nationalism* (pp. 286-288). New Brunswick, NJ: Transaction Publishers.

Strand, E. A. (1999). Uncovering the role of gender stereotypes in speech perception. *Journal of Language & Social Psychology, 18*(1), 86-100.

Sundhaussen, H. (1982). *Geschichte Jugoslawiens, 1918-1980* [Yugoslavian history, 1918-1980]. Stuttgart: W. Kohlhammer.

Sugar, P. (2001). Fascism and nationality. In A. Motyl (Ed.), *Encyclopedia of nationalism: Fundamental themes* (Vol. 1, pp. 285-296). New York: Academic Press.

Suny, R. (2001). History. In A. Motyl (Ed.), *Encyclopedia of nationalism: Fundamental themes* (Vol. 1, pp. 335-358). New York: Academic Press.

Vodopivec, P. (1994). Seven decades of unconfronted incongruities: The Slovenes and Yugoslavia. In J. Benderly & E. Kraft (Eds.), *Independent Slovenia: Origins, movements, prospects* (pp. 23-46). New York: St. Martin's Press.

Wachtel, A. (1998). *Making a nation, breaking a nation: Literature and cultural politics in Yugoslavia*. Stanford, CA: Standford University Press.

Woolard, K. A., & Schieffelin, B. B. (1994). Language ideology. *Annual Reviews Inc, 23*, 55-82. Retrieved from http://www.annualreviews.org/

Young, A., & Hélot, C. (2003). Language awareness and/or language learning in French primary schools today. *Language Awareness, 12*(3/4), 234-246.

Yuval-Davis, N. (2001). Gender relations and the nation. In A. Motyl (Ed.), *Encyclopedia of nationalism: Fundamental themes* (Vol. 1, pp. 297-314). New York: Academic Press.

CHAPTER 8

"POLICY BORROWING" AND COMPATIBILITY:
Critical Discourse Analysis on the CEFR, CEFR-J, and JF Standard

Shinji Kawamitsu
University of Massachusetts-Amherst

Introduction

Since the enactment of the Common European Framework of Reference (CEFR) in 2001, the Framework has been used worldwide and is now available in thirty-nine languages (Council of Europe, 2012). Integrating the Framework into a Japanese-as-a-foreign-language (JFL) context, instructors in Europe and the Japan Foundation developed their own framework in 2010, called the JF Standard. A number of educational institutions in and outside of Japan are integrating the JF Standard into their curriculum and using it as an assessment tool that provides teachers and students with communicative competence (Arai et al., 2012; Fujinaka & Nakao, 2013; Komatsu & Yokoyama, 2012; Kumano, Ito & Hachisuka, 2013; Shibuya, 2013). This "policy borrowing" can be seen not only in a JFL context but also in an English-as-a-foreign-language (EFL) setting in Japan. A handful of scholars in Japanese universities established a project team, discussing an "import" of foreign countries' language policy. In 2012, they developed the framework for the EFL context in Japan, with extensive financial support from the Japanese Ministry of Education, Culture, Sports and Technology (MEXT). This CEFR-J has now been adopted by more than 1000 institutions in Japan, including both formal educational schools and other private language institutes.

The two literacy approaches, JF Standard and CEFR-J, have accomplished the process of "borrowing" and "importing" supranational language policy into their own programs. However, a number of practical issues have emerged recently, including a strongly rooted notion of "English is the only foreign language," an ignorance of plurilingualism, and difficulties in integrating the CEFR with pre-existing courses resulting only in a "can-do" assessment (Haida, 2012; Rappleye, Imoto, & Horiguchi, 2011). This present study was designed to reexamine the compatibility of the CEFR in the two Japanese literacy approaches and to discuss theoretical and political issues for educational policy practices and the national development of language ideology[1]. Fairclough's critical discourse analysis or CDA (1989; 1992; 2003) is used as a theoretical framework for this study. This paper also employs systemic functional linguistics (Halliday & Matthiessen, 2004; Martin & White, 2005; Martin & Rose, 2007) as an analytical tool, especially for the description of the texts. This study argues that the newly established national language practices has the potential to be used as a tool to restructure the existing symbolic power and to further sustain the dominant position of one language and language ideology.

Background

CEFR is a framework of reference that describes what language learners have to learn in order to use a language for communication and what skills they have to develop to act effectively in a particular context (Council of Europe, 2001). It was designed by the Council of Europe in 2001, in an attempt to provide a transparent, coherent and comprehensive basis for language syllabuses, curriculum guidelines, teaching and learning materials, and the assessment of foreign language proficiency. One of the most influential sections of the CEFR is the can-do descriptor that defines learners' language proficiency with six common reference levels. Those proficiency levels have been used not only in education but also in the field of traveling and business all over the world.

Plurilingualism is the core political concept in the CEFR. It is a term used to discuss situations in which a person has communicative abilities in more than one language. Plurilingualism is different from multiculturalism, where multiple languages exist side-by-side in a society but are used separately. Garcia (2009, as cited in Canagarajah, 2009) graphically represents multilingualism and plurilingualism as in Figure 8.1. According to Canagarajah, multilingualism refers to separate, whole, and advanced competence in the different languages, almost constituting two or three separate monolingualisms where each language is kept distinct from the others. In contrast, in plurilingual competence, the directionality of influence is much more diverse. The languages may influence each other's development, and competence in the language is integrated, not separated (Canagarajah, 2009).

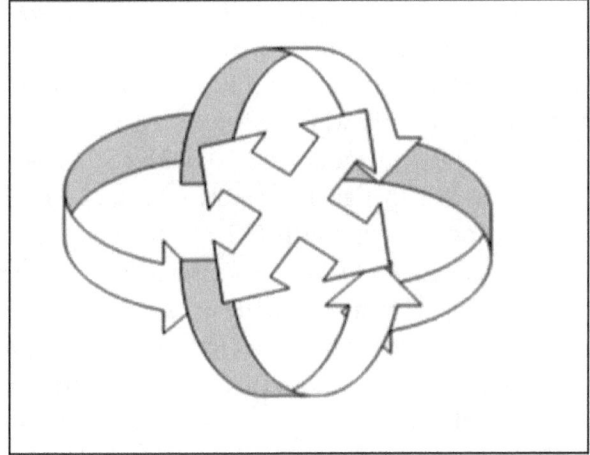

Figure 8.1. Plurilingualism and multilingualism. Source: Garcia, O. (2009). Bilingual education in the 21st century: A global perspective (p. 119). Oxford: Wiley-Blackwell. Used with permission.

Conceptualizing plurilingualism, the Council of Europe mentions their literacy approach in the CEFR as follows: "[the aim of language education] is no longer seen as simply to achieve 'mastery' of one or two, or even three languages, each taken in isolation, with the 'ideal native speaker' as the ultimate model. Instead, the aim is to develop a linguistic repertory, in which all linguistic abilities have a place" (Council of Europe, 2001, p. 5). For an open and flexible characteristic of the Framework, descriptions of individual languages have been developed after the enactment of the CEFR.

In 2010, the CEFR was designed specifically for Japanese-as-a foreign/second language (JFL/JSL) and developed as the JF Standard by the Japan Foundation. The Japan Foundation is an administrative agency independent from the Japanese Ministry of Foreign Affairs, and "Japan's only institution dedicated to carrying out comprehensive international cultural exchange programs throughout the world" (Japan Foundation, 2013, p. 2). While not much information is available regarding why and how the Japan Foundation integrated the CEFR into the JF Standard, the organization briefly describes its connection with the CEFR as follows: "The development of the JF Standard was based on the concepts that support the CEFR. By using the JF Standard, it is possible to see Japanese-language proficiency levels in a way that is based on the CEFR" (Japan Foundation, 2010, p. 6).

In 2012, the CEFR was also adapted in the field of EFL in Japan. A handful scholars and educators who have received the JSPS Kaken grant have borrowed the CEFR and modified it as CEFR-J. According to Tono and Negishi (2012), two of the leading scholars in the CEFR-J enactment, CEFR was borrowed and brought to the EFL setting in Japan because of the "undeniable fact that Japanese EFL learners' proficiency levels are extremely low among major developed countries in the world" (p. 6). In order to create clear attainment goals for the current education system and to provide motivations for language learners to learn English for true communicative purposes, the CEFR was brought into a setting with an urgent need of a "solution" (Rappleye, Imoto, & Horiguchi, 2011; Tono & Negishi, 2012).

Data Analysis

Drawing on Fairclough's CDA (1989; 1992; 2003), in this study, the documents of CEFR, CEFR-J, and JF Standard are deconstructed for: first, *description of text*; second, *interpretation of text and interaction*; and third, *explanation of interaction and social context*, in order to examine their theoretical and political compatibility with the CEFR. Since each of the three documents has a framework layout in the first three chapters, segments from those chapters are used as the primary data for this study. The following sections briefly illustrate the three stages in Fairclough's CDA procedure for each stage.

Stage I: Description of Text

Stage I is text analysis. Text is linguistically analyzed and deconstructed into formal data in this stage. Following are ten questions that Fairclough (1989) provides for the text analysis:

1. What experiential values do words have?
2. What relational values do words have?
3. What expressive values do words have?
4. What metaphors are used?
5. What experiential values do grammatical features have?
6. What relational values do grammatical features have?
7. What expressive values do grammatical features have?
8. How are (simple) sentences linked together?
9. What influential conventions are used?
10. What large-scale structure does the text have?

For questions one through four, text is deconstructed at a vocabulary level. According to Fairclough, examining ideologically contested vocabularies (i.e., synonymy, hyponymy, antonymy) allows us to see how vocabularies "ideologically 'place' a text" (p. 113). For the next four questions (five to eight), text is analyzed at a grammar level. Sentence is the unit of analysis, and multiple grammatical features (i.e., verbs and participant types, nominalization, conjunction, speech functions, etc.) are focused in these questions. For the last two questions (nine to ten), text is deconstructed for textual structures. Text type/genre is examined here, and elements in a text are "interpreted in accordance with what is expected at the point where they occur, rather than in terms of what they are" (Fairclough, 1989, p. 138).

In order to have delicate linguistic analysis, this present study modifies these ten questions and reorganizes them in terms of field, tenor, and mode based on Halliday's description of systemic functional linguistics (SFL). Following Halliday's notion of register, questions five and eight are reconceptualized in terms of field (i.e., experiential and logical meanings). Through this perspective of field, a text is deconstructed by transitivity analysis and causality analysis in order to see social action that is taking place (Halliday & Hasan, 1989). The following is a sample analysis of transitivity.

> The Common European Framework provides a common basis for the elaboration of language syllabuses, curriculum guidelines, examinations, textbooks, etc. across Europe. (Council of Europe, 2001, p. 1)

In the example above, the clause is labeled as a material clause, which construes "the procedure as a sequence of concrete changes" (Halliday & Matthiessen, 2004, p. 179). The doer of the change *provide* is *CEF*, which functions as an actor, and the object of the action is *a common basis* that is labeled as a goal. In this stage, clause type and participant are examined for every clause in the text, and emergent themes or patterns are highlighted.

Table 8.1
Sample analysis of transitivity

Clause	Process (Verb) Type		Participant		Participant		Participant (Range)		Circumstance
1	material	*provides*	actor	CEF	goal	a common basis	beneficiary	*for the elaboration*	across Europe

Along with this transitivity analysis, field is also examined by causality analysis. Every clause that has causal meaning, regardless of whether it is explicitly or implicitly, is deconstructed as cause and effect (or purpose and result) to see the logical connection in the texts. The following is a sample analysis of causality.

74. As there is such a variety of purposes,
75. there is no need for everyone to learn Japanese in the same way. (Japan Foundation, 2010, p. 9)

Table 8.2
Sample analysis of causality

Clause	Items	Cause	Effect
74-75	As	there is such as variety of purposes	there is no need for everyone to learn Japanese in the same way.

In the example in Table 8.2, the conjunction *as* functions as a causal marker that connects the two "there is" clauses. In this stage, how causality positions the framework and how the positioning of the framework further positions the text are examined.

The questions one, two, three, four, six, and seven are reorganized as tenor, the contextual parameters that construe interpersonal meanings. For tenor, speech function (declarative, interrogative, or imperative) and modality (e.g., can, might, must) are examined to see the kind of role relationship among participants that appears in a text (Halliday & Hasan, 1989). This current study also uses appraisal theory for tenor to see how a text evaluates oneself or others (Martin & White, 2005). As the last modification for this study[2], clause is used as a minimum unit of analysis instead of sentence, in order to see how the doer of particular actions in a clause is linguistically positioned, or sometimes, excluded or hidden in the texts. Field and tenor analysis are conducted on all of the clauses, and the data obtained from the text analysis is interpreted in the following stage.

Stage II: Interpretation of the Relationship Between Text and Interaction
This stage discusses how to interpret a text. According to Fairclough (1989), interpretations in CDA "are generated through a combination of what is in the text and what is in the interpreter, in the sense of the member's resources" (p. 141). Therefore linguistic features of the text are "cues" that activate elements of interpreters' member resources, and the interpretations are generated through the dialectical interplay of cues and member resources. This stage also examines intertextuality that examines discourses and texts from a historical perspective, and is often described as "the source of much of the ambivalence of texts" (Fairclough, 1992, p. 105). Conceptualizing Bakhtin and Kristeva's notion of intertextuality, Fairclough draws the inherent historicity and heterogeneity of texts into his notion of intertextuality that "highlights the diverse and often contradictory elements and threads which go to make up a text" (p. 104).

Stage III: Explanation of the Relationship Between Interpretation and Context
This last stage aims to depict discourse as part of a social process and social practice. Fairclough (1989) describes this stage as "detailed sociological

analysis" (p. 166), and the dialectic relation of how discourse is determined by social structures and how the social structures are determined by the discourse is examined in this stage. This dialectic relation is investigated at the social level, the institutional level, and the situational level, and there are multiple ways to examine a discourse depending on which level is the focus. Following this analytical procedure, the next section illustrates the results of text analysis on the three documents.

Findings

Stage I: Description
CEFR.

Field. The transitivity analysis shows that the CEFR text prefers employing material processes (action verbs). Followed by the second predominant "A is B" clause (42/154), more than half of the clauses are used as material clauses (83/154). What is prominent in this text is that most of the actors of material clauses are missing or unclear because they are excluded by passivizing the clauses. The following is a sample of material clauses that is structured with an unclear actor in the CEFR text (process is bolded).

> 78. Multilingualism **may be attained**
> 79. by simply **diversifying** the languages ..., or
> 80. by **encouraging** pupils to learn more than one foreign language, or
> 81. **reducing** the dominant position of English in international communication. (Council of Europe, 2001, p. 4)

In the example above, the doer of the process *may be attained* is linguistically hidden by passivizing the clause, and the following three subordinate clauses (#79-81) do not have actors either. Preference for an unclear doer is constructed by bulleted lists as well as passive clauses. Especially in section 1.2 "The aims and objectives of Council of Europe language policy," a number of doers of political and educational actions are unclear due to the itemization.

The causality analysis shows the text employs implicit causal markers more than explicit ones. Particles and conjunctions such as "to," "by," and "when" are frequently employed instead of typical causal conjunctions such as "because," "therefore," and "since." In addition, similar to the findings in the transitivity analysis, the text prefers infinitive phrases with an unclear effect. For example, specific motivations and purposes such as "to apply…" and "to aver the danger…" are raised, but their consequential effect or their expected result is not, at least explicitly, mentioned in the document. Therefore it does not show clearly what is expected by taking those particular actions. As seen in the transitivity analysis, who does what is not very clear either.

Tenor. The CEFR text uses dialogue to construct meanings. In each heading of the chapters, the document has an interrogative clause such as "What is the CEF?" and "What is plurilingualism?" which is answered within the chapter. As for modality, few modal items are used; however, the text occasionally employs mental clauses such as *serve, reflect, require*, that can possibly construe a hierarchical notion of the governmental system. The following examples are mental clauses that reflect the organization structure of the CEFR and Council of Europe (mental process is bolded).

> 27. CEF **serves as** the overall aim of the Council of Europe
> 28. as **defined** in Recommendation R (82) 18 and R (98) 6 of the Committee of Ministers (Council of Europe, 2001, p. 2)

In the examples above, mental processes such as *serves as* and *defined* depict the CEFR in service to particular agencies and purposes, and readers of the text are aware of the discourse participants and organization in the CEFR text. Similarly, appraisal items are rather indirectly used in the document. Implicit appraisal verbal groups such as "the CEFR is intended to overcome the barriers to communicate…" are employed to implicitly evaluate the Framework. What is prominent in terms of evaluative language use is that, while the text avoids direct evaluation of the Framework, it prefers explicit and direct evaluative language of the consequences of using the Framework:

> 98. From this perspective, the aim of language education is **profoundly** modified. (Council of Europe, 2001, p. 5)

In the example above, the adverb *profoundly* is used to insert a manner into the process *is modified*. This appraisal pattern, that is, evaluative language is used not for the Framework but for the possible consequence of using the Framework, emerges recursively in the CEFR text.

JF Standard.

Field. Similar to the CEFR text, the JF Standard text also prefers material processes (55/99). More than half of the clauses are action verbs, followed by the second predominant "A is B" clause (27/99). What is different from the CEFR is that the goal or grammatical object of the action verbs is often the Japan Foundation or their products.

> 33. By using **the JF Standard**,
> 34. it is possible to see the level of proficiency by what and how well the learner can do things in Japanese. (Japan Foundation, 2010, p. 6)

In addition to having the JF Standard or their products as a grammatical object, the text also prefers having them as a doer in a clause:

> 94 **The JF Standard Tree** depicts the relationship between communicative language competences and communicative language activities. (Japan Foundation, 2010, p. 9)

The causality analysis also shows the difference between the CEFR and JF Standard. While the CEFR does not have a clear effect or result in the text, the JF Standard almost always has a clear and positive effect. The following is an example of the JF Standard's positive productivity as its effect.

> 15 By using the same framework to describe language proficiency …,
> 16 **learners and teachers of the Japanese language around the world can see the level** at which they are learning or teaching,
> 17 wherever they are in the world. (Japan Foundation, 2010, p. 1)

What is found significant in this causality analysis is that when a positive effect occurs, the JF Standard or their products are positioned as its cause almost all the time. In the example above, with an implicit causal marker *by*, JF Standard is positioned as the grammatical object and construed as the cause of the positive effects.

Tenor. While the CEFR text uses dialogue to construct meanings, the JF Standard text uses monologue. All of the sentences are declarative, simply providing information. As for modality, a number of potential *can* verbs are used. What is unique in the text is the implicit causality such as *by using the framework...*, which is also highlighted as an indirect evaluation in appraisal analysis because of its positive productivity.

CEFR-J.

Field. The transitivity analysis of the CEFR-J text reveals a difference from the other two texts. While the CEFR and JF Standard texts prefer material clauses, the CEFR-J text prefers "A is B" verbs, or relational processes in SFL terms. Almost half of the processes are relational processes (33/78), followed by material clauses with unclear doers (25/78) and "there is" clauses (10/78). The following is an example of a relational process in the CEFR-J (translated into English by the author).

1. 外国語教育のための共通参照枠として開発されたCEFRは、欧州評議会の外国語教育政策の中心的柱となっている。(Tono, 2013, p. 92) (The CEFR that was developed for a common reference for foreign language education is a fundamental basis of the Council of Europe's foreign language education policy.)

This relational clause captures sequence and action, and can "encode meaning about *states of being*" (Eggins, 2004, p. 237). In the CEFR-J text, nominalization is frequently weaved into the relational processes, which embeds experiential and logical meanings into a nominal group and enables the authors to exclude their modality from a process. This way of nominalization, that is, to construct a clause that has a potential to be a sequence but embeds it as part of nominal group or adverbial phrase and captures it as the state, increases the number of content-carrying words in a clause and make the text linguistically dense. The nominalization and relational clauses can thus create less space for readers to negotiate and contributes to the construction of an authoritative voice in the text.

The difference from the other two texts is also seen in the causality. While the CEFR and JF Standard involve themselves or their member groups in their cause and effect, the CEFR-J text often employs the CEFR in its causality:

16. ...欧州でのCEFRの受容とその影響力を看過できない現状から、CEFRの日本における適用に関しての研究を行うことがまずは急務である、
17. という結論に達したのである。(Tono, 2013, p. 93) (Because the influence of the CEFR and its acceptance in Europe cannot be overlooked, we

concluded that research on adopting the CEFR into English education in Japan was an emergent need.)

Tenor. Similar to the CEFR text, the CEFR-J text uses dialogue to construct meanings. Every section has one question in the heading, which is answered in the chapter. There are also a small number of modal items. Similar to the CEFR text, this text constructs authoritative voice through the choices of nominalization of relational clauses and passivation. Similar to the CEFR and JF Standard, the CEFR-J has a small number of appraisal items in the text. What is unique, however, is that positive evaluations are used not on the CEFR-J but withdrawn from the CEFR (appraisal items are bolded):

> 59. オリジナルのCEFRでも、教育経験や直観によるチームでのCAN-DOディスクリプタ作成は**効果的である**、と書いてある…. (Tono, 2013, p. 94) (In the CEFR, it is written that making Can-do descriptors based on teaching experience and intuition is **effective**.)

Stage II: Interpretation

As seen in Stage I, the CEFR text has linguistically hidden doers and unclear effects. The hierarchical notion of their organization is instantiated through mental verbs, and possible outcomes of the CEFR are explicitly appraised. With this register, this study interprets its discourse as *instituting policy* discourse type at the *society* level that aims to promote plurilingualism within Europe with the CEFR. The CEFR text integrates several documents instituted by other ministries (i.e., Committee of Ministers, Council of Cultural Co-operation, etc.), and shows how the CEFR is associated with their initiatives and political summits. This register and intertextuality construct an authoritative voice, and readers of the text would be rightly lead to believe that the CEFR is not a small-scale framework developed in a short period, but has been well planned, discussed, and enacted by the governmental institutions in Europe through a number of conferences and summits. The situational context of the CEFR always resides within Europe, and interrelated texts are never withdrawn from outside of Europe.

The JF Standard, which is found does not share most of the linguistic cues with the CEFR, is interpreted as *advertisement* discourse type at the *situational* level that aims to promote the JF Standard for globalizing Japan and the Japanese language. The positive causality makes it clear what teachers and students can do with the JF Standard, and the repetitions of certain phrases (i.e., *By using the JF Standard, it is possible* ...) may attract Japanese teachers and learners to use the framework in their settings. Since the target of advertising the framework is language teachers and learners, the discourse type is situated at the micro context where the discourse is accessible for teachers and learners. Similar to the intertextual context of the CEFR, the context of the JF Standard also resides within the circle of the Japan Foundation, with the very small number of the citations of the CEFR. What is different from the intertextuality of the CEFR text is that the research reference for the JF Standard is very vague. While the CEFR text names very specific documents such as "Recommendation R (82) 18," the JF Standard has less detailed references, instead referencing such vague terms as "the numerous research findings," and "an enormous amount of advice." These abstract words, resources for readers' appraisal, allow the text to speak highly of the JF Standard, and further render the text to function as an advertisement.

The CEFR-J, which constructs an authoritative voice and positions the CEFR in its causality, is interpreted as *resource* discourse type at the *institutional* level that shows how the CEFR and CEFR-J are both similar and different. The sections in the CEFR-J book are constructed as question-and-answer, and readers can easily find the information they need using the index. As the original aim of importing foreign countries' language policy was "to have a consistent English education (from primary to higher education)" (Tono, 2013, p. 92), and as the CEFR-J was planned to be used as a reference for schools to have an action-oriented literacy approach, the CEFR-J text targets schools and administrators, especially those who are interested in or already have a continued education system (*Ikkan Kyooiku*). The intertextual context of the CEFR-J is significantly different from the other two. As opposed to the CEFR and JF Standard text where the employment of texts mostly resides within their contexts, the CEFR-J employs the CEFR as its main source. The CEFR is cited a number of times, and half of the questions in the headings are references to concepts about the CEFR (i.e., "What is the historical context of the CEFR?"). Also, the CEFR-J cites its research with JSPS Kaken grant, which further adds historicity and trustworthiness to the CEFR-J.

Stage III: Explanation

As "Japan's only institution dedicated to carrying out comprehensive international cultural exchange programs throughout the world" (Japan Foundation, 2013, p. 2), the Japan Foundation contributes to Japan's diplomacy to a great extent. For instance, when in 1983 Prime Minister Nakasone oversaw the "Welcoming 100,000 Students From Overseas" project for the purposes of "education," "friendship," and "international cooperation," the Japan Foundation cooperated with other agencies and made the Japanese-Language Proficiency Test (JLPT) to certify the Japanese proficiency of non-native speakers. The project was achieved in 2003 with the JLPT and other agencies' contribution; however, it left the government with a number of future tasks. The report by MEXT suggests that the vast increase of students from overseas caused problems for the systems of accepting them in Japanese universities and decreased the quality of exchange students (MEXT, 2003). In 2008, by reviewing and reflecting on these issues, the government announced another project: the "Welcoming 300,000 Students From Overseas" project. As a specific strategy, the government promoted "one-stop service" for independent administrative agencies overseas to provide a consultation service for international students. This integrated window service, still in use today, allows them to quickly provide information about studying in Japan and make the invitation process smooth. It would not be surprising, in the process of "one-stop service," if the JF Standard became a functional certificate for learners to show what they can do with the language, and as criteria for agencies to accept them in Japanese universities. It would make the process smooth and increase the quality of exchange students, which is what the government has been concerned with from the enactment of the first project to increase the number of foreign students in Japan. However, what may be questioned is that the use of the JF Standard as part of the enactment of the policy, more specifically, for globalizing Japanese and the Japanese economy, seems to be against the original aim of the CEFR. As the CEFR was developed for plurilingualism and communicative competence, and for reducing the notion of the dominant position of one language, using the Framework to globalize one language for one country may not fit the conceptual framework of the CEFR. Although the JF Standard can make sense within the context of the project, people engaging in this enactment should be aware that they run the risk of losing the project's original aim of using the CEFR through the process of policy borrowing. What may be beneficial about this project stems not from using the Framework, but rather from the knowledge gained by privileging one language as a certificate to determine what learners can do in Japan.

The original aim of the CEFR seems to be lost in the process of its importation into the EFL setting in Japan. Because English education in Japan needed a common framework for learning, teaching and assessment, the CEFR was borrowed as a "solution" (Negishi, Takada, & Tono, 2011; Rappleye, Imoto, & Horiguchi, 2011). This import of foreign language policy influenced the MEXT's five proposals for promoting English proficiency for international communication (Tono & Negishi, 2012), and it seems that the CEFR-J holds much potentials to become a very useful tool to achieve the MEXT five proposals. However, while the CEFR-J is expected to function as the "solution" in English language teaching in Japan, this present study suggests that it would also function as a "brand" for particular schools. Since the reform of *Hojinka* (semi-privatization of national universities) in 2004, national universities were separated from MEXT. The reform required national universities to distinguish themselves from other universities in order to attract more students due to the recent demographic decline, and led to pressure for "a search for innovation and efforts in branding"(Rappleye, Imoto, & Horiguchi, 2011). Integrating the CEFR-J into their curriculum and proposing continued English education through primary to tertiary education may serve to brand universities, especially those offering continued education. If this is the case, English will still be taken for granted as the de-facto foreign language, losing the Council of Europe's ideology of unity in diversity, and the CEFR-J would function merely as a *resource* to brand particular universities in a micro-political context.

Through CDA and SFL, this paper attempts to unpack national motivations and language ideology embedded in this "policy import" of the CEFR. Although a number of practical issues have emerged recently, theoretical and political gaps seem to still be unexploited. This study is concerned that the CEFR, which was designed for unity in diversity and plurilingual competence, would be integrated by particular language ideologies and misused as a national certificate to restructure existing symbolic power structures. If the JF Standard and CEFR-J are to be used as an advertisement or resource to brand particular schools and to gear dominant positions of one language, this policy borrowing has left vast space to discuss national language ideology and existing symbolic power structures. Further studies are needed in these newly established language practices and policy import.

Notes

1. The purpose of this paper is thus not to criticize these literacy approaches. Rather, this paper questions what is going on in the policy borrowing, who is involved in the dialogue, and what kind of knowledge is selected and privileged by who for what, which is, what the author believes, fundamental philosophy of CDA.
2. In this study, mode is not included mainly because of two reasons. The first reason is that, while the CEFR and JF Standard are written in English, the CEFR-J is written in Japanese. Since the construction of theme and rheme and thematic variation are linguistically different, comparing theme progressions between the two languages is often ineffective. The second reason is that since three of the texts are all written text, the medium of language is the same. Since mode focuses on the role of language reveals the way the text participates in the social activity, this present study posits that an analysis through mode perspective is unnecessary.

References

Arai, Y., Waki, K., Ishigami, A., Ishida, M., Kourakata, R., & Sekizaki, H. (2012). Task-gata oral test ni okeru Can-do Statement wo mochiita hyoukahouhou no ichishian [An application of Can-do statements in evaluating students' oral performance on a task based test]. *Nihongo Kyouiku Ronshu, 27*, 81-103.

Canagarajah, S. (2009). The plurilingual tradition and the English language in South Asia. *AILA Review 22*, 5-22.

Council of Europe. (2012). *Activities of the Committee of Ministers*. Retrieved from http://www.coe.int/t/cm/Home_en.asp

Council of Europe. (2001). *Common European Framework of Reference for Languages: Learning, teaching, assessment*. Retrieved from http://www.coe.int/t/dg4/linguistic/Source/Framework_EN.pdf

Eggins, S. (2004). *An introduction to systemic functional linguistics*. London: Pinter Publishers.

Fairclough, N. (1989). *Language and power*. London: Longman.

Fairclough, N. (1992). *Discourse and social change*. Cambridge: Polity Press.

Fairclough, N. (2003). *Analysing discourse: Textual analysis for social research*. London: Routledge.

Fujinaga, K., & Nakao, Y. (2013). JF Standard wo riyoushita "Kyoushi muke nihongo kouza" kaizen no kokoromi [An attempt to improve "Japanese language courses for teachers" by using the JF Standard]. *Kokusai Kyouryoku Kikin Nihongokyouiku Kiyou 9*, 89-107.

Garcia, O. (2009). *Bilingual education in the 21st century: A global perspective*. Oxford: Wiley-Blackwell.

Haida, K. (2012). Nihon no daigakugengokyouiku ni okeru CEFR no juyou—genjou, kadai, tenbou—EU oyobi nihon no koutoukyouiku ni okeru gaikokukyouiku seisaku to gengonouryokuhyouka system no sougoukenkyu [The acceptance of CEFR in Japanese universities' language education—present situation, future tasks, and prospect: Research on foreign language education policies and language assessment system in higher education in EU and Japan]. *Kagakukenkyuhihojokinkibankenkyu B Kenkyu Project Houkokusho*, 93-103.

Halliday, M. A. K., & Hasan, R. (1989). *Language, context, and text: Aspects of language in a social-semiotic perspective*. Oxford: Oxford University Press.

Halliday, M. A. K., & Matthiessen, C. (2004). *An introduction to functional grammar* (3rd ed.). London: Arnold.

Japan Foundation. (2010). *JF Nihongo Kyouiku Standard* [*JF Standard for Japanese-Language Education*]. Retrieved from http://jfstandard.jp/summary/ja/render.do#docs

Japan Foundation. (2013). *About the Japan Foundation*. Retrieved from http://www.jpf.go.jp/e/about/outline/about_01.html

Komatsu, T., & Yokoyama, N. (2012). "JF nihongokyouiku Standard" Seminar no houkoku to hyouka—Sankasha ni yoru gengojukutatudo no kijutu kara—[JF Standard: seminar report and evaluation—an analysis on participants' description on language achievement]. *Nihongengobunka Kenkyukai Ronshu*, 8.

Kumano, N., Ito, H., & Hachisuka, M. (2013). JFS/CEFR ni motozuku JFS nihongokouza level ninteishiken (A1) no kaihatsu [Development of JFS Japanese course certificate examination (A1) based on JFS/CEFR]. *Kokusai Kyouryoku Kikin Nihongokyouiku Kiyou*, 9, 73-88.

MEXT. (2003). *Aratana Ryugaku Seisaku no Tenkai ni tsuite: Ryugaku Koryu no Kakudai to Shitsu no Kojo wo Mezashite* [About the development of exchange student policy: increasing communication of exchange students and quality]. Retrieved from http://www.mext.go.jp/b_menu/shingi/chukyo/chukyo0/toushin/03121801/009.pdf

MEXT. (2008). *"Ryugakusei 30 mannin Keitaku" Kosshi* [The main points of the project of welcoming 300,000 students from overseas]. Retrieved from http://www.kantei.go.jp/jp/tyoukanpress/rireki/2008/07/29kossi.pdf

Martin, J. R., & Rose, D. (2007). *Working with discourse: Meaning beyond the clause*. London: Continuum.

Martin, J. R., & White, P. R. R. (2005). *The language of evaluation: Appraisal in English*. Basingstoke: Palgrave/MacMillan.

Negishi, M., Takada, T., & Tono, Y. (2011). *A progress report on the development of the CEFR-J*. Retrieved from http://www.alte.org/2011/presentations/pdf/negishi.pdf

Rappleye, J., Imoto, Y., & Horiguchi, S. (2011). Towards "thick description" of educational transfer: Understanding a Japanese institution's "import" of European language policy. *Comparative Education*, 47(4), 411-432.

Shibuya, M. (2013). Thai no kyouikugengashien to shite no JF Standard dounyu [An introduction of the JF Standard as a support of educational sites in Thailand]. *Kokusai Kyouryoku Kikin Nihongokyouiku Kiyou* 9, 109-120.

Tono, Y. (2013). *Eigo totatsudo shihyo sefuāru jei gaidobukku: The CEFR-J Handbook: Kyandu risuto sakusei katsuyo* [The CEFR-J Guide book: making and using Can-do list]. Tokyo: Taishukan Shoten.

Tono, Y., & Negishi, M. (2012). The CEFR-J: Adapting the CEFR for English language teaching in Japan. *The JALT FLP SIG*, 8, 5-12.

CHAPTER 9

THE "OTHERS" FIGHT BACK:
Struggles for Language Rights in Japan

Tamara M. Chung Constant
University of Massachusetts - Amherst

Within the last couple of decades, globalization and global flows of people have created space where a range of social networks, social movements, and organizations have developed at the transnational level. In this new economic environment, the global has been influencing the local as the world economy is becoming more integrated as a civic society at this transnational level (Batliwala, 2002); old and new economies and financial institutions are working across borders. These institutions are helping shape policies internationally and nationally in the form of the World Bank, the Internationally Monetary Funds, the World Trade Organizations, and other regional organizations such as the North American Free Trade Agreement, the European Union, and the Association of Southeast Asian Nations (Batliwala, 2002).

Due to the economic interconnection and interdependence of nation states through the global economy, technological accounts of globalization have focused on the rapid growth of information networks and on the flows of information that are causing the nation state to become less dominant while leading to a "world without borders" (Ohmae, 1990; Wriston, 1992, as cited in Waks, 2006). Social and cultural accounts focus on relations beyond national borders and their consequences within national borders. These relationships create a degree of cultural homogenization and with it a global language, English, which has been interpreted by many theorists such as Robertson (1997) as the world becoming more unified because of the complex connectivity, forms of heterogeneity such as hybridization, language (English), and globalization as part of the multiple linkages.

These developments influence the education process. This means there has been a great impact in the way people gather information, learn, and communicate because finding information has become easier since one has access to worldwide information at the click of a mouse (Schaffner, 1999). The developments in globalization have influenced the education process in many countries in terms of population diversity and language rights. The education of linguistic minorities has become an important component within globalization discourse. Transnationalism, due to globalization, has had a great impact on the Japanese population as a result of Japan's growing need for cheap labor in the 1980s. To meet this need, the Japanese government reached out to *Nikkeijin* who are people of Japanese descent living outside of Japan. This group is now a part of the Japanese education system and society where their educational needs along with other immigrant and minority groups have to be addressed by government officials.

The formation of transnational citizen activism is the direct result of the lack of accountability on the part of many of these institutions and national governments. These new transnational movements have changed the meaning of "grassroots movements" over the last decade. Grassroots movements were once considered small rural communities and urban environments where the common man and woman, who composed of the basic building block of society, lived as they provided the foundation a society needed to function. Freire (1974) used grassroots movements to signify the poor, laboring class, and working class people in rural and farming communities that were fighting against the dominant elites who were stripping them of their rights, especially the right to be formally educated. It appears that grassroots movements have a slightly different meaning at the national and the global levels. Grassroots have recently been perceived as relative, depending on the context, and referred to those whose daily material lives have been severely affected by their conditions.

For the purpose of this chapter, grassroots movements are examined at the local level where the context is part of people's lives affected by their conditions in society. Specifically, this chapter aims to answer the question: What modes of action for education are being used by local communities for language minorities in Japan? In the past, the Japanese government used assimilation policies in the public education system to strip ethnic minorities of their language as well as their cultural heritage. Today, it has no policies in place to help marginalized groups that are living within its borders either to maintain or to revive the language practices of ethnic minorities and immigrant groups. The chapter is organized to address: (1) the struggle for national policies to meet the economic and educational needs of minorities; (2) the development of language education grassroots movements within each ethnic minority group; (3) the successful language education models use by grassroots movements in other parts of the world; and (4) recommendations based on models found within the ethnic minority groups in Japan and in other parts of the world for new immigrants in Japan.

The Buraku's Struggle to Change National Policies

The Buraku people of Japan has taken up the legal battle to provide economic, social, and educational opportunities to minorities within Japan. The struggle began when those in power during the Meiji era (1886-1912) made political activism very difficult for any group because the government did not want the influence of "dangerous liberals and socialist ideas" (Neary, 1997, p. 57). Thus, conciliation discussion groups that were initiated by the Buraku communities were always under the watchful eyes of the government. Some local government even provided some funds to alleviate some of the poverty in Buraku communities to prevent activism (Neary, 1997). After the Rice Riot of 1918, many Buraku people were accused of violence. However, documents indicate that very few actually participated in the riot as they were constantly being watched by the government. This turn of events led to the formation of the social movement organization, Suiheisha.

Suiheisha was dissembled during the Pacific War and then reintroduced after the war under the name the National Committee for Buraku Liberation (NCBL) and later to be renamed Buraku Liberation League (BLL). The occupation by the U.S. under the Truman administration hampered enthusiasm for Buraku liberation as the incorporation of human rights, land reform, and education into the constitution suggested a full democratization of Japan that would eliminate discrimination (Neary, 1997). Interestingly, the U.S. brought the concept of democracy to Japan, when the country practiced institutionalized racism and discrimination within its own borders, and some of these discriminatory practices where part of the military forces that occupy Japan at the time.

In 1959, the BLL was able to convince the Japanese government to publish a report that provided the history of the problems faced by Buraku communities and surveyed the current state of Buraku communities (Neary, 1997). The report revealed the living situation of Buraku people as "ghetto like" because of the quality of homes and lack of available public services (Neary, 1997, p. 63). Moreover, Buraku people were trailing the general population in educational achievement, which was far lower than the national average, and in lifetime employment positions with major firms. As a result, the Buraku people were far more likely than the general population to depend on government assistance (Neary, 1997). The report recommended the government address and eliminate issues that plagued the Buraku communities by introducing legislation that would allow the government to concentrate on the social deprivation described in the report.

The proposed legislation was eventually written into the Law of Special Measures, devising a ten year plan which was divided into seven categories that included: human rights protection; education; social and employment protection; support of small and medium size businesses; promotion of agriculture and fisheries; physical environment; social and public welfare (Neary, 1997). Although this legislation was proposed, it was vague and open to interpretation regarding the recipients of these benefits. A complication was that many Buraku communities had absorbed poor Japanese whose ancestors had not been outcasts during the Tokugawa period (1603-1886). The question was whether these poor Japanese should benefit simply because they live in Buraku communities.

Aside from this issue, Buraku communities faced more discrimination with the development of family records during the Meiji era (1886-1912). Local government officials made certain that Buraku people could be easily identified by marking the family registration in a special way or by forcing them to take on a last name that differentiated them from the general public (Neary, 1997). Later, these documentations were sold to various institutions and organizations that used them to exclude Buraku people from being able to fully participate in the society.

Near the end of the twentieth century, the government argued that discrimination against Buraku communities was no longer part of the system and, therefore, there is no structural foundation for discrimination (Neary, 1997). However, the government did not want to acknowledge a systemic history of discrimination against Buraku communities. This tactic was used by activists to argue that Buraku people could not utilize any legislation or system for compensation since they have equal opportunity in education, employment, and marriage.

This argument was used again in the 1990s when politicians argued that there was not a need to provide special treatment to Buraku communities even though studies showed that Buraku people trailed the general population in standard of living, education, and income. Buraku communities continue to remain heavily segregated from the general public through the late 1990s. According to Neary (1997), 41.4 percent of Buraku people lived in designated areas, 20 percent of Buraku children obtain higher education (compared to 40 percent from the general population), and 10.6 percent of Buraku people were employed by businesses with more than 300 employees (compared to 23.3 percent of the general population).

Although younger Buraku people have assimilated into Japanese homogeneity by erasing their Buraku identity in order to acquire stable jobs and better education, Buraku neighborhoods have not possessed much economic vitality (Nishimura, 2013). According to Brown (2013), the Dowa policies that benefited Buraku people were not renewed as national policies in the 1990s because the government discovered that "9.5 percent of the Japanese population were living below the minimum standard housing" (p. 20). Some non-Buraku Japanese believe Dowa housing promoted reverse discrimination since some non-Buraku Japanese also lived in substandard housing and lower social conditions. Many questions have arisen with the discontinuation of these policies, considering the struggles of Buraku people against centuries of racialization using different ideologies, tactics, and strategies that is based on the legacy of a caste system. Current discrimination practices against Buraku people have taken a more subtle approach and continue to be an insidious problem in Japan because the practices of anti-Buraku discrimination is deeply rooted in Japanese belief systems and social institutions.

Discrimination against Buraku communities has not disappeared but has manifested itself in different forms over time, which is why the BLL has recently placed emphasis on human rights. This dimension creates a shared bond with other minority communities within Japan and across the globe that face discrimination within a nation state border (Neary, 1997). The BLL has been focused on convincing the Japanese government to ratify the International Convention on the Elimination of All Forms of Discrimination. However, government officials have responded by placing an emphasis on domestic laws, arguing the convention conflicts with the Japanese constitutional right to free speech and press. Nonetheless, the effort to implement human rights into the fight against discrimination in Japan has led to the creation of the regional organization Asia Pacific Human Rights Information Centre (Neary, 1997). This organization aims to provide information about human rights activities in the Asian Pacific, promote research in Japan and in Asia, and provide human right education to ethnic groups in order to fight against discrimination.

Grassroots Movements in Education

Grassroots movements in language education have been using human rights rhetoric to ensure ethnic minorities have the right to retain their cultural and linguistic heritage in Japan (Hornberger, 1998; Mandell, 2011; Skutnabb-Kangas 2000). Grassroots movements in language education have a long history in Japan since many immigrants were expected to provide education for their children as Japanese education was developed for Japanese citizens. Many ethnic minorities in modern times have used this argument to develop their own educational institutions, in order to address the linguistic and cultural needs of their people.

Ainu Language of Hokkaido

Around the 1920s, young Ainu people formed a movement that would address the social issues of the Ainu people. The movement focused on the Protection Act, which referred to Ainu people as a "dying race." In the 1930s, the first Ainu organization formed under the name Ainu Kyokai. It was operated under the Social Section of the Hokkaido government and served as an important forum for young Ainu people from isolated communities to come together (Siddle, 1997). Ainu people remained proud of their heritage by helping to create a new, but fragile, sense of what it means to be Ainu under the Japanese narrative of homogeneity and superiority. This narrative continued to shape their lives by denying those who continue to identify with their heritage the opportunity to participate in the economic and political systems.

After World War II, the Ainu Kyokai was renamed Utari Kyokai since Japanese use the term Ainu in a derogatory manner. Under the new name, the organization began an assault on the Japanese government's assimilation policies. Similar to other colonized indigenous groups around the world, Ainu people reactivated cultural symbols and a sense of identity by creating an Ainu nation with its own symbols, history, and concept of homeland legitimizing the existence of the Ainu people and their claim to opportunities in Japan (Siddle, 1997).

In 1961, against a backdrop of rampage poverty and division within Ainu communities, the Utari Kyokai organization received criticism from poor Ainu people who were suspicious of the motives of the organization and from those who did not want to identify with the group and thought the organization was perpetuating an illusion of the existence of the Ainu people (Siddle, 1997).

This new organization was able to pressure the government to create a welfare package that would meet the needs of Ainu communities. The organization functioned as an arm of the government, which provided financial and personnel assistance (Siddle, 1997). The welfare package showed that the Ainu people's position had changed little since pre-war Japan, although Japanese society had undergone change. Moreover, Siddle (199) writes that the Ainu people remained wards of the state under the Protection Act that was established in the 1930s.

According to Siddle (1997), several events took place between 1968 and 1970 that glaringly showed the continuing marginalization of Ainu people. The first event took place during the celebration of Hokkaido's history where neither the Ainu people nor Japan's colonization of Hokkaido was mentioned in order to continue to cast Japan's colonialism in term of "the application of the beneficial effects of 'progress' to a 'natural' extension of Japanese territory" (p. 29). The second event was the call to abolish the Protection Act as part of government streamlining of bureaucracy. Still another event was the government placing blame on Ainu people for unlawful incidents such as domestic terrorism. These are just a few examples provided by Siddle (1997) that contributed to the increase politicization of Ainu communities as their marginalized status was brought to the surface.

By this time, Ainu activists were looking beyond domestic movements by minority groups such as the Buraku communities and Japan's radical political left to more global movements. Therefore, in the early 1970s, they began forming links to indigenous and minority people outside of Japan (Siddle, 1997). Ainu activists became knowledgeable on indigenous activism that was taking place around the world through media channels as well as personal contacts. These contacts with worldwide indigenous people were very important in shaping Ainu nationhood. At the international level, according to Stavenhagen (1990), laws protecting the rights of indigenous people had not been established, specifically the right to self determination, but such concepts were being articulated by indigenous groups around the world.

Contacts between Ainu and other indigenous groups increased after a visit with native Alaskans and other native people in North America. By 1981, an Ainu representative attending the World Conference of Indigenous Peoples and took part in the discussions on the restoration of indigenous people's rights and the celebration of indigenous cultures (Siddle, 1997). These interactions allowed the sharing of political strategies and an underlying aboriginality based on similar historic lifestyle and experiences of colonization (Siddle, 1997). At the same time, Ainu activists strengthened their domestic alliances, finding common causes within the language of universal human rights framework with a variety of movements, especially minority groups who have experienced institutionalized and social discrimination. The tactic of using nationhood and human rights as narratives struck at the core of the government's attitude and policies towards Ainu people; however, from the government's point of view, Ainu people were no longer in existence in homogeneous Japan (Siddle, 1997).

Ainu activists along with Utari Kyokai (with caution since it was directly linked to government and government funds) began a New Law campaign (Siddle, 1997). This New Law aimed to increase Ainu access to capital in the society "for the benefit of a constituency defined in terms of a distinct ethnic identity and not merely by the extent of its relative deprivation" (Siddle, 1997, p. 41). Under the new campaign of ethnopolitics, identification became a tactic in the political struggle. Although described under ethnic pride and human rights, Siddle (1997) writes that the New Law had its origins in Japanese welfare policy introduced by the Utari Kyokai. With the abolition of the Protection Act, the New Law would strengthen welfare policies. However, many Ainu people expressed doubt that these policies would or could narrow the standard of living gap between Ainu people and Japanese people.

Utari Kyokai's adoption of the New Law indicated a clear development in Ainu ethnopolitics as many Ainu people, regardless of their myriad of identities and political opinions, perceived themselves as being linked by history and culture as an indigenous nation (Siddle, 1997). Since 1987, Ainu leaders increasingly became involved with Japanese civil rights groups and human rights activities, by participating in international forums dealing with indigenous groups, and assembling with indigenous peoples' movement and its language of indigenous rights. Ainu people have been partially successful on the international level. However, within Japan, the dominant narrative of homogeneity and peaceful development of Hokkaido has remained secured despite growing support internationally and within Japan. The general Japanese public continues to have very little knowledge of Ainu people or have any interest in their plight.

For the Ainu people who have been trying to restore their language that has slowly been eradicated, bilingualism is not their objective goal. However, according to Anderson and Iwasaki-Goodman (2001), bilingualism should play a central role if language revitalization is to be successful. Fishman (1991) advocates language revitalization through the conscious use of various languages or dialects in different social environments. For the Ainu people, Japanese would be their language of choice for the dominant society, and Ainu would be the language of the family and community.

In 1983, an Ainu language movement was officially founded in Nibutani, Hokkaido. However, Honda (1997) writes that these revitalization movements began earlier in the 1970s with Ainu language and culture groups forming throughout Hokkaido. This eventually led Utari Kyokai to respond to the growing interest in Ainu language and culture by establishing untraditional classrooms for the transfer of traditional knowledge and language (as cited in Anderson and Iwasaki-Goodman, 2001). These language and culture programs slowly emerged in various parts of Hokkaido, and as a consequence, there were various methods being used to teach from the Ainu language textbook. According to Anderson and Iwasaki-Goodman (2001), some programs focused on conversational skills while others focus on both conversational skills and cultural transference.

The Nibutani program is a program that places emphasis on language and culture relationship. Nibutani is a small town known for having the highest concentration of Ainu people in Hokkaido: approximately 70 percent of its 478 inhabitants consider themselves to be Ainu. Craig (1992) writes that the Nibutani language program has led the way to the revitalization of the Ainu language. According to Kayano (1994), the program in Nibutani began with Shigeru Kayano an Ainu leader who became bilingual in Ainu and Japanese as a child (as cited in Anderson and Iwasaki-Goodman, 2001). In 1983, he began teaching children, mostly relatives, the Ainu language. When the number of children slowly grew, he considered establishing a daycare for Ainu children where they could learn the Ainu language and culture. Instead, he decided to start a language program for children because the Japanese government did not approve of his plan (Kayano, 1994, as cited in Anderson and Iwasaki-Goodman, 2001).

Later, the Ainu language program grew into different components for children and adults. The original program for children was divided into two separate parts: one targeting younger children and the other older children. According to Anderson and Iwasaki-Goodman (2001), the program in Nibutani is the only Ainu language program that started as a program for children and has retained its separate program. Krauss (1992) stressed that children are the key to language maintenance. The language program in Nibutani focuses on language within the cultural context it is spoken, so children can understand the interconnectedness of the language to the culture.

In 1998, this program registered a total of 18 children. This low number is due to the adoption of Ainu culture and language as part of the regular curriculum at the Nibutani Elementary School, which indicates that the success of the program has influenced the local school system (Anderson and Iwasaki-Goodam, 2001). With the success of the program focusing on traditional Ainu culture, many recognize that the program should not only focus on the past but also the future. That is, the language needs to adapt to the culture and lifestyle of Ainu people living in this century.

Okinawan Dialect?
One group that is taking into consideration modern culture and lifestyle in its language use is the people of Okinawa. The Ryukyuan language has experienced a language shift and resurgence in use because of the younger generation. Youth in Okinawa have created their own language with the mixture of Okinawan languages, standard Japanese, and English known as

uchinaa-yamatoguchi, which has transformed the image of Okinawa. Since the reversion of Okinawa in 1972, the people of the island have gradually begun asserting their identity and pride in their cultural and linguistic heritage. According to Midori (2001), the Japanese broadcasting network, NHK, has played a major role in providing the Okinawan culture respectability in the eyes of mainland Japanese by highlighting Okinawan cultural distinctiveness. Aside from the television network, diasporic Okinawans and their children are returning to Japan to attend universities or other language institutions; many of which have maintained the Okinawan languages. These two major events have helped Okinawans reclaim their pride and identity as Okinawan people.

With renewed confidence, the people of Okinawa have revived traditional arts and cultural practices and have even exported some to mainland Japan with the help of well-known born Okinawan celebrities in sports, music, and other entertainment areas (Midori, 2001). In spite of their difference, many Okinawan celebrities have become successful in mainstream Japan, which has helped the confidence levels of Okinawan youth. With this new found confidence and self-assurance, many Okinawans began to reconsider the importance of their language (Midori, 2001). Midori writes that Okinawan speech contests and recitation of folk tale in the various Okinawan language dialects started taking place to encourage the use of the Okinawan language dialects. Furthermore, radio talk shows would feature talk in Okinawan languages sometimes with standard Japanese. In addition, the mixture of Okinawan language dialects and standard Japanese was also very prominent in comedic routines as well as literature.

Midori (2001) asserts that the survival of a language depends heavily on the speakers of that language and how they try to preserve the culture and tradition attach to the language in order to maintain their identity. It seems that the people of Okinawa are trying to preserve their language through the culture.

Old Immigrants: Chinese, Taiwanese, and Koreans
The Chinese is another group that has been trying to preserve and maintain its culture and language in the context of Japan's homogeneity and monolingualism. As the Chinese population increased in certain areas in Japan, merchants began forming associations that sponsored the

construction of new schools, temples, hospitals, and other service buildings due to the growth of the Chinese immigrant community in subsequent years (Vasishth, 1997). There was an absence of Taiwanese immigrants in the more traditional associations, which led them to expand in a range of occupations from construction to medicine, causing Taiwanese entrepreneurship to become larger than that of Chinese.

With new governments in place in mainland China and Taiwan, both the People's Republic of China (PRC) and Taiwanese Republic of China (ROC) competed for the loyalty of overseas Chinese, including those in Japan, by sponsoring schools and other cultural activities. This caused a split amongst overseas Chinese and the associations. According to Vasishth (1997), in Japan, Chinese schools either supported PRC or ROC, which resulted in Chinese parents sending their children to Japanese schools in order to stay out of the conflict. Nevertheless, provincial associations continued to play an important role in the lives of overseas Chinese immigrants in the form of advisement on education, ethnic education, marriage, and employment (Vasishth, 1997).

Interestingly, there has been limited interaction between new immigrants from PRC and established Chinese community associations as these associations now mainly serve and maintain the interest of the privileged Chinese. These wealthy and privileged Chinese who participated in the Chinese associations participated in the exclusion of Chinese laborers in Japan.

While the Chinese were perceived as model minorities, the Koreans have traditionally asserted their Korean identity. For Koreans, there has always been a relationship between language and culture. This relationship and the desire to retain their culture has been considered important by all Korean immigrant groups. For Koreans, language has always been associated with ethnicity, which was reinforced during colonial time when Korean was prohibited from being used by the subjects under Japanese rule as well as those on mainland Japan. For Koreans living in Japan, teaching the language to the younger generation has been used as a method to teach them about Korean culture and a method to resist assimilating into Japanese culture.

A major goal of the Korean schools established after World War II was to undo Japan's assimilation policy. The Chongryun school in Matsumaya is dedicated to providing education to Korean children within their community.

Cary (2001) asserts that their conviction is based on the Universal Declaration of Human rights which states that "education shall be free, that parents have the right to choose the kind of education that their children receive and the right of ethnic, religious, or linguistic minorities shall not be denied to them" (p. 115). The Chongryun school has developed its curriculum to provide its students with a broad range of knowledge, to promote a love for their homeland and culture, and to help them live in Japan as apposed to their native country and its destiny (Cary, 2001). The curriculum along with the textbooks used by the school is based on the philosophy of independence, scientific correctness, and realistic objectivity (Ryang, 1997).

During the elementary years, the important task is teaching the basic elements of Korean since it takes students about two years to learn the language as the medium of instruction (Cary, 2001). Then, the students learn ethnic education focusing on Korean language, math and science, and foreign language education in junior high school. When they reach the high school level, much of the same subjects taught in junior high school are emphasized at a higher level with the addition of cultivating a proper world view. At the university, students can take the available traditional courses with the option of training for those interested in being employed by the Chongryun organization. Since the school was founded, textbooks have gone through two revisions. Early textbooks were developed with the intention of students eventually returning to Korea. Contemporary textbooks and curriculum were revised because students are more than likely to live permanently in Japan (Ryang, 1997).

An important factor in the maintenance of one's mother tongue is language use in the home. A questionnaire survey of Korean heritage homes conducted by Cary (2001) revealed that Japanese was used at least part of the time for communication between family members. Out of 22 families surveyed, one respondent indicated that Korean was used more frequently between the elementary school age children while another reported more Korean used between a mother and grandparents. One mother reported using mostly Korean with her children while another reported using mostly Japanese, and one father used mostly Korean when speaking with his children. Amongst the 22 respondents with school age children in the 12 families, only two children were reported as speaking only Japanese in the home. Based on these results, Cary (2001) concludes that Japanese is the language that is most often used in the home and children in the youngest grades speak mostly Japanese, unlike older school-age children who can speak both Japanese and Korean. This supports the two-year plan for the students to learn Korean. Children are trained to be bilinguals through the school's immersion style instruction in Korean. They acquire Korean after they have acquired the Japanese language as their first language. This is a case of school bilingualism rather than natural bilingualism, which is distinguished by Skutnabb-Kangas and is referred to as consecutive childhood bilinguality (Hamers and Blanc, 1989).

New Immigrants: Japanese Brazilians
Japan's growing new minority, Japanese Brazilian *Nikkeijin*, have developed language maintenance models to emulate within the new social context of homogeneity and monolingualism. The reasons most Japanese Brazilian *Nikkeijin* come to Japan to work is to save money (Ishii, 2000, as cited in Riordan, 2005). The wage disparities between Japan and Brazil means that Japanese Brazilian *Nikkeijin* can make up to five times the income in Japan compared to Brazil even if they are doing unskilled factory work in Japan (Tsuda, 2003). Since many *Nikkeijin*'s goal is to save money, most usually take opportunities for overtime work, and regular work week composes of six days; moreover, workdays are usually long which means they have very little time for language study to improve or supplement their prior Japanese knowledge (Linger, 2001).

A survey conducted by Ishii (2000) of 369 Japanese Brazilian parents who have children attending elementary and junior high schools in the Kanto region revealed that parents usually spoke Portuguese at home and in the community with their children, and Japanese when the conversation is initiated from the child(ren). Japanese Brazilian parents did reveal that Japanese and Portuguese are used equally when the children spoke to friends (as cited in Riordan, 2005). The survey further revealed that the respondents rarely encountered Portuguese speakers; almost 30 percent claimed to have no contact with Portuguese speakers which may be due to a lack of Japanese Brazilian *Nikkeijin* in the area. Moreover, the respondents indicated that they were exposed to more Japanese mass media than Brazilian Portuguese, and the children had very little contact with written Japanese outside of the school environment.

Ishii's (2000) findings indicate that the linguistic environment for the children of Japanese Brazilians in the Kanto region who are isolated from other Japanese Brazilian *Nikkeijin* may not be well-suited for children to acquire and maintain Portuguese (as cited in Riordan, 2005). The survey also revealed parents expectations of their children becoming bilingual in both Japanese and Portuguese despite the lack of bilingual education available to Japanese Brazilian *Nikkeijin* children in the school system. Ishii (2000) concludes that Japanese Brazilian *Nikkeijin* parents were unaware of the ways the linguistic environment for their children affected their language development, and the parents did not know what they needed to do to make sure their children developed proficiency in both Japanese and Brazilian Portuguese (as cited in Riordan, 2005).

Many Japanese Brazilian *Nikkeijin* seem to be settling in Japan permanently despite their marginalized status in the society. As for Japanese Brazilian *Nikkeijin* children's adaptation in Japanese society, the prospects are not uniform. According to Tsuda (2003), children of Japanese Brazilian *Nikkeijin* face the greatest challenge of integration in later elementary and middle schools compared to children in the earlier years of elementary schools because of the challenges of learning Japanese early (Tsuda, 2003). Additional barriers are the Japanese educational system, which sets very high academic standards and also has an examination system that begins to separate students early on based on students' academic merit. In addition, these students encounter social pressure to conform to Japanese norms from both adults and peers, which can eventually lead to social alienation. Tsuda (2003) asserts that these children go through what he calls "identity diffusion" where they tend to identify with Brazilian culture but are faced with Japanese culture (p. 393). Unlike their parents, these children cannot easily dismiss Japanese culture as they participate in it every day through the school system. This leads many of these older students to join their parents in manufacturing and construction work.

Tsuda (2003) is more optimistic for the younger Japanese Brazilian *Nikkeijin* students in the public school system compared to Sekiguchi (2003). Tsuda (2003) writes that young children are at an advantage since they are at an age where they have the ability to acquire a new language. Moreover, they enter the educational system with their peers who have not learned too much in the form of reading and writing. Tsuda (2003) believes this is the period that emphasizes group work rather than competing as individuals academically. Younger children are able to quickly adapt to their new environment by accepting many of the cultural norms and some even see themselves as Japanese who are no different from their peers who are born and raised in Japan (Tsuda, 2003).

On the other hand, Sekiguchi (2003, as cited in Riordan, 2005) concludes that this may be the case for those in lower elementary schools, but when students reach junior high and high schools they are at an even greater academic disadvantage because they do not have a proficient first language. In many cases involving children who are born in Japan or who came to Japan at an early age, these children do not have the exposure to more than the abstract use of Japanese in the higher levels. Furthermore, their parents lack the language knowledge to support the children's studies at home, and neither Japanese nor Brazilian Portuguese are studied at home causing both languages to remain at a conversational level, never advancing.

Sekiguchi's (2003, as cited in Riordan, 2005) study reveals cases of Japanese Brazilian parents using their older children as caretakers of younger children while they work or sometimes want their older children to begin work in order to make more money before they return to Brazil. These cases along with the linguistic environment of the children make becoming bilingual difficult since education is not heavily emphasized in Japanese Brazilian *Nikkeijin* homes which results in underdeveloped study habits (Sekiguchi, 2003, as cited in Riordan, 2005).

Nevertheless, Brazilian Portuguese language education continues to be demanded by many Japanese Brazilian *Nikkeijin*. As a result, a distance education program was developed which made it possible for Japanese Brazilian *Nikkeijin* students to fulfill the Brazilian curriculum requirements while in Japan (Ninomiya, 2002, as cited in Riordan, 2005). The Ceteban Project for Distance Education allows the children of Japanese Brazilians *Nikkeijin* to take examinations in order to obtain credentials from primary and secondary schools. This distance education program allows for the establishment of Japanese Brazilian schools. According to Ninomiya (2002), the Pythagoras group is the most-well known for maintaining schools for Brazilians in countries around the world with a few of their schools located in Japan, and, so far, only a few hundred Japanese Brazilian *Nikkeijin* children within Japan are attending such schools (as cited in Riordan, 2005).

Aside from these big companies establishing schools for Japanese Brazilian *Nikkeijin* children, concerned Japanese citizen and Japanese Brazilian *Nikkeijin* have established schools to meet the needs of these children. In Hamamatsu city, where Japanese Brazilian *Nikkeijin* number about 15,899, they represent 60 percent of the non-Japanese population (Sugino, 2006). A Brazilian school was founded in 1996 by the principal of the school that purchased and remodeled an old company dormitory that has a main building for classes and a smaller area for sports. According to Sugino (1996), the school caters to approximately 100 students from lower elementary (age six) to high school (age 17). Although the local government in Hamamatsu provided immersion bilingual programs in the schools and aid outside of school in the form of pull-out programs, some Japanese Brazilian *Nikkeijin* parents prefer to send their children to private Portuguese medium schools that ask for high tuition with less sophisticated facilities (Sugino, 2006). Sugino (2006) emphasizes that this school in Hamamatsu is not accredited by the Japanese government, but is accredited by the Brazilian government, which means they use the same texts book as the school system in Brazil.

It seems that the approach to language maintenance in Japan varies depending on the historical context of a linguistic minority. The Ainu people of Hokkaido are in the process of revitalizing their language, which had nearly died out due to the forceful assimilation process used to unify Hokkaido with Japan where Japanese people outnumbered the Ainu people. The Ryukyuan people of Okinawa were also colonized by Japan, but the country had a stable government for many years that established a national language even though the islands had many dialects. The Ryukyuan population was relatively high compared to the Japanese population making it easier to maintain aspects of the language. Even though the language is going through a shift, aspects of it are being maintained by the younger generation in a new form. As for the Korean and the Chinese population in Japan, like other established immigrant populations, these languages are being maintained through school bilingualism. Is the situation of Japanese Brazilian *Nikkeijin* similar to previous immigrants in Japan?

Successful Grassroots Movements in Other Parts of the World
The reversal of language shift has been on the agenda of many organizations around the world. Fishman was the first linguist to focus on language loss,

although philologists and linguistic anthropologists have been trying to recreate languages that are considered "dead" or working to preserve languages through a few minority speakers for many years (Spolsky, 1995). According to Fishman (1989), the most tragic situation in the study of language is the death of smaller languages, and the most successful is the revival of a language that was considered moribund. He suggests that societies need to maintain multiple languages to provide for social consciousness, a core concept in the field of sociolinguistics.

There are many issues that are involved in language maintenance. The issue that seems the most difficult concerns the passing of a language from parents to children as the mother tongue. Spolsky (1995) refers to this as informal intergenerational transmission, which is a key component in language maintenance. Fishman (1991) asserts that when this chain is broken, it will take a major effort if not a miracle to repair it. This type of language maintenance through the process of reversing language use may be referred to as language revitalization. Spolsky (1995) writes that "it can be defined as the restoration of vitality…to a language that had lost or was losing this attribute" (p. 178). Language revitalization ensures intergenerational transmission which is critical to language vitality.

Language Revitalization Model
For the purpose of examining successful grassroots in other parts of the world, the language revitalization model within second language acquisition explored by Spolsky (1991) is used as a foundation for language maintenance and spread in cases of second language learning. The model suggests that context is important to language learning in determining learning opportunities (formal or informal), and the attitude and goals of the learner. Spolsky (1991) adds that this model depends on the decision of caretakers to speak the moribund language to the younger generation. Moreover, the level of knowledge on the part of the language source has a strong effect so limitation in fluency and in lexicon on the part of the language source can hamper revitalization or maintenance. Other social factors can be grouped into two categories: pragmatic or instrumental and ideological or integrative. Spolsky (1991) argues that in order for language revitalization to be successful both informal and formal forms of language use must be part of the learning process. Spolsky's model focuses on informal intergenerational language

transmission, not other forms of transmission such as ethnoreligious or cultural-religious which are transferred through formal educational systems. Furthermore, the model is not concerned with efforts to raise the vernacular language to the dominant standard language. The purpose of the model is to isolate the conditions that are important to language maintenance, which encourages new generation of speakers.

The language revitalization and eventual maintenance of Maori and Hebrew are examples of this model. The following description and analysis which focus on elements that would be helpful to Japanese Brazilians in maintaining the Brazilian Portuguese in Japan where bilingual education is in its infant stage.

The Revitalization of Maori and Hebrew
The shift away from the use of Maori began after the New Zealand land war in the early nineteenth century and the use of English became the language for medium of instruction in Maori schools (Spolsky, 1991). Later, many Maori people worked towards preserving their language, culture, and identity and insisted that their language be taught in the secondary schools. However, language loss continued, especially when Maori people began moving to the cities and then returning to the villages bringing with them the English language.

Sociolinguistic surveys between 1973 and 1978 shows the progressive loss of the Maori language which began as early as 1915. As a result of policies, by the 1970s, there were no signs of the new generation of children learning the language which made the prospects of the language surviving become dimmer (Spolsky, 1991). The movement of revival and revitalization appeared in the 1980s with external civil rights concerns when it was proposed that children learn the language before going to school (Spolsky, 1991). Therefore, the Department of Maori Affairs sponsored Maori language pre-schools where fluent speakers of the Maori language conducted programs entirely in Maori to make up for parents inability to speak the language. Although the Department of Maori Affairs provided financial support and encouragement to the community, the responsibility and implementation of the program fell on the community. Fishman (1991) indicates that such a movement in reversing language shift has potential since it started without any child speakers. Spolsky (1989) conducted a survey in 1987 on the situation of Maori bilingual education where he noted three types of schools: older bilingual programs, immersion programs with Maori speaking instructors presenting a full syllabus, and Maori philosophy schools where both instruction and curriculum are in Maori.

According to Spolsky (1991), Maori philosophy schools serve over just one percent of Maori children and another 12.5 percent of children receive some form of bilingual education by 1993, with 335 schools offering some form of Maori medium instruction. Benton (1991) asserts that the language revitalization movement was producing around 3,000 speakers yearly with bilingual and immersion primary school programs that continued into secondary school and beyond. Benton (1991) is concerned about the success of language reversal and resources that are being drained to teach Maori language and culture to non-Maori students. This concern emerged with the report by the New Zealand Ministry which reported that 93 percent of children in Maori medium education are Maori or of Maori descent, but 50 percent of students who are studying Maori at the secondary schools are not Maori or of Maori descent, and Maori students are about 18 percent of the students who attend Maori culture programs in 1993 (Benton, 1991).

Spolsky (1991) writes that programs that teach Maori as a New Zealand language instead of an ethnic language use resources that are needed for language revitalization programs that targets transmission from caretakers to young children. The actual level of Maori knowledge and use is still low even with students in immersion programs. In bilingual programs, the teachers are generally second language speakers of Maori most of who have low fluency and restricted knowledge of the language, resulting in Maori being restricted to the classroom space in teacher and student communicative interactions while the students continue to communicate with each other in English. Nevertheless, the efforts that have been made have not led to a drastic change in language use but can be said to count as successful revitalization.

Another language that has used this model of transmission for revitalization through second language acquisition is Hebrew. Hebrew is a language that has not been spoken as a native language in daily conversation for hundreds of years, but it has maintained it status in almost all Jewish communities around the world as a language to be read, written, pray, and study. Also, the language was used in nonreligious texts such as the law, science, and philosophy. Moreover, books were written in Hebrew throughout the period the language was not spoken, so new vocabulary and terminologies were being added to meet the needs of the changing world and culture (Spolsky, 1991). Spolsky (1991) writes that the language domain was restricted to liturgical, scholarly and literary functions. However, it is not to assume that the language was incapable of dealing with daily life before revival methods. Glinert (1987) provided evidence that showed a semi-vernacular religious Hebrew already available and in daily use as it covered the life and other aspects which were dictated by religious law. This semi-vernacular religious Hebrew was taught in the traditional Jewish elementary schools in Palestine and Europe.

Based on the evidence, it appears that Hebrew was a language with the potential for modern usage, and Jewish people with a strong education in Hebrew would have the opportunity to start speaking the language. Weinreich (1980) argues that Hebrew needs to be separated from the diaspora and from Yiddish that represents the diaspora in order for revitalization to take hold. The Jewish people who began arriving to Palestine in the 1880s were mostly from Eastern Europe, and they began embracing the idea of using Hebrew as a national language. For revitalization to take place, Nahir (1988) proposes four steps which he has coined the "Great Leap": (1) instilling linguistic attitude in the children in the community; (2) presenting a model of language use in school; (3) using and speaking Hebrew in and outside of school as a second language; (4) using Hebrew as the language of communication with their own children who can then grow up as native speakers. This language-learning model clarifies the relationships between the various factors involved in the revitalization process.

Hebrew was instilled in young students by using the direct method which involved teaching Hebrew in Hebrew. This method was used for five years with all studies explained in Hebrew in kindergartens and preparatory schools (Fellman, 1973). These two modes became the main instrument for developing Hebrew fluency. According to Fellman (1973), the Hebrew Teachers Association adopted Hebrew, with Sephardic pronunciation and Ashkenazic script, as the medium of instruction and the direct method as the technique of instruction.

Spolsky (1991) writes that the program was slow at leading language use in the beginning because graduates of these Hebrew schools stopped speaking Hebrew or used a mixed variety with another language after they left school. Harshav (1993) supposes that the first two decades of the revival movement provided disappointing results. The movement saw breakthrough with the second wave of Jewish immigrants who came to work in Israel from Eastern Europe; this group of immigrants were better educated and ideological in their outlook. Although small in numbers, the group held an intense ideological stance for a Hebrew land, Hebrew work, and Hebrew language (Spolsky, 1991). The first successful efforts were seen within these small groups.

However, there were some developments that lead to this success. First, the Minister of Education stepped down from his position, which allowed Hebrew to replace French which was the dominant language (Spolsky, 1991). Also, Hebrew was introduced as the language in which all public business was to be conducted. Spolsky (1991) asserts even though the revitalization process began in the 1880s, the change to the use of Hebrew took place between 1906 and 1914. Bachi (1956) reports that the 1916 census showed that 40 percent of Jewish people in Eretz-Israel claimed Hebrew as their mother tongue, and this figure has jumped to 75 percent since that time. Based on Spolsky's model, it appears that the process of revitalization of Hebrew took approximately twenty-five years even though the language may need to be further developed as a full modern spoken and written language.

The revitalization and maintenance efforts of Maori and Hebrew have illuminated the possibility for revitalization and maintenance. However, the situation of the two languages was very different. According to Spolsky (1991), Hebrew is a language that had not been spoken for many years, while Maori was spoken by older native members of the Maori community. Moreover, Hebrew has had a literary history in many forms with a volume of written material that tracked the change of the language with time by shaping the language to changing intellectual and practical needs (Spolsky, 1991). On the other hand, Maori relied on an oral tradition, with only a portion recorded in written form in the 19th century. In addition, the Hebrew revitalization movement wanted to add spoken functions to a language whose literacy was already established, while the Maori movement wanted to add literacy functions and formal status function to a spoken variety of a language, standardizing the language (Spolsky, 1991).

The Hebrew and Maori efforts were the results of small-scale grassroots movements where activities of ethnic-based ideologies were working to establish new identities which had to do with physical, demographic, social, and cultural dislocation. Although Hebrew has succeeded, the results have turned out somewhat differently from what was envisioned, especially with the complaints of normativists who claim the language has become unrecognizable (Spolsky, 1991). Hobsbawm (1996) writes that when a language moves from the oral to reading and writing or any combination (the case of Hebrew) that language changes in character. As for the Maori campaign, Spolsky (1991) writes that the issue has not been decided even though the revitalization and maintenance process has reached a critical state.

Recommendations

In this environment of transnationalism where the world is becoming more unified, the role of educational institutions needs to be reconsidered and renegotiated, as the serving population shifts because of economic pressure. According to Henry, Lingard, Rizvi, and Taylor (1999), globalization discourse often proclaims that the market has triumphed over the state, and the world economic system has become so complex that no single nation state can control what is taking place within its jurisdiction. Due to this globalization, education has gone through a restructuring process in various forms, including: "commitment to market based provision of services; encouragement of an individualized consumerist ethos; and a derisory view of the 'nanny state'" (Henry, Lingard, Rizvi, and Taylor, 1999, p. 88). Furthermore, public and private spheres are becoming more separated with the privatization of education. Nation-state educational institutions that were once an entry point for disadvantaged students now operate within the training market. In other words, education is affected by all changes relating to globalization in terms of structure, policy, practice, and the experiences students bring with them to their education.

In this new environment, it seems that the Japanese government cannot invest in educating students whose futures within the country are uncertain. As government officials have stated in the past, education in Japan is there to serve Japanese citizens (Vaipae, 2001). In other words, it is there to serve people who will later help the country compete globally. Therefore, the government may not see the need to provide language education to ethnolinguistic minorities whose languages cannot help them compete in the global economy including *Nikkeijins*.

In the past and present, Japan has invested in the English language, which has been viewed as the language of the market since the early 1900s. Many scholars and educators in the past saw English as the language of the future and advocated for the language. Today, English is widely studied in the secondary levels and in higher education in Japan (Maher, 1997). There has been an increasing importance placed on English literacy in Japan, especially in professional or occupational positions where English is considered the working language.

It seems that multiple migrations are preventing economic success, and, according to Tsuda (1999), Brazilian *Nikkeijin* continuously migrate between Japan and Brazil for economic reasons. Multiple migration patterns prevent them from accumulating wealth generationally and create educational problems for children. Maori people who moved back and forth from the reservations to the city also created educational problems for their children. In their dilemma as transnational people, the Japanese Brazilian community has approached the problem of cultural education and language maintenance similarly to other ethnic minorities in Japan, by establishing schools that provide instruction in the ethnic minority language.

These schools appear to be utilizing a weak form of bilingual education, the separatist form, where the child is part of the language minority and is learning the minority language in the classroom by choice (choice between Japanese public school and private language school). This method aims at societal and educational detachment and/or autonomy, leading to limited bilingualism (Baker, 2006). This separatist form of bilingual education has been used to maintain ethnic minority languages by Chinese and Taiwanese immigrants, ethnic Koreans, and other colonized ethnic minorities in the revitalization of their languages. However, this approach is only feasible for those ethnic minorities who can afford it. As for Japanese Brazilian *Nikkeijin*, many have come to Japan for economic reasons, so other solutions need to be made available to those who cannot afford to send their children to private Brazilian schools. On the other hand, there are members of the Brazilian *Nikkeijin* community in Japan that migrated for reasons other than economics.

The preservation of collective group identity may be one of many reasons why ethnic groups see language as an important aspect in the preservation of their culture. According to Nida (1993), language is an elemental part of culture, with its semantic component related to entities, events, states, processes, and relations within culture, and culture depends on language to perpetuate itself. Language expresses the cultural realities of groups and allows members to refer to common experiences and knowledge about the shared world, but language is also used to create experiences (Kramsch & Widdowson, 1998). For ethnic minorities in Japan, language maintenance is perceived as important for the continuation of the group's cultural identity.

In response to the Japanese government's lack of action on behalf of ethnic minority groups, many grassroots movements began to emerge at the local levels in the hope of preserving (Chinese, Korean, Brazilian Portuguese) and revitalizing (Ainu and Okinawan languages) the languages, but also in the hope of changing educational policies (Buraku). These movements have been taking place through the establishment of private schools for ethnic minority students; teaching the general population about the language and the culture; and placing pressure on the government to acknowledge inequality in education amongst the general population and minorities. One of the first grassroots movements for recognition as an ethnic minority group began with the Buraku people, who wanted the government to be aware of the hardship and discrimination this group had suffered. The Buraku's movement provided a starting point for other minorities. The Ainu people have used some of the same arguments in the fight for their own recognition as an ethnic minority group that possesses its own language, culture, and identity.

Grassroots movements among the ethnic minorities in Japan have emerged to specifically address the language needs of people within these ethnic groups who want to maintain the linguistic aspect of their identity. However, it seems that these movements have used weak forms of the bilingual education model to address the needs. That is, the movements have utilized a separatist model that targets the minority language child and aims at limited bilingualism (Baker, 2006). For example, the ethnic Koreans used a separatist model to implement consecutive biliguality in the schools, as early consecutive bilinguals have been reported to have the same level of proficiency as simultaneous bilinguals. The position of ethnic Koreans in Japan make this the preferable model for the group, even though younger Koreans do not generally retain the language due to social circumstances

(Ryang, 1997). The Ainu people have also used a separatist model to revitalize the Ainu language. The model focuses on the generational transfer of the language from older Ainu speakers to younger ones.

Grassroots movements outside of Japan have used intergenerational transmission for the purpose of language revitalization, as in the cases of Hebrew and Maori. However, the forms of bilingual education used for these programs differ from the ones that are being used in Japan. In the case of Hebrew and Maori, it seems that a strong form of bilingual education was used to address the issue of Hebrew and Maori language loss. The immersion program within Spolsky's (1991) language revitalization model was utilized in the revitalization and maintenance efforts of Hebrew and Maori. Language majority children were bilingual within the classroom but with an emphasis on the second language (Hebrew or Maori) with the goal of developing bilingualism and biliteracy.

Based on the success or lack of success of these bilingual education programs with different models that are being used by these grassroots movements, Japanese Brazilians have different options in how to approach bilingual education as transnational people. Similar to other migrants living in Japan, Japanese Brazilians have established private schools for their children, some of which are accredited by the Brazilian government. These Japanese Brazilian schools could emulate the consecutive bilingualism model that has been in use by ethnic Koreans, but with a strong form of bilingual education since the language outcome would be bilingualism and biliteracy rather than limited bilingualism. I would recommend the use of the consecutive bilingualism model with the maintenance and heritage language (MHL) or the two-way and dual (TWD) language program for language minority children. The children would use both the majority and the minority languages in the classroom for TWD, or place an emphasis on the first language for MHL, with the common goals of bilingualism, biliteracy, pluralism, and cultural enrichment since these children participate in a cyclical migration pattern that is influenced by the economy.

Even though Brazilian Portuguese is not a dying or dead language, Spolsky's model of revitalization can be used as it provides a foundation for language spread in second language learning. The model would allow Japanese Brazilian children to maintain and strengthen the dominate language through intergenerational transmission, in a community setting with the help of volunteers, while acquiring Japanese in the public school system to be functional within Japanese society. The Japanese Brazilian volunteers could use the maintenance and heritage language program within Spolsky's model. This would open up an option for Japanese Brazilian parents who cannot afford to send their children to expensive private schools. This approach may also allow the Brazilian and Japanese governments to play a role in the maintenance of Brazilian Portuguese in the Japanese Brazilian community, through the funding of community language programs. In other words, the governments could provide the funding while allowing the community to implement the language education program, similarly to the Maori revitalization programs. That is, if these two nations decide to have a vested interest in the minority community maintaining both languages, even though the evidence suggested that it is only in the interests of the minority communities to maintain their mother tongue or first language and learn the dominant language. These approaches have been suggested because of the social context and position of Japanese Brazilians as transnational people who migrate back and forth for economic reasons between Japan and Brazil.

Grassroots movements can be used to address the language education problem within the Japanese Brazilian community in Japan, since they have been successful in the revival of languages in other ethnic minority communities in Japan. The Okinawans have revived the use of their language through a language shift process, and the Ainu people in Hokkaido have revitalized a modified version of their language and have begun to transmit the language to the younger generation. This intergenerational transmission has been successful in other parts of the world, specifically New Zealand and Israel. Spolsky's model of language revitalization within second language acquisition has been successful in Israel for Hebrew but is questionable in the case of Maori, which may be due to sociohistorical and political position of the group.

Regarding the political context of Japanese Brazilians in Japan, the Japanese national government appears hesitant to address the problem, even though they are benefiting from the contribution of Japanese Brazilians' labor. The Japanese Brazilian *Nikkeijin* community may need to become more involved in their children's education because of the weak response by the national and the local governments to the problem of language education and education. This involvement would require that parents provide a strong first language base to their children in the home environment at the same time as the children are learning the majority language in school. That is, parents need to learn to pass down the Brazilian Portuguese language to the next generation by developing a more language-friendly environment and becoming more involved in their children's education.

As a consequence of globalization, Brazilian and Japanese schools need to develop two tracks: one for children whose parents plan to stay in Japan and another for children whose parents want to return to Brazil as the economy changes.

References

Anderson, F. E., & Iwasaki-Goodman, M. (2001). Language and the culture revitalization in a Hokkaido Ainu community. In M. G. Noguchi & S. Fotos (Eds.), *Studies in Japanese bilingualism* (pp. 45-67). Sydney: Multilingual Matters ltd.

Baker, C. (2006). *Foundations of bilingual education and bilingualism*. London: Multilingual Matters.

Batliwala, S. (2002). Grassroots movements as transnational actors: Implications for global civil society. *Voluntas: International Journal of Voluntary and Nonprofit Organizations*, 12(4), 393-401.

Benton, R. A. (1991). *The Maori language: Dying or reviving?* Honolulu: East West Center.

Brown, E. S. (2013). Racialization in a 'homogenous' society? The case of Buraku people in Japan. *Asian Ethnicity*, 14(1), 1-28.

Cary, A. B. (2001). Affiliation, not assimilation: Resident Koreans and ethnic education. In M. G. Noguchi & S. Fotos (Eds.). *Studies in Japanese bilingualism* (pp. 98-132). Sydney: Multilingual Matters ltd.

Fellman, J. (1973). Concerning the 'revival' of the Hebrew language. *Anthropological Linguistics*, 15, 250-257.

Fishman, J. (1989). Language spread and language policy for endangered languages. In J. Fishman (Ed.), *Language and ethnicity in minority sociolinguistic perspective* (pp. 389-402). Clevedon: Multilingual Matters.

Fishman, C. A. (1991). *Reversing language shift: Theoretical and empirical foundations of assistance to threatened languages*. Clevedon, UK: Multilingual Matters.

Freire, P. (1974). *Pedagogy of the oppressed*. New York: The Seabury Press.

Glinert, L. (1987). Hebrew-Yiddish diglossia: Type and stereotype implicatios of the language of Ganzfried's Kitzur. *International Journal of the Sociology of Language*, 67, 39-56.

Hamers, J. F., & Blanc, M. H. A. (1989). *Biliguality and bilingualism*. Cambridge: Cambridge University Press.

Harshav, B. (1993). *Language in time of revolution*. Berkeley: University of California.

Henry, M., Lingard, B., Rizvi, F., & Taylor, S. (1999). Working with/against globalization in education. *Journal of Education Policy*, 14(1), 85-97.

Hobsbawm, E. (1996). Language, culture, and national identity. *Social Research*, 65(4), 1065-1080.

Hornberger, N. H. (1998). Language policy, language education, language rights: Indigenous, immigrant, and international perspectives. *Language in Society*, 27(4), 439-456.

Kayano, S. (1993). Ainu ethnic and linguistic revival. In N. Loos & T. Osanai (Eds.). *Indigenous minorities and education: Australian and Japanese perspective of their indigenous peoples, the Ainu, Aborigines and Torres Strait Islanders* (pp. 360-367). Tokyo: Sanyuasha Publishing Co.

Krauss, M. (1992). The world's languages in crisis. *Language, 68(1)*, 4-10.

Kramsch, C., & Widdowson, H. G. (1998). *Language and culture.* Oxford: Oxford University Press.

Linger, D. T. (2001). *No one home: Brazilian selves remade in Japan.* Stanford, CA: Stanford University Press.

Maher, J. (1997). Linguistic minorities and education in Japan. *Educational Review, 49(2)*, 115.

Mandel, B. (2011). Putting theory into practice: Using a human rights framework and grassroots organizing to build national revolutionary movement. *Columbia Journal of Race & Law, 1*, 402.

Midori, O. (2001). Language and identity in Okinawa today. In M. G. Noguchi & S. Fotos (Eds.). *Studies in Japanese bilingualism* (pp. 68-97). Sydney: Multilingual Matters Ltd.

Nida, E. (1993). *Language, culture, and translating.* Shanghai: Shanghai Foreign Language Education Press.

Nahir, M. (1988). Language planning and language acquisition: The 'Great Leap' in the Hebrew revival. In C. Bratt Paulson (Ed.). *International handbook of bilingualism and bilingual education* (pp. 275-295). New York: Greenwood Press.

Neary, I. (1997). Burakumin in contemporary Japan. In M. Weiner (Ed.), *Japan's minorities: The illusion of homogeneity* (pp. 50-78). London: Routledge.

Nishimura, Y. (2013). Reconstruction of minority identities in the 21st century Japan. *Global Ethnographic, 1*, 1-8.

Riordan, B. (2001). *Language policy for linguistic minority students in Japanese public schools and prospects for bilingualism: The nikkei Brazilian case* (Doctoral dissertation). Bloomington: Indiana University.

Robertson, R. (1997). Social theory, cultural relativity and the problem of globalization. In A. King (Ed.), *Culture, globalization and the world system* (pp. 69-90). Minneapolis: University of Minnesota Press.

Ryang, S. (1997). *North Koreans in Japan: Language, ideology, and identity.* Boulder, CO: Westview Press.

Schaffner, C. (2000). Globalization, communication, translation. In C. Schaffner (Ed.), *Translation in the global village* (pp. 11-28). Clevedon: Multilingual Matters Ltd.

Siddle, R. (1997). Ainu: Japan's indigenous people. In M. Weiner (Ed), *Japan's minorities: The illusion of homogeneity* (pp. 50-78). London: Routledge.

Skutnabb-Kangas, T. (2000). *Linguistic genocide in education or worldwide diversity and human rights?* London: Lawrence Erlbaum.

Spolsky, B. (1991). Maori bilingual education and language revitalization. *Journal of Multilingual and Multicultural Development, 9(6)*, 1-18.

Spolsky, B. (1995). Conditions for language revitalization: A comparison of the case of Hebrew and Maori. *Current Issues in Language and Society, 2(3)*, 177-201.

Stavenhagen, R. (1990). *The ethnic question: Conflicts, developments, and human rights.* Tokyo: United Nations University Press.

Sugino, T. (2006). *Linguistic challenges and the possibilities of immigrants: In case of Nikkei Brazilians in Japan.* Country Note on Topics for Breakout Session 4 Japan, Yokosuka: National Defense Academy.

Tsuda, T. (1999). The motivation to migrate: The ethnic and sociocultural constitution of the Japanese Brazilian return-migration system. *Economic Development and Cultural Change, 48*(1), 1-32.

Vaipae, S. (2001). Language minority students in Japanese public schools. In M. Noguchi & S. Fotos (Eds.), *Studies in Japanese bilingualism* (pp. 184-233). Clevedon: Multilingual Matters LTD.

Vasishth, A. (1997). The Chinese community: A model minority. In M. Weiner (Ed), *Japan's minorities: The illusion of homogeneity* (pp. 50-78). London: Routledge.

Waks, L. J. (2006). Globalisation, state transformation, and educational restructuring: Why postmodern diversity will prevail over standardization. *Studies in Philosophy of Education, 25*, 403-424.

Weinreich, M. (1980). *History of the Yiddish language* (trans. J. Fishman and S. Noble). Chicago: University of Chicago Press.

CHAPTER 10

WAR, PEACE, AND LANGUAGE

Charles Kowalski
Tokai University

Does language learning contribute to world peace? Most language teachers would probably answer "yes", but is there any way to prove this assertion empirically? Anyone who compares the most "peaceful" societies in the world and the most linguistically diverse ones might be forgiven for having some doubts. Among the ten most "peaceful" societies, according to the 2013 Global Peace Index[1] (Vision of Humanity, 2013), more than half score towards the bottom of the Greenberg diversity index[2] (Lewis, 2009), as seen in Table 10.1.

Considering the GPI ratings of the world's most linguistically diverse nations (Table 10.2), we find that half of the most linguistically diverse nations have a GPI ranking in the bottom third, while only one (Australia) is in the top third. For anyone trying to establish a positive correlation between linguistic diversity and a peaceful society, these numbers are rather depressing. It seems to support the viewpoint of "monolingualist" movements such as the "English Only" movement in the United States, which takes its rallying cry from former President Theodore Roosevelt: "We have room for but one language here, and that is the English language" (Roosevelt, 1919, p. 2).

If we are looking for evidence that multilingualism and linguistic diversity lead to an increase in peace, where do we start? This paper will begin by examining the inverse proposition: that the suppression, misinterpretation, and distortion of language lead to an increase in violence. It will then explore the role of the linguist in conflict, including some ways that the language learner is uniquely equipped to act as a peacemaker.

Table 10.1
Linguistic diversity in the world's top 10 "peaceful" nations

GPI rank	Country	Number of languages	Diversity index (rank /199)
1	Iceland	2	(no data)
2	Denmark	19	0.096 (163)
3	New Zealand	24	0.280 (125)
4	Austria	18	0.122 (157)
5	Switzerland	22	0.556 (78)
6	Japan	13	0.036 (186)
7	Finland	19	0.121 (158)
8	Canada	172	0.601 (66)
9	Sweden	23	0.153 (147)
10	Belgium	28	0.697 (53)

Table 10.2
GPI rankings of the world's most linguistically diverse countries

Rank	Country	Languages spoken[3]	Diversity index	GPI rank (/162)
1	Papua New Guinea	837	0.988	99
2	Indonesia	706	0.815	54
3	Nigeria	527	0.891	148
4	India	449	0.913	135
5	United States	420	0.334	99
6	China	301	0.511	101
7	Mexico	287	0.108	133
8	Cameroon	280	0.972	108
9	Australia	244	0.211	16
10	Brazil	224	0.054	81

Violence Resulting from Suppression of Language

Galtung (1969) set a standard for peace research by classifying violence into two broad types: direct violence (overt and visible forms of violence, such as war), and indirect or structural violence (systemic denial of human rights and basic needs). By this definition, any attempt to restrict a person's use of language is a form of structural violence.

The Universal Declaration on Linguistic Rights (UNESCO, 1996) affirms this, stating in the Preamble that "in order to ensure peaceful coexistence between language communities, overall principles must be found so as to guarantee the promotion and respect of all languages." These include:

- All people have the right to use their own language in public and private (Article 3.1).
- Discrimination against any language community is inadmissible (Article 10.2).
- Everyone has the right to be multilingual (Article 13.2).
- Everyone has the right to learn any language (Article 23.4).
- All language communities have the right of free access to education in their own language (Articles 24-29).

Violation of these rights is a form of structural violence that has been known to escalate into direct violence. One example is the *Shahid Minar* ("Language Martyrs") of East Bengal (the eastern part of Pakistan, now Bangladesh). In 1952, Sir Khawaja Nazimuddin, the second Prime Minister of Pakistan (and ironically, the first one from East Bengal) issued a declaration that "Urdu and only Urdu" would be the state language of Pakistan. This set off a wave of protests by native speakers of Bangla, who comprised about 54% of the population. On February 21, a general strike was called, and demonstrations were held throughout Dhaka, centered on the University of Dhaka campus. Police responded first with tear gas, then with live ammunition. Five students were killed that day, and several more in the riots that ensued throughout the city (Bari, 1998). This is widely held to be one of the incidents that set Bangladesh on the path to declaring independence in 1971. The incident also led UNESCO, in 1999, to designate February 21 as International Mother Language Day.

Violence Resulting from Misinterpretation of Language

There are also occasions where the misinterpretation of language, or a historical shift in the interpretation of words away from their original senses, paves the way for an increase in violence. Since religions, particularly the Abrahamic religions of Judaism, Christianity, and Islam, receive more than their share of blame for the conflicts in the world, it seems fitting to take examples from the languages of their sacred scriptures, biblical Hebrew and classical Arabic.

In the Hebrew Bible, the sixth of the Ten Commandments (Exodus 20:13, Deuteronomy 5:17) is expressed as "You shall not *rtsh*" – a Hebrew verb that can be translated as either "kill" or "murder." The interpretation of this one word has profound implications for modern-day Judeo-Christian societies. One interpretation would take it as a prohibition only against cold-blooded murder, but leave latitude for the execution of criminals or the killing of enemies in battle. The other would forbid the taking of any human life under any circumstances.

As we see in Table 10.3 (based on Bailey, 2005), for the first five centuries of Biblical translations into English, the "kill" translation was used almost exclusively. The shift toward "murder" came at the beginning of the twentieth century, often called "the bloodiest in history."

It has been persuasively argued that the shift toward "murder" has less to do with linguistic accuracy than with the influence of the times (Bailey, 2005). If this is the case, it would strongly suggest that the earliest Christians like St. Maximilian of Tebessa[4], who committed themselves to nonviolence even at the cost of their own lives, were right, and everyone who has tried to justify war in Biblical terms, from St. Augustine[5] to Donald Rumsfeld[6], was wrong.

In a similar vein, two words from the Arabic of the Qur'an have become infamous for their use in inciting young Muslims to violence (often self-destructive), as a result of distortions of their original meaning: *jihad* (commonly translated "holy war") and *shahid* (commonly translated "martyrdom"). For *jihad*, a better translation might be "sacred struggle". In the Qur'an, this word frequently appears in the phrase *al-jihad fi sabil Allah*, "striving in the path of God", and embraces many activities other than armed struggle (which is also referred to by a separate word, *qital*), such as study and spiritual practice (Asfaruddin, 2010). A well-known hadith (post-Qur'anic teaching story) has Mohammed saying upon return from a military campaign, "We have returned from the lesser *jihad* to the greater *jihad*" (Nakamura, 1973, p. 176, as cited in Asfaruddin, 2010).

Table 10.3

Historical comparison of English translations of Biblical Hebrew rtsh.

Century	"Kill" versions	"Murder" versions
16th	1535: Coverdale 1560: Geneva 1568: Bishops' Bible	
17th	1609: Douay 1611: King James Version	
18th	1752: Richard Challoner	
19th	1853: Isaac Leeser 1856: Samuel Sharpe 1890: John Nelson Darby	1885: English Revised 1898: Young's Literal Translation
20th	1901: American Standard 1952: Revised Standard Version 1985: New Jerusalem Bible	1960: New American Standard 1982: New King James Version 1989: New Revised Standard
21st		2001: English Standard Version 2004: Holman Christian Standard 2011: New International Version

"Martyrdom" (Arabic *shahid*) is another word that has recently acquired connotations that would have surprised the earliest Muslims. In the Qur'an, a *shahid* is simply a "witness", without the connotation of dying for one's faith. The interpretation of *shahid* as "martyrdom" in the English sense is post-Qur'anic, and one of the earliest works to define the concept, the *Musannaf* of 'Abd al-Razzaq (744-829), defines a martyr as "one who, if he were to die in his bed, would enter heaven" (*Musannaf* 5:268, cited in Asfaruddin, 2010, p. 54). The *Musannaf* lists several examples of how martyrdom might be attained, including the plague, dying in childbirth, drowning, or dying of diarrhea. Significantly, there is no mention of death by violence. It is only later collections of hadith, like the *Sahih* of Muhammad al-Bukhari (810-870), that include dying on the battlefield on equal terms with death by disease or accident (Asfaruddin 2010).

And it was not until the "bloody" twentieth century that the word *shahid* began to be interpreted, mainly by Shi'a theologians in Iraq and Iran in the 1960s-70s, to include death as the result of a deliberate act of self-destruction (e.g., a suicide bombing) (Freamon, 2003). This interpretation goes against a long-standing prohibition against suicide in Islam. The Qur'an is ambiguous on the matter; verse 4:29 has been interpreted variously as "do not kill yourselves" and "do not kill one another.". The hadith, however, are full of clear condemnations against acts of self-destruction. Al-Bukhari tells numerous stories of the Prophet refusing to pray for the souls of men wounded on the battlefield who chose to end their suffering by taking their own lives, saying that for taking it upon themselves to do what belongs only to Allah to do, they will be sent to a Hell where they will be punished by having to relive endless repetitions of the moment of death (23: 446, as cited in Hare, 2010). Muslim ibn al-Hajjaj (817-874) also records the story of a group of soldiers who angered their commander, and as punishment, were ordered to enter into a fire. They refused, and when the matter was reported to the Prophet, he said: "If they had entered into the fire, they would have remained there until the Day of Judgment. There is no obedience in disobedience to Allah" (20:4535, as cited in Hare, 2010).

In short, according to the sources closest to the Prophet, anyone who strives daily to be a better person qualifies as a *jihadi*, and anyone engaged in this struggle at the moment of death qualifies as a *shahid* (martyr). If these original interpretations were more widely known today, one wonders whether the orchestrators of suicide bombings would have quite as large a pool of recruits to draw from.

Violence Resulting from Distortion of Language

If "the first casualty of war is the truth"[7], then surely language must be the first instance of "collateral damage." Orwell (1946) decried the use of language in wartime as "the defence of the indefensible" (p. 261). In his view, politicians whose real aims were at odds with their declared aims turned to vagueness and euphemism "instinctively…like a cuttlefish squirting out ink" (p. 262).

He offers these examples:

> Defenceless villages are bombarded from the air...this is called *pacification*. Millions of peasants are robbed of their farms and sent trudging along the roads with no more than they can carry: this is called *transfer of population* or *rectification of frontiers*. People are imprisoned for years without trial, or shot in the back of the neck or sent to die of scurvy in Arctic lumber camps: this is called *elimination of unreliable elements*. (p. 261)

His conclusion was that the political language of his day was "designed to make lies sound truthful and murder respectable, and to give an appearance of solidity to pure wind" (p. 265). To his mind, this degeneration of language, if left unchecked, would lead to the "Newspeak" of his novel 1984, an artificial variety of English constructed to make it impossible to say anything against the interests of the totalitarian government.

An observer of modern-day political language may conclude that, although the "cuttlefish" may not have blackened the ocean as completely as Orwell feared, consumers of news are still being served generous portions of *nero di seppia*. Examples abound of how governments in wartime use language like the two ends of a telescope, to magnify atrocities on the other side and minimize their own. "Torture" on their side is "enhanced interrogation techniques" on ours, "brutal slaughter of innocent civilians" on their side is "collateral damage" on ours, and so it goes.

Some of the most notorious examples of such language distortions, of course, came from Nazi Germany. The trial of Adolf Eichmann brought to light the "language rules" governing all official correspondence, strictly regulating what could or could not be said. According to Arendt (1964, p. 85), "The prescribed code names for 'killing' were 'final solution' (*Endlosung*), 'evacuation' (*Aussiedlung*) and 'special treatment' (*Sonderbehandlung*)."

This type of evasion serves a dual purpose. One, of course, is to conceal from the general public the true nature of the actions described. Naturally, those in the know are under no illusions about what these words refer to, but as Arendt (p. 87) continues: "The net effect of this language system was not to keep people ignorant about what they were doing, but to prevent them from equating it with their old, 'normal' knowledge of murder and lies."

When Eichmann visited a concentration camp, saw the gas chambers being prepared, and heard the camp commandant explain how they were going to be used, he discovered that the linguistic defenses that had been constructed for him were, as Arendt says, "not a foolproof shield against reality" (p. 87). In his own words:

> For me, this was monstrous. I am not so tough as to be able to endure something of this sort without any reaction.... If today I am shown a gaping wound, I can't possibly look at it. I am that type of person, so that very often I was told that I couldn't have become a doctor. I still remember how I pictured the thing to myself, and then I became physically weak, as though I had lived through some great agitation. (Arendt, p. 87)

In Eichmann's case, the fence that the "language rules" built around his mind, to keep out clear pictures of the actions that the words represented, allowed him to go complacently about his business of coordinating a process that, if he had seen it firsthand or even been able to form a clear image of it in his mind, would have horrified him.

Can something as simple as changing a word bypass the human conscience so completely? The testimony of Vietnam veteran Allen Nelson would suggest so. Nelson went to Vietnam a rough-and-ready Marine and came back a Quaker peace activist, and could point to the exact moment when the transformation came. While his platoon was passing through a village, they suddenly came under attack, and he took cover in one of the improvised bunkers that many houses had, only to find that he was sharing it with a teenage girl who was at that very moment going into labor. When he saw the baby emerging from the girl's body, he reflects, "I realized that the Vietnamese were human beings" (Nelson, 2003, p.18). That thought had not occurred to him until he saw incontrovertible physical evidence, because: "We never called the people of Vietnam the Vietnamese. We only called them 'gooks' and 'communists', and we were trained to think that gooks and communists were not humans" (p. 18).

The Linguist in Conflict

In Nelson's case, the simple act of changing the name moved the Vietnamese into a different mental category from ordinary human beings. But what about the linguist in wartime? Could someone who speaks the language of "the enemy" still be vulnerable to the kind of manipulation that led Nelson to believe that the Vietnamese were something other than human?

In the case of another Vietnam veteran, military intelligence officer Peter Martinsen, his Vietnamese language ability gave him no scruples about using cruel interrogation tactics, even staging a mock execution[8]:

> When I learned to speak Vietnamese, I was able to intimidate the Vietnamese. I was able to tell them in their own language, 'I know you're lying'...I had a man dig his own grave, with a gun at his head, and I counted off the minutes that he had to live, in Vietnamese so he knew I wasn't kidding (Oral testimony from the Vietnam War Crimes Tribunal, recorded in Limqueco and Weiss 1971, pp. 253, 260).

Other testimonies from a more recent war corroborate this. Erik Saar enlisted in the U.S. Army in the hope of going into military intelligence and learning Arabic, because he had "been fascinated by the complexities of Middle Eastern politics and culture for years" (Saar, 2005, p. 11). When the September 11 terror attacks struck shortly after the end of his language training, it gave him the opportunity to "think about what it now meant to be in military intelligence and to know the language of the enemy" (p. 3). His conclusion at the time was:

> Now the hatred would be coming right back at [al-Qaeda], with all the military might of the combined U.S. armed forces, and I was eager to be called into action...I kept hearing [intelligence community] chatter that we were about to pull out all the stops, not only in Afghanistan but around the Muslim world. As far as most of my friends in the military and I were concerned, we couldn't go after them soon enough. (pp. 3-4)

Saar was caught up in the wave of martial fervor, and anger towards the entire Muslim world, that swept the country after September 11. His knowledge of Arabic, rather than providing any protection, became instead a weapon in his arsenal.

Former U.S. Army interrogator Tony Lagouranis has a similar story. He joined the Army in peacetime primarily because it afforded the opportunity to pursue his interest in the Arabic language, and after September 11, found himself unexpectedly called into action in Iraq. Over time, as his superiors ordered him to use increasingly harsh interrogation techniques, his qualms diminished, until the point where he thought, as he walked into a detainee's cell:

> Khalid was right where I left him, calm and serene. I never saw a hint of resentment or fear in his eyes. When I looked at him, the anger surged…A thought flashed through my head: *Chop his* [expletive] *fingers off.* (Lagouranis 2007, p. 127)

This also proved to be a watershed moment for Lagouranis, as he goes on to reflect:

> Something very wrong had happened here. The idea of cutting his fingers off was something I quickly dismissed, but the fact that it even crossed my mind… Here was a signal that it was time to pull myself out of this abyss. (p. 130).

Testimonies such as these suggest that language learning is not necessarily an effective vaccine against the dark forces that take over the mind in wartime and cast the other side as something less than human.

In some cases, however, we can see a ray of light. Both Saar, with his gung-ho attitude at the beginning of the war, and Lagouranis, whose qualms about torture fell by the wayside during his tour of duty, left the service with grave misgivings about the war itself and their own role in it. Lagouranis' story also offers a counter-example, in the case of a friend who had joined the Army as a political conservative and unquestioning soldier, and left it as a conscientious objector:

> His experience learning Arabic and following the news and constantly talking to and challenging other people changed him…One of the early influences on his transformation was Al Jazeera. We watched this station constantly at [the Defense Language Institute], and I remember him starting to see that Middle Eastern issues were actually very complex. That the Palestinians had legitimate grievances, that the Saudis weren't always the best allies, that everyone did not see America as a paragon of virtue. (Lagouranis, 2007, pp. 144-145)

Presumably this is not the return that the Department of Defense hopes for on its investment in language training. It does offer a note of hope, however, that language learning—and more importantly, the voices from "the other side" that can enter the soldier's mind through the gate of a new language—can help protect the human soul from the corrosion to which it is so often prone in wartime.

The Linguist as Mediator

The story above illustrates how language learning can help even soldiers at war to move past seeing the conflict in terms of "us vs. them", and perceive the other side as human beings. Having come to this realization, the linguist in wartime is also uniquely placed to intervene between the two sides and reduce bloodshed.

Several examples can be found in the testimonies of United States Navy and Marine Corps linguists, who deployed to the Pacific Theater after intensive study of Japanese. For them, the process of change began in language school:

> By the end of the second trimester, regular contact with their teachers in and beyond the classroom wiped away any 'race theories' the students may have had. Their teachers became friends who bore little resemblance to the racial stereotypes of Japanese so prevalent in wartime American society…[The students] were learning to look beyond the barriers of race and prejudice to see persons of Japanese ancestry as individual human beings not so very different from themselves. (Dingman, 2009, pp. 47-48)

When these linguists were sent into combat in the Marianas, the units they accompanied often needed to assist fleeing civilians while staying wary of soldiers waiting in ambush. This frequently involved the dangerous task of "cave-crawling": entering into the caves that dotted the islands, not knowing whether they would find frightened civilians or armed soldiers inside. Many Marine commanders preferred to resolve this issue simply by shooting all Japanese on sight, or blanketing an entire area with napalm or hydrogen phosphorous. It fell to the linguists to persuade their leaders to hold fire and give the civilians a chance to surrender, even if the linguists had to risk their lives by taking the task of cave-crawling on themselves.

In and out of the caves, the linguists had to negotiate with Japanese soldiers and civilians who had been told by their government that suicide was preferable to surrender. "As time passed…the Marine interpreters got better at producing happier results. They would try to wait out civilians, who after they came out of their hiding places and received decent treatment, would urge soldiers still in hiding to surrender themselves" (p. 88).

It also fell to the linguists to make sure that captives really were treated decently, in spite of ramshackle prison camps, scarce resources, and leaders often indifferent to the suffering of the prisoners, such as the overtly racist commander of one Navy base who insisted that "Japanese" be written with a lower-case "j" and noted on a report about an accident involving a Japanese worker, "Too bad it didn't kill him" (p. 213). One linguist reminded medical personnel that they needed to care for the sick and wounded among the captives as well as the soldiers, and scrounged rice for sick and malnourished prisoners. For this, he was threatened with a court martial at the time, but later received a commendation (p. 181).

For the persuasiveness that helped them reduce further bloodshed, these linguists were recognized as highly valuable assets to the armed forces. Four Marine linguists were awarded Bronze Stars for their "innovative and courageous work in broadcasting surrender appeals and rescuing civilians. The 24th Regiment intelligence officer reported that 'the value of Japanese linguists cannot be overestimated'" (p. 89).

It would be encouraging to be able to share similar success stories from military linguists in more modern wars, like Afghanistan and Iraq. Such stories, however, are hard to come by. By the most generous estimates, fewer than 1,000 of the 130,000 U.S. troops stationed in Iraq, less than 1% of the total force, had even a rudimentary knowledge of Arabic (Guidère, 2008; Tan, 2008).

One of the ways the U.S. military tried to remedy this deficiency was by trying actively to recruit American citizens or permanent residents (offering the latter the enticement of a fast track to citizenship) from an Arabic-speaking background as linguists under the "09-Lima" designation (Tan, 2008). The attrition rate in this program, however, was around 40%, partly because of the discrimination these recruits often faced in the Army. One recruiting sergeant recalls his own experience being called "raghead" or "Taliban" by his fellow soldiers (Elliott, 2006), about which he presumably kept silent when talking to potential recruits.

Another way was through the use of contract interpreters recruited from among civilians in the theater of operations. These interpreters frequently proved to be indispensable to the military, as one Army platoon leader recounts:

> What I have come to understand since patrolling the streets of Baghdad day after day is that [our interpreter] is one of our most valuable assets for bringing peace

to Iraq. He understands the mindset of civilians with whom we interact on a daily basis. He lends his support well beyond that of just translation by providing recommendations on projects that are sustainable based on the framework of local government and the precarious rule of law in the city. (quoted in Inghilleri 2010, p. 189)

But the coalition forces' recognition of the interpreters' value did not necessarily extend to protecting them adequately. Over 300 civilian interpreters working for American and British forces were killed during the Iraq War (Hawksley, 2008), targeted as enemy collaborators by insurgents and sometimes even by their own families (Associated Press, 2010). In many cases, the policies of the Pentagon made the interpreters easier targets. Interpreters were not issued body armor. They were not allowed to use priority lanes to enter the Green Zone, having instead to wait in long lines under constant threat of sniper attacks. Requests for asylum often languished in interminable bureaucracy. At one point, Army commanders forbade interpreters to wear the face masks that kept their identity secret from other Iraqis, until pressure from within the Army compelled them to rescind that decision (Hawksley, 2008; Packer, 2007).

How does the U.S. military expect to "win hearts and minds" if it has to borrow ears and tongues? Perhaps this problem is what U.S. President Barack Obama (2009) had in mind when he said, "In the 21st century, military strength will be measured not only by the weapons our troops carry, but by the languages they speak and the cultures they understand" (para. 40). If this statement indicates a shift from bullets to words as the U.S. military's weapon of choice, it is to be welcomed. On the other hand, it would also suggest that the military-industrial complex perceives language learning as no threat to its continued existence.

In addition to serving as a mediator between opposing forces in wartime, the linguist can also play a valuable role in defusing an intra-state conflict before it escalates into civil war. We can see evidence of this in one final example: the transition from apartheid to democracy in South Africa.

At the conclusion of the Truth and Reconciliation Commission hearings, commissioner Archbishop Desmond Tutu wrote that reconciliation was an ongoing process, "a national project to which every South African makes a contribution" by many means including "learning the language and culture of others" (Tutu, 1999, p. 274). In matters of language, he can be assumed to know whereof he spoke, because part of his job as commissioner was coordinating simultaneous interpretation among all of South Africa's eleven official languages—a logistical challenge that makes the U.N. General Assembly, with its six official languages, look easy.

Usually, at high-profile public events, interpreters are relegated to the sidelines—heard but not seen. After the Truth and Reconciliation Commission hearings, however, the "Truth in Translation" project set about trying to discover the interpreters' points of view on the proceedings, with an eye towards a dramatic performance in which the interpreters would take center stage. Part of this project was a symposium for the former interpreters, convened in 2003 and archived on video on the project's website (Truth in Translation Project, 2003). The interpreters' reflections included:

- "The interpreter was the sponge that absorbed all the pain throughout the entire process." (Sphithi Mona, Swathi/Sepedi/Sesotho/Afrikaans/ English)
- "I'm interpreting for a white Afrikaans-speaking male as a perpetrator. I didn't have to live myself into the role of the perpetrator, because I grew up with it. It's a new process of holding a mirror up to my face." (Louis Nel, Afrikaans/English)
- "We would go into the booth, and just interpret. And there would be no communication, no interaction, with these white men who were the perpetrators. So many people viewed them as monsters. And the only people that they could really communicate with, talk to, whom they felt would at least be neutral or objective, were the interpreters." (Nomusa Zulu, Zulu/Swazi/Afrikaans/English)

The reflections of these interpreters suggest that they saw their function not only as interpreting from one language into another, but also as being neutral mediators between victims and oppressors, who could play a vital role in the healing of the nation.

Conclusion

From the small and disparate sampling of evidence examined here, what conclusions can be drawn? An increase in language learning may or may not lead to an increase in peace, but the inverse is certainly true: denial or suppression of language leads to an increase in violence. Being able to learn, use, and be educated in the language of your choice is a basic human right, and interference with that right is a form of structural violence that may become the spark that ignites direct violence.

Governments at war, and the "religious" leaders who support them, are masters at manipulating language to serve their own ends. In such situations, linguists (those who know another language, or are trained to analyze the use of their own) are better equipped to draw from the original sources of their guiding principles, and see past the propaganda of the "cuttlefish" who distort language for the sake of political expediency.

The mere fact of learning a language does not necessarily make the learner more predisposed toward peace, nor does it confer immunity from the cruel impulses that affect so many soldiers in wartime, as the testimony of the military interrogators from Vietnam and Iraq indicates. At the same time, other testimonies show that people who have taken the time and trouble to learn the language of "the enemy" cannot help seeing them as fellow human beings, however strong the pressure may be to cast them in the role of demons or monsters. They are also uniquely equipped to be mediators, helping to prevent conflict from escalating into open war, reduce bloodshed during war, and ease the transition to a stable peace after war.

Language learning in itself may or may not contribute directly to the peace of the world. But it is clear that, if we agree with Quaker peace activist Gene Knudsen Hoffman's (1997) maxim that "An enemy is one whose story we have not heard," then language learning opens the doors to hear the stories of the other side, whereupon it becomes harder to see them as "the enemy". And language learners who then take upon themselves the role of persuader or mediator will find that their language learning is a powerful tool to make them agents of peace.

Notes
1. A ranking of 162 countries from most to least peaceful, based on 23 criteria broadly categorized into: militarization, ongoing international and domestic conflict, and safety and security in society.
2. The probability that any two randomly chosen inhabitants of a country will have different mother tongues.
3. This was chosen as the main criterion in order to give a more global view. All the highest scorers on the Greenberg index, except Papua New Guinea, are in sub-Saharan Africa.
4. St. Maximilian of Tebessa (274-295) was the first known conscientious objector

to be martyred, claiming that "I cannot serve in the military; I cannot do evil; I am a Christian." (*Acta Maximiliani*, BHL 5813, cited in Wood, 1999.)
5. St. Augustine of Hippo (354-430), originator of the "Just War Doctrine", later expanded by Thomas Aquinas (1225-1274) into the version currently recognized by the Catholic Church.
6. U.S. Secretary of Defense 2001-06, who liked to embellish the cover pages of his "Worldwide Intelligence Updates" with quotations from Scripture.
7. Commonly attributed to U.S. Senator Hiram Warren Johnson (1866-1945).
8. At the time, this interrogation technique was not specifically banned under the Geneva Conventions, but it has since been included under the prohibited category of "cruel and degrading treatment", and it was named in a WHO report as an unacceptable form of "organized violence" (World Health Organization, 1987).

References

Arendt, H. (1964). *Eichmann in Jerusalem: A report on the banality of evil*. New York: Viking Press.
Asfaruddin, A. (2010). Recovering the early semantic purview of jihad and martyrdom: Challenging statist-military perspectives. In Q. Huda (Ed.), *Crescent and dove: Peace and conflict resolution in Islam* (pp. 39-62). Washington, DC: U.S. Institute of Peace Press.
Bailey, W. A. (2005). *"You shall not kill" or "You shall not murder"? The assault on a biblical text*. Collegeville, MN: Liturgical Press.
Bari, M. (1998). *A brief history of the Bangla language movement*. Retrieved from http://www.virtualbangladesh.com/history/ekushe.html
Dingman, R. (2009). *Deciphering the rising sun: Navy and Marine Corps codebreakers, translators and interpreters in the Pacific War*. Annapolis, MD: Naval Institute Press.
Elliott, A. (2006, Oct 7). For recruiter speaking Arabic, saying "Go Army" is a hard job. *The New York Times*. Retrieved from http://www.nytimes.com/2006/10/07/us/07recruit.html
Freamon, B. K. (2003). Martyrdom, suicide, and the Islamic law of war: A short legal history. *Fordham International Law Journal, 27*(1), 299-369.
Galtung, J. (1969). Violence, peace, and peace research. *Journal of Peace Research, 6*(3), 167-191.
Guidère, M. (2008). *Irak in translation: De l'art de perdre une guerre sans connaître la langue de son adversaire* [Iraq in translation: The art of losing a war without knowing the language of one's adversary]. Paris: Éditions Jacob-Duvernet.
Hare, J. B. (2010). *Internet sacred text archive*. Retrieved from http://www.sacred-texts.com/index.htm
Hawksley, H. (2008, Dec 6). Iraq translators' mask ban dropped. BBC News. Retrieved from http://news.bbc.co.uk
Hoffman, G. K. (1997). An enemy is one whose story we have not heard. *The Journal of the Fellowship of Reconciliation*, May/June. Retrieved from http://www.coopcomm.org/gkh_essay05.htm
Inghilleri, M. (2010). "You don't make war without knowing why": The decision to interpret in Iraq. *The Translator, 16*(2), 175-196.
Lagouranis, T. (2007). *Fear Up Harsh: An Army interrogator's dark journey through Iraq*. New York: New American Library Caliber.

Lewis, M. P. (Ed.) (2009). *Ethnologue: Languages of the world* (16th ed). Dallas: SIL International. Retrieved from http://www.ethnologue.com

Limqueco, P., & Weiss. P. (Eds.) (1971). *Prevent the crime of silence*. London: Bertrand Russell Peace Foundation.

Nakamura, K. (1973). *Ghazali on prayer*. Tokyo: University of Tokyo Press.

Nelson, A. (2003). *You don't know war: Allen says it's because of Article 9*. Kyoto: Kamogawa Shuppan.

Obama, B. (2009, August 17). *Fulfilling America's responsibility to those who serve*. Address to Veterans of Foreign Wars, Phoenix, AZ. Retrieved from http://www.realclearpolitics.com

Orwell, G. (1946). Politics and the English language. *Horizon, 13*(76), 252-265.

Packer, G. (2007, March 26). Betrayed: The Iraqis who trusted America the most. *The New Yorker*. Retrieved from http://www.newyorker.com

Roosevelt, T. (1919, January 5). *Address to the President of the American Defense Society, New York*. Retrieved from http://msgboard.snopes.com/politics/graphics/troosevelt.pdf

Saar, E. (2005). *Inside the wire: A military intelligence soldier's eyewitness account of life at Guantanamo*. New York: Penguin.

Tan, M. (2008, June 21). Army sweetens re-up deal for linguists. *Army Times*. Retrieved from http://www.armytimes.com/news/2008/06/army_09Lima_062108w/

Truth in Translation Project. (2003). TRC interpreters' conference [Video file.] Retrieved from http://www.truthintranslation.org/index.php/v2/video#video2

Tutu, D. (1999). *No future without forgiveness*. New York: Image Doubleday.

United Nations Educational, Scientific, and Cultural Organization (UNESCO). (1996). *Universal declaration on linguistic rights*. Retrieved from http://www.unesco.org/pv_obj_cache/pv_obj_id_64A2F5B271ADB276B4B9BF514A1E84ACA9A60000/filename/linguistic.pdf

Vision of Humanity. (2013). *The 2013 global peace index*. Retrieved from http://www.visionofhumanity.org/gpi-data/

Woods, D. (1999). St. Maximilan of Tebessa. In *The military martyrs*. Retrieved from http://www.ucc.ie/milmart/Maximilian.html.

World Health Organization (WHO). (1987). *Health hazards of organized violence*. The Hague: Distribution Center of Government Publications, Ministry of Welfare, Health and Cultural Affairs.

Yacoub, S. N. (2010, June 18). Iraqi interpreter for U.S. Army shot dead by family over his job. *Huffington Post*. Retrieved from http://www.huffingtonpost.com/2010/06/18/iraqi-interpreter-for-us_n_617359.html

LANGUAGE, CULTURE, AND SOCIETY

CHAPTER 11

IDENTIFYING AND IDENTIFIED—IN VAIN:
Autoethnographic Inquiry into Language, Gender, and Identity

Aya Kitamura
Tsuda College

Ethnographer's Dilemma and Autoethnography

In qualitative research, the relationship between the researcher and the researched has long been problematized as essentially unilateral, asymmetrical and thus unrequited. While some scholars claim that their studies work to empower the research participants, others are more skeptical, raising the issues of appropriation and exploitation that the unequal relationship causes in the research field. Critical questions such as "For whom?", "In what voice?", and "By whom?" (Fine et al., 2003) are now inevitable when one ventures to represent others in an academic text. One should also be reminded that what she or he depicts is nothing but a "partial truth—committed and incomplete" (Clifford, 1986, p. 7), far from something captured from a transcendent viewpoint.

Feminist ethnographers and native ethnographers—and those who identify themselves as both—have most acutely confronted this issue of ethnographic representation. The researcher, sharing the same gender, racial, ethnic and/or cultural background with her research participants, risks exploiting and betraying those who regard her as "one of them." No matter how intimate the encounters are, the end result is, more often than not, an impersonal and wordy text that is meant to circulate only in the academia. Those represented are unlikely to have access to it, and even if they do, they may not recognize themselves in the text. Ruth Behar (1996), Judith

Stacy (1991) and Lila Abu-Lughot (1991), all acutely aware of their complex position as a feminist and/or native ethnographer, speak of the dilemmas in which they find themselves.

> Our methodology, defined by the oxymoron "participant observation," is split at the root: act as a participant, but don't forget to keep your eyes open. Lay down in the mud in Colombia. Put your arms around Omaira Sanchéz. But when the money runs out, the summer vacation is over, please stand up, dust yourself off, go to your desk, and write down what you saw and heard. Relate it to something you've read by Marx, Weber, Gramsci, or Geertz and you're on your way to doing anthropology. (Behar, 1996, p. 5)

> The lives, loves, and tragedies that fieldwork informants share with a researcher are ultimately data—grist for the ethnographic mill, a mil that has a truly grinding power. ... In this sense, too, elements of inequality, exploitation, and even betrayal are endemic to ethnography. (Stacey, 1991, pp. 113-4)

> Both halfie and feminist anthropologists are forced to confront squarely the politics and ethics of their representation. There are no easy solutions to their dilemmas. (Abu-Lughot, 1991, p. 469)

I, a Japanese woman researching Japanese women, am a "halfie," in Narayan's (1993) sense of the term, meaning not just that I am bilingual/bicultural but also that I am half researcher, half researched. And I have had my fair share of the ethnographer's "dilemma." On the one hand, I feel it my responsibility to represent Japanese women as a Japanese woman myself; on the other hand, I find it impossible to do so when my research participants differentiate and distance themselves from me. The women I talk to at times seem like comrades while some of them speak as if I were an outsider—or worse, an enemy. The intimacy we cultivate during interviews could easily evaporate, a reminder that the ethnographic rapport can be imaginary. The partial truth I depict is, at best, contentious and fragmentary.

Autoethnography is among others a method that attempts to tackle, if not resolve, the dilemma that stems from the ethnographer's split positionality.

> Autoethnography is an autobiographical genre of writing and research that displays multiple layers of consciousness, connecting the personal to the cultural. Back and forth authoethnographers gaze, first through an ethnographic wide-angle lens, focusing outward on social and cultural aspects of their personal

experience; then, they look inward, exposing a vulnerable self that is moved by and may move through, refract, and resist cultural interpretations. ... As they zoom backward and forward, inward and outward, distinctions between the personal and cultural become blurred, sometimes beyond distinct recognition. (Ellis & Bochner, 2000, p. 739)

Here, the distinction between the observer and the observed is also blurred. An analytical gaze is now turned at the researcher herself, and not only the research participants' but also the researcher's stories become the "grist" for ethnography. She is now a "vulnerable observer" (Behar, 1996) who cannot stay behind the academic fortress of objectivity, neutrality and generalizability. The self-reflexive process is what the method focuses on, and the researcher's emotional experiences, traditionally regarded as irrelevant and even a taboo, become the central data of inquiry.

Therefore, autoethnography is not a mere collection of backstage anecdotes. Nor is it a self-indulgent, self-absorbed narrative by a researcher, which, as often accused, mutes the research participants' voices in turn. It is a methodology that turns personal accounts into "*a critical, performative practice*, a practice that begins with the biography of the writer and moves outward to culture, discourse, history and ideology" (Denzin, 2014, p. x, emphasis added). While individual autoethnographies can take on varying, unorthodox forms including poetry, theater and visual arts, the "critical, performative practices" commonly aim for subversion. Some may explicitly violate academic norms, using "I" in every sentence or referring to their sexual encounters in their research fields. Others—often researchers in socially vulnerable positions themselves—would challenge dominant power structures, drawing on their senses of misery, sorrow and anger. In the introduction to *Critical autoethnography*, the editors, professing, "We write as an Other, and for an Other" (p. 15), say:

> Autoethnography is oftentimes serendipitous, occurring when we are going about our everyday lives. Autoethnography is also therapeutic, embodied, performartive, and queer, speaking from, for, and to the margins. (Boylorn & Orbe, 2014, p. 18)

Reflecting this methodological paradigm, this paper offers an autoethnographic account of a complex, conflicting and thus impossible identification process of a bilingual Japanese woman researching other bilingual Japanese women. I will discuss my dilemma, my "halfie-ness," recounting and examining concrete experiences that I had with specific others in particular contexts. The "epiphanies" (Denzin, 2001, 2014) I delineate here involve both personal troubles and sociopolitical issues, the connected nature of which is the central focus of exploration.

Is English a Savior for Women?: The Project
My sociological inquiry revolves around language, gender and identity in Japan, a society in which the English language has a curious position. It is said to be idolized and coveted—an object of *akogare*—especially among women, who, arguably, are victimized in the male-dominated society. Japanese women are therefore said to dream of liberation through the acquisition of English, or in some cases, an English-speaking man (Kelsky, 2001, 2008; Kobayashi, 2002; Takahashi, 2013). Women in Japan have been therefore depicted in their fervent pursuits of "Western dreams" (Kelsky, 2001).

How it Started
As a bilingual woman in Japan, teaching, researching, presenting and writing in both Japanese and English, I have always agonized over such prevailing images. I was once a learner of English. Yes, I was quite impassioned. But I don't associate myself with the naïve *akogare*-infatuated women I often encounter in scholarly discourses. I used to say I liked English when I was young, but I am not sure exactly in what sense. I don't recall having any specific goals or hopes at that time; I just enjoyed getting high marks in school exams, didn't I? Did I fantasize about an English-speaking Prince Charming? Did I envision liberation through English? Liberation from what? I have been unable to locate myself in the seemingly established discourse.

Nevertheless, at present, I may look like an embodiment of the "Western dreams," with my international, intercultural and interlinguistic work and marriage; however, I have never been comfortable with such a label, either. The dominant image of successful and contented bilingual woman, circulating both in journalistic and academic writings, always disturbs me. Whenever I try to speak of myself, in a hospital, hair salon or real estate agency, I have to fight people's (well-meaning) words of compliment and adoration. It is as if the stereotype of the bilingual woman encapsulates me, denying my personal experiences and feelings, some bitter and worrisome.

My predicament also comes from my dual background as a sociologist and an English teacher. The former identity sheds a critical gaze at so-called "English dominance" (Tsuda, 1990) in Japan. In class, I critique the Japanese government's empty slogans of internationalization and globalization, which in fact mean only Anglicization (Kubota, 2002). I passionately lecture on language politics from our everyday language discrimination to worldwide linguistic imperialism (Phillipson, 1992). However, in my English language classes, I teach grammar, correct students' sentences and thus mold their imaginative writings with academic norms. I am indeed a part of the "global education" fad, supported by the Japanese government's "Project for Promotion of Global Human Resource Development." I am feeding my students into the political apparatus of which I am so critical. I know I contradict myself.

Exasperated, I strive to pursue critical pedagogy and feminist pedagogy, firmly believing that the students' learning processes involve not only static acquisition but also participation in the language community and appropriation of the language (Block, 2003). I teach them how feminist and postcolonial writers have appropriated and subverted the language of men and colonialists, dislocating their authority. I encourage them to do the same, to read English academic articles critically and to question, examine and deploy the language for their own ends. I try to promote such active and subversive learning. However, whether I am successful in this pursuit remains a question. I often catch myself drowning in my self-consciousness, never content with my bilingual and bi-disciplinary self.

Such personal discomfort has been the backdrop of my sociological project since 2008. I had to look into how other bilingual women deal with their identities, negotiating their relationship with the language of *akogare*. I have been interviewing forty female translators, interpreters, English instructors and corporate employees using English at work in the Tokyo Metropolitan area, periodically meeting with several of them for follow-ups. Their ages range from twenty-four to fifty-nine, and most of the women I interview are highly educated, some with graduate degrees earned overseas. In 2011, I published an interim part of the longitudinal project, a Japanese book entitled, *Eigo wa onna o sukuu noka* (*Is English a Savior for Women?*) (Kitamura, 2011).

How it Developed

In the beginning of each interview, I tell the research participant that I am curious as to whether English actually rescues women in Japan, as we often hear in the media, and that I would like to hear her opinion. I ask participants to reflect upon their past experiences and present situations with regard to the question. I conduct an "active interview" (Holstein & Gubrium, 1995, 2003), interactively taking part in the dialogue, rather than statically posing questions and quietly listening. That is, contrary to the traditional objective interviewer, I react to—often empathize with—what the women have to say. I also refer to my own experiences, disclosing who I am and what I think, to receive both agreeing and disagreeing remarks. The resulting data therefore is co-constructed through our interaction.

> Respondents' responses are not viewed as reality reports delivered from a fixed repository. Instead, they are considered for the ways that they construct aspects of reality in collaboration with the interviewer. (Holstein & Gubrium, 2003, p. 79)

Actively interviewing other bilingual Japanese women has been assuring and agitating at the same time. Assuring because I learned that I was not the only one with mixed feelings towards English, our reputed savior. While some women immediately brushed off the myth of English salvation, other women at first exhibited a well-crafted story of their successful English endeavors. Although those stories of proud achievements resemble the "personal testimony" (Seargeant, 2009) articles prevalent in English-celebrating magazines in Japan, quite a few of the stories I heard involved twists as they progressed. As I spoke of my own reservations towards the popular images of the English language and bilingual women, the women started to disclose some of the troubling aspects of their lives too. For example, a Japanese-English translator gradually spoke of the hardship she underwent on a daily basis juggling childcare and demanding job orders that poured in during the evening and that needed to be completed by the next morning. An English language textbook editor more noticeably changed her tones in the middle; after a coherent speech on how she had gained her present status, she told me that the job required extraordinary physical and mental commitment, which at times exhausted her. She also lamented that her friends outside the English-related industry never seemed to understand her predicament and only repeated that they envied her. The grass is always greener on the other side, we concurred.

Simultaneously, as I collected such intriguing stories, I was distressed by what little vocabulary was available to speak of the complex, even incoherent, identities of bilingual women in Japan. During interviews, we were tongue-twisted describing ourselves. The working-mom translator significantly slowed down when reflecting upon her day-to-day burdens, while her speech was much smoother, as if reciting a story, in describing her career course. The textbook editor spoke of the difficulty to communicate with her friends about her conflicts, and she seemed to be experiencing just the same at the interview, pausing and sighing, "I don't know" many times. Transcribing the data, I caught myself stammering too to make sense of myself. They—and I—were struggling to break out of the stereotypes of liberated and empowered bilingual women. And yet, we also tried to escape from the miserable picture of disillusioned *akogare*-pursuer, victimized in the persistent gender, racial, ethnic and linguistic hierarchies. We fought to detach ourselves from both, finding no secure position.

As an academic, I was expected to yield a thesis out of the interviews, an answer to the question whether the English language rescues Japanese women. It would have been easier if I had drawn a simple conclusion that, say, Japanese women's English dreams were after all doomed. However, was it such a simple story that we exchanged over a three-hour lunch, sipping coffee that had gone cold? Didn't we keep searching for words that described what we had in our mind, albeit to no avail? How could I capture the sense of frustration that was so palpable at the interviews?

The conclusion—tentative and indefinite—I drew for the book, *Is English Savior for Women*? was that English sometimes saves Japanese women, and it sometimes does not. What more could I have said after hearing—in fact, collaboratively constructing—those rich, complex narratives? Instead, I questioned the question itself, challenging why it is that we need a simple answer, a linear story, to begin with. I focused on the multiplicity of women's experiences and the complexity of their relationships with English, reexamining the surrounding discourses simultaneously.

In the course of the analysis, I criticized the ready-made vocabulary such as *akogare*, liberation and empowerment for shaping the diverse women's experiences into a monolith. I used alternative key terms such as "ambivalence" and "desperation." I demonstrated, through quoting and analyzing the women's narratives, how it was not a simple either/or question. The women held mixed feelings towards the English language, and the language at times left the women despairing in their realities that couldn't be farther from its glamorous image.

In fact, I did not use the clumsy, ill-fitting Japanese translations for those terms (*ryōgisei* for ambivalence and *zetsubō* for desperation). I instead put them in katakana (a type of Japanese syllabic writing mainly used for foreign-borrowed words) as *anbivarensu* and *desuparēshon*, explicating at length what they connote. The choice reflects my bilingual identity, that is, how I always mix two languages and create a hybrid tongue. The research participants did the same in the interviews too. Of course the katakana-laden text exposed me to criticism that I was an elitist English imperialist; however, I chose to venture the language hybridization in a firm belief that my readers, even if they were not English speakers, would familiarize themselves with those new concepts given the ample examples from interviews along with my explanation. I thought that avoiding new terms assuming that "lay (monolingual) people" wouldn't understand them was in fact elitist. I attempted to offer a new set of vocabulary that helped us see beyond what had already been told.

Therefore, the seemingly simple inquiry in fact encompassed political motives, revealing hidden aspects of bilingual women's realities for one and re-narrating the women's identities in an alternative way for another. The voices of forty other bilingual Japanese women made it possible to do so. The book was therefore a fruit of our collaborative endeavor—or so I thought.

Ethnographer's Dilemma Deepening: The Representation Politics

My findings that bilingual women's admittedly successful lives could actually be precarious and disillusioning and that many of them were ambivalent about their "savior" were, as I said, a revelation enabled through animated conversations based on our similarities in background. I often spoke of my dilemma of educating female elites, who may not always be able to climb up the social ladder as a racial, linguistic and gender Other, just like many of the women and I had experienced. Our exchanges deepened, eliciting more and more of the English realities that had been shed little light on.

In 2010, a Tokyo publisher offered to include *Is English a Savior for Women?* in a series that they had recently launched. The series had produced books with social-science themes but written for a more general and younger (twenties to forties) readership. They would design my book in such a way as to attract young women, allegedly an untapped market for such a genre. I was going to represent the hidden realities of bilingual career women to a larger world. I would bridge women separated by the English divide.

As I prepared my book manuscript, I asked each research participant to read over the parts where they were quoted. I had promised each research participant to do so before anything went in print; however, many were surprised at my request because, in fact, such procedure is rather unusual in Japan. Unexpectedly, revisiting what we had discussed at the interviews yielded even further findings. Some took the opportunity to reflect upon their lives once again while others noticed that their opinions had changed since the interviews. They told me more stories, some of which, upon their consent, I added to my manuscript. Fortunately, everyone agreed with how I presented them in the book, some taking interest in my findings and others agreeing with my theses—everyone except one.

This person was angry. She wrote me a long email saying that I used her words against her. I included too much of her personal troubles that she had told me only informally, over a couple of glasses of wine. Her husband would divorce her if he read my book. What would her friends think? Her colleagues? In-laws? She had expected to be presented in a certain way, which couldn't be more different from my manuscript. She wanted out. All I could do was to apologize and agree to edit her words out.

Apparently, my promise to protect the participants' privacy and my explanation before and during the interview that everyone would be treated anonymously in the book were not successful or sufficient. At the interviews, in order to induce a candid atmosphere, I presented myself not so much as a researcher but as a friend's friend. I did not present a formal consent form or have them sign on it, but took the consent only orally. The anonymity part hence had slipped out of the woman's mind, and she thought that her identity would appear in the book. My apologetic explanation afterwards did not help change her mind. Her decision to participate in my research had involved not only me writing about her but also her showing the book to her friends and families.

My personal skills as a researcher were certainly to blame, and the lack of ethical codes in Japanese academia may be called into question too. And yet, this should not be regarded merely as personal misconduct, a cautionary tale for researchers. For, the woman's expectation was, I would argue, socioculturally constructed. As discussed earlier, women's magazines are filled with positive, inspirational images of "real-life" bilingual women. It is not surprising if she, and possibly some others, thought that I was writing something like those magazine articles. If so, she had every right to be angry when I focused on the parts where she revealed the somewhat harsh realities of her professional and personal lives, which, according to her, she would not have mentioned in a formal setting. That is, she drew a line between what should be disclosed in an informal chat and in a published context. I then violated the boundary, trying to drag all the pieces into the public light.

There was in fact one more participant who withdrew, saying that her husband was against her presenting her life story in a book, albeit anonymously. She said that her husband thought it was embarrassing for an ordinary person to brag about her life. I explained to her once again that my aim was to share with readers what she had experienced, ordinary or not, but in vain. She, and her husband, had a clear idea of who should be represented in the media and who should not. I was trying to debunk the stereotype of bilingual Japanese women being extraordinary; and yet, the very ideological construct interfered with my interaction with some research participants. I was trapped.

I felt deflated by these experiences, and my confidence in what had seemed a good cause collapsed. My apparent successes at the other interviews started to trouble me. The vivid, at times poignant, stories were private and sometimes cast an unflattering light on the women. Who would want to see themselves represented in a book ranting about their present work conditions or disclosing their physical and mental illnesses caused by a stressful job? Especially when the high-careered women I interviewed were proud of their achievements at the same time? Who was I to expose them against their will?

There was one participant whose story I was aware that I used in a way she never imagined. She was an aspiring literary translator and kept saying during the interview that what she had to tell me was irrelevant because she was "inferior to all those great achievers out there." Therefore, upon reading the manuscript, she was beyond belief that I quoted her in more than ten lines, in which she articulated her intriguing relationship with English. She was learning English translation, but not out of professional ambition. She emphasized that she only took pleasure in the learning process—"any type of learning for that matter"—after her failed attempt to conceive a child. Although her words, taken out of such poignant context, could have been analyzed as a case of English salvation, I discussed her agency instead. Her narrative that she "gave up on a so-called normal life as a woman" and then engaged herself with English learning "but just as a hobby," to me, signifies an evasive identity; she refused to associate herself with the normative "good wife, wise mother" figure or the prevailing "inspirational bilingual woman" story. She created a space of her own, defying both gender and linguistic ideologies in Japanese society.

She commented on my analysis that she was amazed at how "a scholar can transform banal experiences into something significant." I took it as a complement as such deconstructive representation was the original intention of my book. Recalling the exchanges, however, I am not certain to what degree she was comfortable with the way I represented her. I "transformed" her after all. I cannot tell if I did justice to her and the other women who so openly confided with me. And what does it mean to "do justice" in representing the lives, experiences and identities of others? Who can judge that, and how? At the same time, I kept my own "transformation" through the course of writing this book, a trajectory from a researcher to an ally and back to a researcher, behind the scenes. Our relationship remains asymmetrical.

Apparently, the research participants and I were not always able to identify with each other although we shared similar backgrounds in terms of nationality, race, ethnicity, gender and language. As "one of them," I tried to expose the hidden realities of bilingual Japanese women, but some of the research participants may have wanted a different light cast on them. The angry email from the participant who felt she had been misled suggests that women themselves may want to keep some realities in the dark. For an apparent social sanction, they may prefer to be represented just like the successful women in magazines. The withdrawal and hesitation of some participants indicate that the women are well aware of what they are expected to look like as bilinguals, and that they at times feel they fall short of such expectations. It was such sociocultural expectations that I wanted to problematize, but I found myself trapped by the same discourse in the process. Moreover, a few participants backed out in the end, and there may have been others to whom I brought discomfort, or possibly, feelings of betrayal. My attempt to identify with the bilingual women, ultimately, deepened my ethnographer's dilemma.

Epiphanies: What Autoethnography Enables

Being a learner, teacher and researcher of English all at once, I often find myself caught up in split subjectivities. Such emotional experiences have brought a critical insight into the popular images that simplify the lived experiences of us bilingual Japanese women. We are not simply liberated through our study or work abroad experiences, and English does not necessarily open a door to a new, better world. And yet, we are not mere victims of an English-imperialist and male-dominant society. We struggle within the powerful discourses, narrating incoherent and thus subversive identities.

My interactions with some research participants, however, brought into question the notions of "we" and "us." I was at first exhilarated at the commonalities I found with the women but then acutely reminded of the ethnographic authority only I was entitled to. In the midst of conflicting expectations, it was only mine, the author's, that went in print. I was never free from the ethnographer's dilemma. The autoethnography above is thus without an obvious happy ending.

In fact, some ethnographies do conclude happily ever after. There are stories in which researchers at first confront exclusion and refusal from the research subjects, maneuver the social relations in the field, and eventually overcome the difficulties. They may suggest a precaution or two so that other researchers can avoid conflicts in a research field. Typically, they are presented only in the introduction and conclusion of an article (Ellis & Bochner, 2000, p. 734) or as a byproduct of the "real work" of the ethnographer. Such revelation is safe because researchers stay in control and maintain an academic face. The issues they experienced are regarded as personal and thus not described or analyzed extensively. I concur with Fine et al. (2003, p. 170), who say, "Simply briefly inserting autobiographical or personal information often serves to establish and assert the researcher's authority, and ultimately produces texts 'from which the self has been sanitized'" (Okely, 1992, p. 5).

Rather than providing another "sanitized" text, here I have aimed to point to sociopolitical issues that lie underneath my personal experiences. Instead of proposing a how-to-navigate-your-fieldwork method, I discussed how contentious reactions from research participants can enable new possibilities of inquiry; that is, how these moments can be "epiphanies" for researchers.

> Epiphanies ... are interactional moments and experiences which leave marks on people's lives. In them, personal character is manifested. They are often moments of crisis. They alter the fundamental meaning structures in a person's life. ... The critical autoethnographer enters those strange and familiar situations that connect critical biographical experiences (epiphanies) with culture, history and social structure. He or she seeks out those narratives and stories people tell one another as they attempt to make sense of the epiphanies, or existential turning-point moments, in their lives. In such moments persons attempt to take history into their own hands, moving into and through ... liminal stages of experiences. (Denzin, 2014, pp. 52-3)

Had it not been for the rejection, withdrawal and hesitation by my research participants, I might not have taken into account how the stereotypical image of bilingual women affected the women's narratives. I could have assumed as if the interview site were a vacuum in which sociocultural ideologies did not interfere. I would not have noticed the representation politics in which the women and I were embedded. It would not have occurred to me how my political motives could possibly alienate other women. As such, my self-reflexive account "takes us somewhere we couldn't otherwise get to," and "not a decorative flourish, not exposure for its own sake" (Behar, 1996, p. 14).

Such self-reflexive analyses do not necessarily—and should not pretend to—resolve the ethnographer's dilemma. Ethnographers can never cease to reflect upon their experiences from different positions, perpetually crafting new versions of their story. Notably, the process, full of pain and embarrassment, is nothing other than what they put their research participants through. Therefore, vulnerable exposure of researchers should no longer be regarded as a taboo or a mere trend; it is an attempt at reciprocity in the midst of an unequal relationship between the researcher and the researched, which enables an unexpected perspective. Bittersweet as it may be, the resulting epiphany would be the only possible happy ending to an autoethnography.

References

Abu-Lughod, L. (1991). Writing against culture. In R. Fox (Ed.), *Recapturing anthropology: Working in the present* (pp. 466-79). Santa Fe, NM: School of American Research Press.

Behar, R. (1996). *The vulnerable observer: An Anthropology that breaks your heart*. Boston: Beacon Press.
Block, D. (2003). *The social turn in second language acquisition*. Washington, DC: Georgetown University Press.
Boylorn, R. M., & Orbe, M. P. (2014). Introduction: Critical autoethnography as method of choice. In R. M. Boylorn & M. P. Orbe (Eds.), *Critical autoethnography: Intersecting cultural identities in everyday life* (pp. 13-26). Walnut Creek: Left Coast Press.
Clifford, J. (1986). Introduction: Partial truths. In J. Clifford & G. E. Marcus (Eds.), *Writing culture: The poetics and politics of ethnography* (pp. 1-26). Berkeley: University of California Press.
Denzin, N. K. (2001). *Interpretive interactionism*. Thousand Oaks, CA: Sage.
Denzin, N. K. (2014). *Interpretive autoethnography*. Los Angeles: Sage.
Ellis, C. & Bochner, A. P. (2000). Autoethnography, personal narrative, reflexivity: Research as subject. In N. K. Denzin & Y. S. Lincoln (Eds.), *Handbook of qualitative research* (2nd ed., pp. 733-68). Thousand Oaks, CA: Sage.
Fine, M., Weis. L., Wessen, S., & Wong, L. (2003). For whom?: Qualitative research, representations, and social responsibilities. In N. K. Denzin & Y. S. Lincoln (Eds.), *The landscape of qualitative research* (2nd ed., pp. 167-207). Thousand Oaks, CA: Sage.
Holstein, J. A., & Gubrium, J. F. (1995). *The active interview*. Thousand Oaks, CA: Sage.
Holstein, J. A., & Gubrium, J. F. (2003). Active interviewing. In J. F. Gubrium & J. A. Holstein (Eds.), *Postmodern interviewing* (pp. 67-80). Thousand Oaks, CA: Sage.
Kelsky, K. (2001). *Women on the verge: Japanese women, Western dreams*. Durham: Duke University Press.
Kelsky, K. (2008). Gender, modernity, and eroticized internationalism in Japan. In D. B. Willis and S. Murphy-Shigematsu (Eds.), *Transcultural Japan: At the borderlands of race, gender and identity* (pp. 86-109). London: Routledge.
Kitamura, A. (2011). *Eigo wa onnna o sukuunoka* [Is English a savior for women?]. Tokyo: Chikuma Shobo.
Kobayashi, Y. (2002). The role of gender in foreign learning attitudes: Japanese female students' attitudes towards English learning. *Gender and Education, 14*(2), 181-197.
Kubota, R. (2002). The impact of globalization on language teaching in Japan. In D. Block & D. Cameron (Eds.), *Globalization and language teaching* (pp. 13-28). New York: Routledge.
Narayan, K. (1993). How native is a 'native' anthropologist? *American Anthropologist, 95*(3), 671-86.
Okely, J. (1992) Anthropology and autobiography: Participatory experience and embodied knowledge. In J. Okely & H. Callaway (Eds.), *Anthropology and autobiography* (pp. 1-49). London: Routledge.
Phillipson, R. (1992). *Linguistic Imperialism*. Oxford: Oxford University Press.
Seargeant, P. (2009). *The idea of English in Japan: Ideology and the evolution of a global language*. Bristol: Multilingual Matters.
Stacey, J. (1991). Can there be a feminist ethnography? In S. B. Gluck & D. Patai (Eds.), *Women's words: The feminist practice of oral history* (pp. 111-119). New York: Routledge.
Takahashi, K. (2013). *Language learning, gender and desire: Japanese women on the move*. Bristol: Multilingual Matters.
Tsuda, Y. (1990). *Eigo shihai no kouzou* [The structure of the dominance of English]. Tokyo: Daisan Shokan.

CHAPTER 12

DESIRED COMMUNITIES AND CONFLICTING ESL IDENTITIES:
Negotiating Identities Across Composition Classes

Heejung Kwon
Purdue University

The notion of L2 learners' identity has been extensively researched in the context of higher education and secondary education in English-speaking countries. Second language learners' identity has been explored both empirically and theoretically in order to find ways to articulate the relationship between learners' identity and their language learning processes, motivation, and outcomes. It has also been studied as a process of cultural adjustment in U.S. classrooms, their relationships to the second language, a sense of ownership and membership of the language community (Cohen, 2012; Cummins & Davison, 2007; Harklau, 2000; Norton & Kanno, 2003; Pavlenko & Norton, 2007; Thesen, 1997). It has been emphasized that identity can be an important factor in learning a second language and becoming enculturated to L2 environments. Wenger (1998) conceptualized identity by explicating how the learner's identity is constructed in educational settings through theorizing communities of practice. Norton (2001) has used 'imagined community' to further explain what second language learners hope to see in language classrooms or language learning environment. 'Imagined community' coined by Anderson (1991) refers to the abstract image of the community of people that exists in one's mind "bonded with fellow compatriots across space and time" (Kanno & Norton, 2003, p. 231). People form this imagined community to feel a sense of community with the people whom they might see some time in the future. Norton (2001), using this concept of imagined community, has explored and theorized non-participation of L2 learners in classroom contexts in order to better understand the relationship between learners' identity and language learning.

As a way to help the initial adjustment of international students in US higher education settings, many institutions have created ESL composition classes in which students learn basic writing skills with their peer ESL writers in a relatively less stressful environment. The mainstream composition classes have been known to provide challenges to international students as the majority of the students in those classes are domestic students who speak English as their first language. International students who may not feel quite ready to interact and participate in class with domestic students often choose ESL composition classes and those who are highly motivated to immerse themselves in a mixed class environment choose to take mainstream composition classes. However, the placement of ESL students is largely up to institutional decisions depending on students' English proficiency. ESL students whose English proficiency is high enough are given a choice whether to be in ESL or mainstream composition classes.

L2 learners' initial understanding of the given institutional context could affect the way they shape their identity in the long run in an L2 environment. Some of their experiences at the beginning stage of the enculturation in L2 settings can impact the way they form social network, plan their career path, and construct their social and professional identity. International students who speak English as a second language tend to struggle to find a community where they can feel a sense of belonging and gain social support. In the process of locating the communities, some students might want to become part of L2 communities to adjust themselves in the L2 environments sooner and form social networks with English-speaking students, and some students may want to stay in the community in which they can be with other ESL learners. Participating and engaging in any of these activities in the community can greatly contribute to the formation of their identities. These identities can be conflicting if they do not feel accepted or differentiated from other members of the community. ESL students tend to be considered *foreign* students as their identities are often institutionally and structurally assigned. For this reason, students acknowledge their status and often accept that they should maintain a peripheral status in classrooms, departmental and extracurricular activities, and on campus in general (Canagarajah,

2002, 2006). Students' perceptions of their peripheral status may affect the way they learn and participate in classes, or motivation to become part of the L2 community. It is also possible that their desired communities and institutionally assigned communities differ from each other, which may slow down their linguistic and cultural adjustment or shut down their motivation due to the frustration coming from the natural setting where they are already seen as *peripheral, foreign, L2 learners*. Thesen (1997) stated that learners are categorized according to "a limited set of identity markers, which results in a deterministic view of identity in terms of the researcher's imposed categories" (p. 488). Drawing on her case study on an African student in a South African university in Cape Town, she noted that institutional labels must be balanced by opportunities for individuals to speak for themselves (p. 504).

The purpose of this small-scale pilot study is to better understand international students' decision making process in placing themselves in composition courses at the university level in their first year. It explores how they navigate themselves within a variety of different course options and their own perceptions towards them, as well as their initial motivation in taking mainstream courses and reasons for coming back to ESL classes with their peer international students. Rather than drawing a conclusion or strong implications from this study, I would like to further discuss how one might go about studying second language learners with a better understanding of their identity, institutional contexts, and their relationship with language and community in multicultural contexts.

Literature Review

Communities of practice, a notion developed and theorized by Wenger (1998), refer to the concept that everyone belongs to certain communities of practice in which they interact with the members of the community. Members of the communities will participate in certain activities or events, everyday practices and function as a legitimate participant either centrally or peripherally in the community. Practice means any activities in social contexts that can be either explicit or tacit. According to Wenger (1998), meaning is constructed through negotiation in communities of practice, and this process involves *participation* and *reification* which are two fundamental factors of practice. Through negotiation of meaning, people make sense of their world and create narratives of their own communities. In this sense, negotiation of meaning is always "historical and contextual" (p. 54). Wenger illustrated that community requires *mutual engagement*, *joint enterprise*, and *shared repertoire*. These three elements contribute to the formation of a community and help explain how certain members of a community participate, or do not participate in the community.

Wenger (1998) illustrated the ways identity is formed through social actions. Identity is an important notion in explaining communities of practice. Constructing an identity involves negotiation of meanings from "experience of membership in social communities" (p. 145). Wenger explains the concept of identity as follows:

> The concept of identity serves as a pivot between the social and the individual, so that each can be talked about in terms of the other. It avoids a simplistic individual—social dichotomy without doing away with the distinction. The resulting perspective is neither individualistic nor abstractly institutional or societal. It does justice to the lived experience of identity while recognizing its social character—it is the social, the cultural, the historical with a human face. (p. 145)

Identity is a production of continuous work of negotiation of the self and it involves constant participation and reification to be able to construct an identity through experience and consciousness (p. 151). One constructs his or her identity through participating in communities of practice and reifying their ideas and the self.

The relationship between identity and language learning has been an important subject for exploring as many scholars pay attention to the ownership of language, and membership of a community, and individual motivations and frustration experienced in L2 community (Kanno & Applebaum, 1995; Kanno & Norton, 2003; Norton, 2001; Widdowson, 1994). L2 learners' relationship with the language and the community where he or she lives has been known to greatly impact the way they shape their L2 identities in a given setting, which influences their learning processes (Norton & Toohey, 2011). Norton (1995) explored participation and non-participation with a focus on the motivation of learners in ESL classes and professional classes where learners are pushed back from L2 community due to their limited linguistic competence. Kanno (1995) argued that institutional and structural issues could affect the way L2 learners participate in the community and have negative images towards L2 community in the long run.

Imagined communities have been used as a concept to explain how L2 learners understand their social status, their motivation to participate in language classrooms, and construct their identities (Arkoudis & Love, 2008; Kanno & Norton, 2003). Kanno and Norton (2003) reviewed studies on the learners' identity and their life stories to closely examine imagined communities and find implications for educational practices. Kanno and Applebaum (1995) carefully investigated the ways ESL students form their identities by qualitatively looking at participants' cultural and linguistic background and what kinds of educational contexts they have been exposed to. Norton (1997) explored an ownership of English as she reviews five studies on the identities of second language learners. She argued that "English belongs to the people who speak it, whether one is native or nonnative, whether ESL or EFL, whether standard or nonstandard" (p. 427). Norton and Toohey (2001) attempted to redefine "good language learners." They explicated what a success is in language learning, and what kinds of learners can be successful learners of a target language.

> We approach the explanation of the success of good language learners on the basis of their access to a variety of conversations in their communities rather than on the basis of their control of a wider variety of linguistic forms or meaning than their peers or on the basis of their speed of acquisition of linguistic forms and meanings. (Norton & Toohey, 2001, p. 310)

Norton and Toohey (2011) further explained later that the identity studies and its relationship to language learning become more important as many institutions become internationalized and individual students' background become more diversified.

> Such communities include affiliations, such as nationhood or even transnational communities, which extend beyond local sets of relationships. Such imagined communities may well have a reality as strong as those in which learners have current daily engagement, and might even have a stronger impact on their investment in language learning. (Norton & Toohey, 2011, p. 422)

It is interesting to note that imagined communities are changing as the world becomes more globalized. Imagined communities could not only mean one local community, but it could also be global communities.

In addition to the studies on L2 learners' identity in classroom settings, some studies have looked at how graduate-level students negotiate their identities in the US higher education settings. Kenway and Bullen (2003) explored how female postgraduate students negotiate the institutionally created identity and her own identity as a competent researcher in her field. Cho (2004) explored how international graduate students construct their identities through publishing their work for academic communities. By looking into international graduate students' perspectives in publishing in English, she illustrates how they negotiate their identities throughout the publication process. Cho (2009) also noted that international graduate students become enculturated through personal interactions with advisors who are old-timers of specific community of practice in which international graduate students are newcomers, and participating in scholarly conferences. They become part of the discourse communities by actively participating in the interactions with the old-timers and the events in the target discourse community.

Learning English in higher education settings largely means acquiring social skills, academic and professional skills as well. It is only natural that ESL students seek more opportunities to interact in an L2 environment, which will help their professional development as well as their personal growth. In the process of going through pushback and acceptance in a given community, learners construct their identities and gain experiences and insights into the ways to view the world.

Methods

Upon conducting research, two Chinese international students registered in ESL composition classes were recruited for interviews from the class in which the researcher is the instructor. The researcher specifically recruited students who initially registered for the mainstream composition classes and came back to ESL composition classes after two to three weeks of the semester. This study examined their initial motives to be in a mixed class environment and explores their reasons to come back to ESL composition classes and how they viewed their language abilities compared to that of domestic students, their perception of status and positionalities in the campus community. Both participants were given pseudonyms.

Contexts and Participants
The study was conducted in a North American university with a large international student population. All registered undergraduate students needed to take a first-year composition class in order to graduate. International students whose English proficiency was high enough were able to choose between mainstream first-year composition classes and ESL composition classes. Two freshmen Chinese international students were interviewed. They were initially registered in mainstream composition classes and came back to ESL composition classes after they attended those classes for two to three weeks of the semester. Liang and Ji are both Chinese, graduated from high schools in China and came to the US for their undergraduate education. According to the researcher's observational accounts, Liang always sat in the very back row of the classroom and was quiet in class although she had relatively higher oral and written proficiency than her peer ESL students in class. Ji always sat in the front row of the classroom and frequently sat alone, away from other ESL peers. Both Liang and Ji tended to be quiet in class, however, their writing assignments tended to be thorough and well-written. Their oral proficiency was higher than other ESL peers and they did not have much trouble communicating with the researcher.

Interviews
Two interviews were conducted for each participant in order to give participants sufficient time and chances to tell a story of their own in their own words, from their own perspectives (Barkhuizen, Benson, & Chik, 2014; Bell, 2002; Connelly & Clandinin, 1990). The interviews were semi-structured with open-ended questions. The researcher focused on the participants' initial motives to register for the mainstream composition classes and reasons to drop those classes, and choose to take ESL composition classes, as well as their experience in the first two-three weeks in the mainstream composition classes. Their perceived gap between the abilities to speak and write and those of domestic students were explored, and their perceptions towards peer ESL students were also examined.

Results and Discussion

The results from the interviews are analyzed and discussed below thematically. The participants' initial motivation to become part of a mixed-class environment was explored by identifying the reasons contributed to their decisions. The communicative tasks the participants were exposed to in mainstream composition classes seemed to have overwhelmed them in many levels. In addition, they seem to have formed a clear dichotomy between native speakers and ESL learners, rather than ESL learners and native speakers on a continuum of language learning. The data provides a rich description of how they perceive the social structure, their own language abilities, and student communities in a given context.

Desired Communities

Both Liang and Ji seemed to have been very motivated to immerse themselves in L2 community before they came back to ESL writing classes. Liang perceived the mainstream writing classes as a place where she can obtain "useful" skills that she might be able to transfer to become part of the English-speaking community in the near future. There seemed to be specific writing skills that she want to learn, which is to effectively express her opinions in academic tones with more concise forms, perhaps with more complex language, sentence structures to efficiently deliver the opinions while keeping the writing academic and formal. The excerpt below shows what kinds of high-level skills she wanted to learn in the mainstream composition classes.

> It's more like...um...how to....more...concise and concise our writing. Not to use...um...I don't know, to make us more academic I think? To make us fit in the academic paper, you know...um...to become familiar with that. Um...because sometimes when we write paper, we...because there are the limit of the words, like...at least one thousand words, sometimes we used to write long sentences, but that doesn't have much meaning, so um...maybe we should learn how to be concise, and you know, how to get straight to that point, to show our ideas....I don't know how to say that. Because ESL is for just like, this is designed for international students, so native students will never take this class. Yeah. I just feel like that. I mean the native students never take the ESL class....is that true?

Liang also explained how she was concerned about remaining in the mainstream writing class because her close friends who have experience in taking mainstream writing classes have told her that they had spent a significant amount of time and effort but were not able to get a satisfying grade, which is another reason that Liang came to ESL writing classes. In order to earn a good grade in mainstream writing classes, ESL students need to perform as well as L1 students, which might make it much more stressful for ESL students.

> Before I register these classes, I just heard from the junior students, sophomore students, they talk about these two, and all the sophomore students tell me that rhetoric is very very hard, and you pay a lot of time and you get a B, and that's all the information I got, I don't dare to choose this class.

Liang seemed to think that ESL writing classes are largely remedial, and associated the images of ESL writing classes with Asian students. When asked about the image of ESL writing classes, Liang responded as follows.

> It's more like, upset because maybe I try to catch up with the native students but still couldn't, um…but I think that it is common in daily life, because we have Asian faces, and we speak with Asian accents so just try hard not to….

It appears that she started to form certain images and perceptions toward her own ethnic identity based on how her ethnicity is viewed in the given context. Her *Asian* ethnicity might be associated with someone who does not speak proper English, and thus, cannot be part of the mainstream student body. She seems to understand her non-native status but she does not seem to feel right to be judged based on how she looks. This perceived images of herself and peer L2 learners in ESL classes cause non-participation and frustration.

Perceived Gap and Differences in Class
Both Liang and Ji seem to have felt a big gap between themselves and domestic students in their first three weeks of mainstream classes. Their perceived gap between their own abilities to speak and write and those of domestic students seems to be significant enough that influenced their decisions to take ESL writing classes. It can be observed that she might already have felt overwhelmed by the first-day self-introductions and whole class discussion, specifically, the way L1 speakers handle these communicative tasks more

confidently. Many ESL composition classes use these communicative tasks too, but it seems that Liang did not want to be embarrassed in front of L1 speakers in the mainstream composition classes. Liang further pointed out that she was afraid of getting a low grade for that class and was not able to catch up with the pace of the mainstream composition classes. This overwhelming feeling is natural in L2 settings as ESL students might not be used to interactive classrooms that often adopt group work and peer work that generates discussion among students. Liang said,

> Yeah, I found that almost of students were from US, it was a little bit hard to catch up with them, because, you know, English is not my language to use and um….I'm not very good at how to….use them to write… you know write specific ideas…. They can use them as very common… but I still have to practice, so… they already focus on the… ideas and of the passage, but I think I still need to practice more. So I choose back to take ESL class…. yeah, um… before we go to class, we already have assignments. It's like a…. to write… 'what do you expect to learn from class, and you have to prepare for your self-introduction, in the very first class, and during that self-introduction, I already feel the difference between me and US students, um… and the assignments you know…a little bit too much. Um…maybe for international students. I think the class will kind of you know, lower my GPA, so…I don't want this course to lower my GPA, so I dropped it. yeah I don't know how to say that… you do the same assignments, you paying the…you spend the same time, but you will get different grade.

Ji seemed to have the similar overwhelming feelings when he was in the mainstream composition classes. He says that he felt 'pressure' as he had to perform as well as L1 speakers in order to get a satisfying grade. And ESL writing classes seem to give him less pressure because it is easier to follow the instructions and perform better than in the mainstream classes.

> It's kind of….pressure. Yeah because they, the professor treat you as the native speaker. You have to do like some speeches, and you have to record it, listen by yourself…..Yeah (laugh) the group work is also a speech. You make a speech and everybody just listen to and then they make comment on it. So…I realized how difficult it is….so I just quit it….feel pressure. ESL is… it's just kind of less pressure I think. Because ESL class is you know what the instructor will say next, but about other classes, they use kind of specific words, you really have to concentrate on, or you will miss something.

The perceived gap and differences between L1 speakers and themselves, instructors' expectations, interactions with L1 speakers in numerous communicative tasks seem to have given them reasons to go back to ESL writing classes. These ESL students might be carrying these perceived differences which might be bigger than they actually are, into the classroom. Because of the perceived gap, differences, students might often be discouraged to venture into L2 communities. The obvious existing power relations among L1 and L2 speakers in a mixed class environment creates tension, anxiety, and pressure for L2 learners to deal with.

Idealized Native-Speaker Level
It is interesting to note that Ji already formed opinions on the distinction between native speakers and ESL learners, which might already have impacted his views on ESL composition classes. ESL composition classes might seem nothing but a remedial class that assists ESL students' language development, rather than authentic academic and social skills needed in university settings.

> If you want to apply to university, you have to have ability to English, right? I think ESL is kind of a place to um...to improve the English...to those students who are not, I mean...like fully qualified ....or strong...point... as English. They have to get ability to fully express what he wants to say, in the writing. As a native speaker I think. International students, their English cannot be as native speakers. I mean it's impossible, except they were living in US for years. So there's a kind of difference...maybe ESL is kind of ...to clarify the difference between native speakers and the international students.

Ji seems to see the clear dichotomy between native speakers and ESL students, and to him, native speaker-level seems to be something unreachable. Native speaker and non-native speaker distinction might be on the continuum in many different levels and aspects, rather than a dichotomy. The simplistic understanding of native speaker and non-native speaker might lead students to further differentiating themselves from the L2 community, and lower their motivation to advance their language skills. Learning language skills are not necessarily confined to enhancing grammatical accuracy. Rather, language learning skills are closely linked to their abilities to communicate with a variety of English speakers in a variety of communities of practice (Norton

& Toohey, 2001). With a better understanding of what it means to learn a language, learners can move forward to further their knowledge in social and cultural aspects of language.

Students might encounter pushback from L2 communities they desire to be part of due to the preconceived notions towards ESL students, obvious power relations between L1 speakers and L2 speakers in various communicative tasks, and lack of institutional and social support. Students would have to constantly negotiate identities and navigate themselves in a variety of L2 contexts while maintaining their L1 identities. It is important for ESL students to be able to use their experience to construct a positive image about themselves by overcoming stereotypes and socially constructed images of ESL learners. This may also require institutional support from the classroom level to programmatic level. Second language learning is a constant negotiation process and fighting with existing stereotypes towards ESL learners especially for highly motivated ESL learners.

Conclusion

This study explored highly motivated ESL students' initial motives to immerse themselves in L2 community and what expectations and feelings they had in a mixed-class environment. The results suggest that the participants felt pushback from the desired communities due to perceived gap and differences between their abilities to speak and write in L2 and those of L1 speakers, as well as their concerns about academic achievement in those classes.

It is hard to draw any conclusion from this small-scale study and it certainly cannot be generalized to larger international student populations, nor can it inform the current mainstream teaching practices. I do not wish to say anything that this study informs the teaching practices or theories in a significant way. I also acknowledge that the participants interviewed in this study might be a special case in which they struggled to find their classes and communities to pursue their personal motivation and goals. However, I believe that it is possible to see how ESL students actively try to choose desired communities they wish to be part of, while maintaining their peripheral status, and constantly negotiate their identities across different social contexts and communities. Understanding an ESL student as a person with agency that actively makes decisions based on their motivation and experiences will help researchers and practitioners find ways to approach

ESL classes or a mixed class with both L1 and L2 speakers. As students' experiences greatly influence their personal lives, attitudes towards the local community and the world, and their future selves, helping students have positive experiences in the campus communities can help them create positive images towards themselves and maximize their abilities to achieve academic success.

Internationalization of higher education is becoming a common theme that impacts university-wide policies and curricular decisions in North American contexts. Many higher education institutions are admitting more international students who speak English as a second language every year. This movement is not just confined to North American contexts. Higher education institutions in ESL/EFL contexts are also following this globalization movement. Moreover, technological advancement further facilitates the globalization and gives English learners in ESL/EFL contexts greater access to English language and culture. Accordingly, English learners in general are being exposed to more resources to learn about English-speaking culture in their own home countries as well. Thus, English is not so *foreign* to contemporary English learners in ESL/EFL contexts any more. This calls our attention to how contemporary English learners may build a relationship to English language and communities of English speaker, and construct their L2 identities. Their imagined communities might include almost always L1 speakers whom they can communicate together or share resources, and get involved in professional activities.

The present study provides very limited sets of view about specific directions to take or what policies should be made in higher education settings, however, I believe that it sheds light on a more globalized understanding of L2 learners as global citizens who may already think of themselves as part of the English speaking communities in higher education settings. With this understanding of L2 learners and their relationship to English language and desired communities, many institutions might be able to create more accepting and inclusive environment for all members of the student community, which can help them become a truly internationalized institution. Furthermore, more globalized perspectives in language teaching with an understanding of the development of an ownership of a target language and membership of a global society may help researchers and practitioners in the field develop instructional approaches that could facilitate learning in a way that could help L2 learners empower themselves and become successful language learners.

References

Anderson, B. (1991). *Imagined communities* (Rev. ed.). London: Verso.

Arkoudis, S., & Love, K. (2008). Imagined communities in senior school mathematics: Beyond issues of English language ability. *Journal of Asian Pacific Communication, 18*(1), 71-90.

Barkhuizen, G., Benson, P., & Chik, A. (2014). *Narrative inquiry in language teaching and learning research.* New York: Routledge.

Bell, J. S. (2002). Narrative inquiry: More than just telling stories. *TESOL Quarterly, 36*(2), 207-213.

Canagarajah, S. (2002). Multilingual writers and the academic community: Towards a critical relationship. *Journal of English for Academic Purposes, 1*(1), 29-44.

Canagarajah, A. S. (2006). Toward a writing pedagogy of shuttling between languages: Learning from multilingual writers. *College English, 68*(6), 589-604.

Cho, S. (2004). Challenges of entering discourse communities through publishing in English: Perspectives of nonnative-speaking doctoral students in the United States of America. *Journal of Language, Identity, and Education, 3*(1), 47-72.

Cho, S. (2009). Disciplinary enculturation experiences of five East Asian doctoral students in US-based second language studies programmes. *Asia Pacific Journal of Education, 29*(3), 295-310.

Connelly, F. M., & Clandinin, D. J. (1990). Stories of experience and narrative inquiry. *Educational Researcher, 19*(5), 2-14.

Cohen, J. (2012). Imaginary community of the mainstream classroom: Adolescent immigrants' perspectives. *The Urban Review, 44*(2), 265-280.

Cummins, J., & Davison, C. (2007). *International handbook of English language teaching* (Vol. 15). New York: Springer.

Harklau, L. (2000). From the "good kids" to the "worst:" Representations of English language learners across educational settings. *TESOL Quarterly, 34*, 35-67.

Kanno, Y., & Norton, B. (2003). Imagined communities and educational possibilities: Introduction. *Journal of Language, Identity, and Education, 2*(4), 241-249.

Kanno, Y., & Varghese, M. M. (2010). Immigrant and refugee ESL students' challenges to accessing four-year college education: from language policy to educational policy. *Journal of Language, Identity, and Education, 9*, 310-328.

Kanno, Y., & Norton, B. (2003). Imagined communities and educational possibilities: Introduction. *Journal of Language, Identity, and Education, 2*(4), 241-249.

Kanno, Y., & Applebaum, S. D. (1995). ESL students speak up: Their stories of how we are doing. *TESL Canada Journal, 12*(2), 32-49.

Kenway, J., & Bullen, E. (2003). Self-representations of international women postgraduate students in the global university'contact zone'. *Gender and Education, 15*(1), 5-20.

Norton, B. (1997) Language, identity, and the ownership of English. *TESOL Quarterly, 31*(3), 409–29.

Norton, B., & Toohey, K. (2001). Changing perspectives on good language learners. *TESOL Quarterly, 35*(2), 307-322.

Norton, B., & Toohey, K. (2011). Identity, language learning, and social change. *Language Teaching, 44*(4), 412-446.

Norton, B. (1997). Language, identity, and the ownership of English. *TESOL Quarterly, 31*(3), 409-429.
Norton, B. (2001). Non-participation, imagined communities and the language classroom. *Learner Contributions to Language learning: New Directions in Research, 6*(2), 159-171.
Pavlenko, A., & Norton, B. (2007). Imagined communities, identity, and English language learning. In J. Cummins & C. Davison (Eds.), *International handbook of English language teaching* (pp. 669-680). New York: Springer.
Thesen, L. (1997). Voices, discourse, and transition: In search of new categories in EAP. *TESOL Quarterly, 31*(3), 487-511.
Wenger, E. (1998). *Communities of practice: Learning, meaning, and identity*. Cambridge: Cambridge University Press.
Widdowson, H. G. (1994). The ownership of English. *TESOL Quarterly, 28*(2), 377-389.

CHAPTER 13

WHAT MAKES STUDENTS' LIVES CHALLENGING?
Major Educational Issues Facing Japanese Sojourner Students in the Midwestern United States

Reiko Akiyama
Purdue University

Introduction

One of the major challenges facing U.S. education today is the disparity between primarily white, monocultural, and monolingual preservice teachers (Zeichner, 2009) and a growing ethnically, racially, and linguistically diverse student population (Banks, 1991; Causey, Thomas, & Armento, 2000; Spring, 2008). The U.S. population's large number of immigrants and sojourners—people who temporarily reside in the U.S. with their families (Haneda & Monobe, 2009; Hasebe, 1987; Kanno, 2003)—mean that increasing numbers of people are moving to the U.S. and experiencing challenges as they enter the U.S. education system (Crosnoe & Turley, 2011; Zhou, 1997). Japanese sojourners are one example of this phenomenon (Jones, 2012; MEXT, 2009). To address these challenges, we need to better understand diverse students' experiences in U.S. schools.

Over 25,000 Japanese sojourner students[1] resided in North America (i.e., Canada and the U.S.) in 2013 (MOFA, 2013); many of these Japanese sojourner students attended local schools during their stay in the U.S. and experienced challenges such as language barriers and culture shock (Akiyama, 2012-2014; Haneda & Monobe, 2009; Harkins, 2001; Hasebe, 1987; Kanno, 2000, 2003; Spring, 2008). In some regions in the U.S., specifically the Midwest, student demographics show that the population is predominantly white, while Asian and/or Japanese students are an ethnic minority in U.S.

school environments (Endo, 2011; Ileleji, 2008; Kinghom, 2011). Students and teachers in the racial majority (i.e., white) may not have sufficient experience to integrate with these ethnic minority students in classrooms. The lack of understanding of Japanese students means they have to face additional challenges, including further isolation and marginalization, identity confusion, lower achievement, and lower self-esteem (Greenland & Brown, 2005; Hamann, 2001; Iwamoto & Liu, 2010; Kanno, 2000, 2003; Takeuchi, Yun, & Russell, 2002).

In this chapter, I identify the specific set of challenges and issues encountered by Japanese sojourner students, especially those who reside in the Midwest, where school environments are predominantly white and monolingual (Kinghom, 2011) in comparison to larger cities in the U.S. whose schools are more racially, culturally, and linguistically diverse. I also discuss the major known challenges and issues facing adolescent Japanese students within the U.S. education system through a literature review.

Definition of "Sojourner" Students

There is not an established meaning for "sojourner." Thus, through analyzing several scholarly works, I define "sojourner" in a way that is suitable for the theme of this chapter. Several scholarly works deal with sojourner students and their educational issues (Cooke, 1995; Greenland & Brown, 2005; Hamann, 2001; Haneda & Monobe, 2009; Harkins, 2001; Kanno, 2000, 2003). However, some of their definitions of "sojourner" are keenly distinguished from other scholars' definitions; there are even instances of multiple terms used to mean "sojourner" within a single publication. For example, Miyamoto and Kuhlman (2001) used the term *expatriate*. Several scholars used *future returnee students* (Takeuchi, Imahori, & Matsumoto, 2001; Yoshida et al., 2002) and *third culture kids* (Yashiro, 1995, p. 139). For students from Japan in particular, many scholars use the Japanese term *kaigaishijo* in their research (Endo, 2011; Haneda & Monobe, 2009; Harkins, 2001; Hasebe, 1987; INFOE-USA, 2011; Kanno, 2000, 2003; Koga, 2009; MEXT, 2009; Rikyu, 2009)—*kaigai* means "overseas" and *shijo* means "children" or "sons and daughters" (Kanno, 2003, p. 17), so *kaigaishijo* means "overseas sons and daughters." In this chapter, I will use the term "sojourner" to refer to those who temporarily reside in the U.S. with their families (Haneda & Monobe, 2009; Hasebe, 1987; Kanno, 2003).

Haneda and Monobe (2009) defined sojourner students as, "school-age students who reside and study abroad for a number of years because of their parents' jobs" (p. 8). Besides Haneda and Monobe, several scholars described sojourner students as those who: (1) study abroad for a long period of time; (2) reside with their parents (as temporary resident-workers or academic trainees) and siblings in the host countries; and (3) will eventually return to their home countries at the end of their parents' duties (Endo, 2011; Harkins, 2001; Hasebe, 1987; Kanno, 2000, 2003; Matsumoto, Yoo, & Nakagawa, 2008; Miyamoto & Kuhlman, 2001; Takeuchi et al., 2001; Toyokawa, 2005; Yashiro, 1995). Some students return to their home countries earlier than the parents (who need to stay for their duties) when the students meet "a logical dividing point in their schooling (e.g., at the end of middle or high school)" (Kanno, 2003, p. 17). For the sojourn length, the Ministry of Education, Culture, Sports, Science and Technology (MEXT) considers "one year" as a long-term period (2009, p. 6). In sum, the Japanese sojourner students in this chapter include Japanese students who came to the U.S. with their families because of the parents' occupations, who have been living in the U.S. for at least one year, and who plan to return to Japan in the future. Additionally, Koga (2009) described sojourner students as those "who involuntarily study abroad while accompanying their expatriate parents overseas" (p. 1); this means that sojourner students do not come to the host country at their discretion but at their parents', which influences the students' motivation to learn in the host country.

Demographics of Japanese Sojourner Students in the U.S.
The Ministry of Foreign Affairs of Japan (MOFA) reported that approximately 25,540 Japanese sojourner students resided in North America in 2013, compared to 18,445 in 2005 (MOFA, 2013). These statistics suggest that there is an upward trend in Japanese students entering the U.S. educational system. To discuss educational issues faced by Japanese sojourner students, I believe that it is necessary to acknowledge the demographics of Japanese sojourner students in the U.S., particularly in the Midwest.

MOFA (2012) reported that the total number of Japanese sojourners (adults and children) residing in the U.S. in 2012, according to the reports of the Japanese consulates in the U.S., was about 250,000. The number of Japanese sojourners in greater Chicago was approximately 20,000, in greater Detroit 13,000, and in Nashville 6,900. Therefore, the total number of sojourners in those areas was less than 40,000. On the other hand, the New York consulate reported 75,000 Japanese sojourners and the Los Angeles consulate reported 60,000 (MOFA, 2012). These statistics show that there are fewer Japanese sojourners in the Midwest than there are on the East and West Coasts. This fact suggests that Japanese sojourners residing in the Midwest may have limited access to Japanese resources, community services, and school support in comparison to those living in coastal regions or bigger cities (Shibata, 2000). In addition, the smaller population of Japanese sojourners in the Midwest highlights several educational challenges that sojourner students face, such as cultural and linguistic barriers, stereotyping, and a lack of understanding of Japanese sojourner students on the part of teachers and peers (Akiyama, 2012-2014). These issues can happen anywhere, but they are more likely to happen in areas with a small Japanese population because people in such areas tend to lack multicultural and multilinguistic experiences (Endo, 2011; Lucas, Villegas, & Freedson-Gonzales, 2008). In the following section, I will discuss the major issues that Japanese sojourner students face in U.S. schools[2]. Then I will explore issues specific to the Midwest.

Major Educational Issues Facing Japanese Students in the U.S.

Various scholars have researched Japanese sojourner students and found several issues at school during the students' sojourn (Endo, 2011; Haneda & Monobe, 2009; Kanno, 2000, 2003; Koga, 2009; Miyamoto & Kuhlman, 2001; Takeuchi et al., 2001; Yashiro, 1995; Yoshida et al., 2002). There are several prominent issues that adolescent Japanese students often face in the U.S. educational environment. In this chapter, cultural adjustment, language barriers, limited social networks, and preparation as a future returnee are the salient issues. Not only does each issue have a negative impact on Japanese sojourner students' school lives, but these four issues are also connected to each other and consequently cause further challenges such as isolation and marginalization, identity confusion, lower achievement, and lower self-esteem (Akiyama, 2012-2014, 2013; Greenland & Brown, 2005; Hamann, 2001; Iwamoto & Liu, 2010; Kanno, 2000, 2003; Takeuchi et al., 2002).

Cultural Adjustment

One of the first challenges that adolescent Japanese sojourner students face is cultural adjustment or acculturation. This issue most likely happens to all Japanese students who are considered newcomers to the host country (Akiyama, 2012-2014, 2013; Endo, 2011; Greenland & Brown, 2005; Ileleji, 2008; Takeuchi et al., 2002). Acculturation is defined as a process in which individuals negotiate or adjust themselves into different cultures—one culture is dominant, and the other culture is viewed as having less cultural value (Berry, 1995; Yeh, 2003). Harkins (2001) pointed out that acculturation often happens to minority people when they enter the mainstream environment. She also emphasized that the process of acculturation is not the same as assimilation; rather, "acculturation can be a combination of one or more responses, including marginalization, separation, integration, and assimilation" (Harkins, 2001, p. 337).

Harkins (2001), Miyamoto and Kuhlman (2001), Yoshida et al. (2002), and other scholars emphasized that different school systems and cultures strongly affect students' adjustment process in the host country. In the U.S., there are only a couple of *Nihonjin gakko*, or Japanese schools—where Japanese students learn in Japanese based on a Japanese curriculum—which means that most of the Japanese sojourner students usually attend local schools (Hasebe, 1987; MEXT, 2009). This indicates that a lot of Japanese sojourner students suddenly step into school systems and cultures that are vastly different from those in their home country. These different systems, cultures, norms, and values equal various hardships for the students.

Classroom participation is another one of the challenges that Japanese sojourner students encounter in U.S. classrooms. In U.S. schools, students who frequently speak up are seen as active participants who pay attention to and show interest in lessons; silent students are often perceived as passive or indifferent. This educational norm causes teachers to misunderstand Japanese sojourner students' classroom attitudes. Teruhiko Matsumoto, a representative of INFOE-USA or *Kaigaishijo Education Information Center*, noted some concerns of sojourners' parents, in particular that local schoolteachers often expected the Japanese sojourner students to talk more in class in the form of sharing opinions and asking questions. Matsumoto mentioned that these students were regarded as passive participants in class despite excelling at written exams (INFOE-USA, 2011). In addition, a Japanese sojourner student in Akiyama's study (2012-2014) shared a story about an issue she experienced early in her sojourn: she was frequently required to make presentations in class, which required a lot of effort on her part.

These cases represent how Japanese school cultures and values are different from those of the United States. Japanese schools have a hierarchical (Harkins, 2001; Ileleji, 2008; Iwamoto & Liu, 2010; Kanno, 2000) or pyramid (Murakoshi, 1997) system; teachers are at the top of the hierarchy and students are below. This hierarchical system clearly denotes that Japanese teachers are the authority figures. In addition, Japanese (as well as Chinese and Korean) school culture is regarded as collectivist (Greenland & Brown, 2005; Iwamoto & Liu, 2010; Miyamoto & Kuhlman, 2001; Murakoshi, 1997; Spring, 2008; Takeuchi et al., 2002). This means that Japanese classrooms value "*omoiyari* (empathy) and *yasashisa* (kindness)" (Tsuneyoshi, 2001, p. 44), *enryo* (reserve) (Spring, 2008, p. 158), and *wa* (harmony) [added by author] (Endo, 2011; Harkins, 2001). This suggests that the Japanese classroom atmosphere expects students to obey norms, to respect authority, to have humility, and to avoid shame. Some Japanese students regard asking questions as embarrassing, as if they are exposing their insufficient understanding of the lesson; some teachers feel that a student interrupting the lesson to ask questions is disrespectful (INFOE-USA, 2011). Japanese students (and also students from other Asian countries) usually ask questions before or after class, but they do not interrupt the teacher's lesson or lecture (Endo, 2011; Harkins, 2001). Therefore, Japanese sojourner students growing up in such Japanese school structures cannot immediately become accustomed to the U.S. school culture, although many Japanese sojourner students recognize that speaking up in U.S. classrooms is considered active participation.

Culture has a function of creating and maintaining social order (Matsumoto et al., 2008), and the social order can sometimes be unnoticed by or even insensitive to newcomers. This is especially true when considering the hidden curriculum of schooling. Endo (2011) describes the hidden curriculum as "composed of the cultural norms, knowledge, and behaviors, among other tacit rules valued in the dominant school society" (p. 185). The hidden curriculum in a learner's new community may vary significantly from what they were accustomed to in their homeland, such as non-strict dress code, note-taking, little time between classes, and classroom transfer. For example, school uniforms are common in most Japanese secondary school systems, while there are few schools requiring uniforms in the United States. Japanese students are often flummoxed at the beginning of their sojourns in the U.S. because they are not sure what outfits are considered appropriate at their schools (Akiyama, 2012-2014). In terms of note-taking, students in Japan often write down or copy exactly what their teachers write on blackboards, and the teachers explain the content of the writing; on the contrary, students in the U.S. take notes in their own ways (Takeya, 1992). Takeya attended U.S. schools and noted that her teachers rarely used blackboards and provided more oral explanations instead; therefore, she had to summarize what the teachers said in order to take notes. Moreover, in terms of classroom transfer and time between classes, teachers in most Japanese middle school transfer classrooms; however, students in U.S. schools have to move to another classroom between classes, and they are only given a few minutes to do so (Akiyma, 2012-2014; Tsuneyoshi, 2001). Newcomer students from different cultures often encounter such tacit school rules, which they are rarely informed of directly. These new experiences sometimes turn to culture shock that causes anxiety, depression, frustration (Cooke, 1995; Iwamoto & Liu, 2010), insomnia, phobia, homesickness (Okazaki-Luff, 1991), loneliness, and physical fatigue in students (Miyamoto & Kuhlman, 2001).

Several studies have shown that a longer period of sojourn facilitates the sojourner students' cultural adjustment (Akiyama, 2013; Endo, 2011; Kanno, 2000, 2003; Rikyu, 2009; Yoshida et al., 2002). It should be noted that culture shock is also reduced in the process of improving language skills for many students. Cultural adjustment is significantly associated with language proficiency (Cooke, 1995; Endo, 2011; Fillmore, 2000; Haneda & Monobe, 2009; Harkins, 2001; Ileleji, 2008; Kanno, 2000, 2003; Okazaki-Luff, 1991; Takeuchi et al., 2002), where language can influence the school experience positively or negatively.

Language Barrier
The language barrier is a serious matter that many sojourner students, especially newcomers, are very likely to face. Not many Japanese sojourner students have enough opportunities to practice English prior to their sojourns (Koga, 2009); for example, Akiyama's (2012-2014, 2013) participants mentioned that they had been told they were moving to the U.S. only a few months prior to the move. Consequently, they did not have sufficient preparation time for their new lives in the U.S., such as practicing English and obtaining information about their new homes and U.S. culture. Zhou (1997) stated that, "proficiency in English has been regarded as the single

most important prerequisite for assimilation into American society and as a strong social force binding the American people together" (p. 73). On this point, Harkins (2001) pointed out that "*kaigaishijo* [sojourner students], upon arrival, have limited ability to communicate in English" (p. 336). Living overseas without sufficient preparation becomes yet another stressor and puts added pressure on newcomer students.

To overcome these problems, Takeuchi et al. (2002) emphasized that "willingness" of language use and cultural adjustment was essential. Moreover, several scholars addressed the necessity of teachers' and peers' in-depth understanding of Japanese sojourner students; Harkins (2001) and Koga (2009) proposed "sojourner responsible teaching." The sojourner responsible teacher should play an important role in Japanese sojourner students' language-learning as well as cultural adjustment. For example, Koga (2009) argued that, "teachers should know that oral English language proficiency is essential to sojourning students' school inclusion and socioemotional experiences" (p. 294). Harkins (2001), stating that sojourner students are frequently caught between collective (Japanese) culture and individual (U.S.) culture in the classroom, suggested the importance of providing inclusive cultural and linguistic environments in mainstream classrooms so Japanese sojourner students can maintain their cultural and linguistic integrity while participating in the U.S. educational system. In addition, sojourner responsible teaching has several aspects in common with *Linguistically Responsive Teaching* (Lucas et al., 2008), such as giving clear and explicit instructions to linguistic minority students, providing sojourner students with opportunities to use their native languages, and preventing linguistic minority students from being harassed about their accent and errors in speech and writing.

Among sojourner students, the language barrier frequently becomes the issue of greatest concern in the host country during their early sojourn (Akiyama, 2012-2014; Hamann, 2001; Haneda & Monobe, 2009; Kanno, 2000, 2003; Koga, 2009; Yashiro, 1995). Rikyu (2009), which has an informative website for overseas students, introduced some voices of former Japanese sojourner students—"I didn't understand what teachers were talking about" or "we (the student and a native speaker) didn't understand each other." In Akiyama's (2013) study, a Japanese student addressed his intolerable experience—his classmates' curious gazes—when he started his school life in the U.S. He attended a local middle school, and his classmates looked at him as if he were an alien. He noticed that his strangeness came from his poor English proficiency. Also, Kanno's (2003) participant exposed her bitter experience of being asked, "What are you thinking? Are you deaf or ESL?" (p. 157); this student felt that ESL students were considered as handicapped.

Newcomers are very sensitive to being perceived as different (Yoshida et al., 2002). They feel as if ESL students are not respected or accepted (Akiyama, 2013; Kanno, 2003), and they often make efforts to eliminate their language barriers by learning English from native English-speaking tutors (Akiyama, 2012-2014, 2013; Koga, 2009; Miyamoto & Kuhlman, 2001; Yashiro, 1995), reading books written in English, and watching American TV programs (Yashiro, 1995).

The language barrier causes several challenges for Japanese sojourner students. First, language proficiency is the key to students' academic success (Abedi, 2004; DebBurman, 2005; Fillmore, 2000; Hakuta, Butler, & Will, 2000; Miyamoto & Kuhlman, 2001; Okazaki-Luff, 1991; Takeuchi et al., 2002), which includes standardized exams, group discussions, presentations, and so on. Furthermore, the language barrier affects students with developing language proficiency (DLP students) outside the classroom. For example, language-minority students often struggle to understand concepts in homework and thus have to spend extra time to complete their assignments (Ileleji, 2008). The DLP students feel a lot of pressure and stress, and this pressure becomes "language shock" (Ileleji, 2008, p.127), which has symptoms that are very similar to culture shock.

Stereotypical images also affect Japanese sojourner students. Asian students are often regarded as hard workers, high-achievers, problem-free, and able to make it on their own and require less attention within the classroom (Ngo & Lee, 2007; Yee, 1992); for example, these students are expected to be good at math and science (Endo, 2011; Iwamoto & Liu, 2010; Zhou, 1997). In fact, Japanese academic subjects such as math or science are more advanced than those of the U.S. (Endo, 2011; Ileleji, 2008; Rikyu, 2009; Tsuneyoshi, 2001); therefore, several newcomer DLP students can understand the lesson concepts because of their background knowledge. However, the more advanced the lesson content becomes, the more challenging it is to understand for the newcomers (Abedi, 2004; Ngo & Lee, 2007). Yet the teachers are likely to assume that the students do not need assistance; the newcomer students consequently undergo hardships. In reality, one Japanese sojourner student revealed that she had a hard time instantly grasping some technical terms in science class and that the class became challenging to understand (Akiyama, 2012-2014). She concluded that her teacher still had a high expectation of her because of her previous understanding and achievements.

The language barrier strongly affects the DLP students' social lives, making it harder to make friends and integrate with classmates as the DLP students often face fast-paced conversations in the classroom and daily conversations (Rikyu, 2009). For example, a Chinese immigrant student in Fillmore's (2000) study had a difficult time communicating with his classmates because of his insufficient English skills, which resulted in miscommunication and discord. This student came to keep silent and rarely said anything in class (Fillmore, 2000). In the same vein, one Japanese sojourner student could not communicate with anyone; thus, she was a taciturn student at the beginning of her stay in the U.S. (Akiyama, 2012-2014). In addition, newcomer students often have uncomfortable experiences in communicating with peers because of their accents (Endo, 2011; Fillmore, 2000). For example, Endo (2011) witnessed that some classmates teased an Asian immigrant student's accent in a mainstream classroom.

Endo (2011) and Ileleji (2008), who conducted qualitative research on Midwestern public schools where a few Asian (including Japanese) students attended, described the schools they observed as enrolling predominately white students, and that these schools had a great number of Hispanic students in the ESL classes. Their Asian research participants who took ESL classes felt singled out because they represented a very small number and the other students always communicated in Spanish. Furthermore, the ESL teacher sometimes spoke Spanish during class (Ileleji, 2008). The Asian (in particular Japanese) student population in the Midwest is smaller than in coastal areas or larger cities; therefore, Japanese students are identified as an ethnic minority. Students and teachers in such a closed environment are inexperienced in interacting with different ethnicities and linguistic minorities in comparison to those on the West and East Coasts or in larger cities that have more diverse student populations. Endo (2011) and Ileleji's (2008) studies clearly depict the characteristic and serious issues in ESL classes that newcomer ethnic minority students in the Midwest face.

Limited Social Network

Social networking is an important element for adolescent Japanese students because becoming part of a community helps them find physical and emotional support and security (Shibata, 2000). In particular, adolescents are very sensitive about their sense of belonging, and many adolescents are aware that relationships with others influence their lives (Akiyama, 2013; Kanno, 2000, 2003; Moss & Davis, 2008). Thus, establishing a social network is a significant component that Japanese sojourner students are highly concerned with. However, ethnic minority students, including Japanese sojourner students, often face challenges or difficulties in interacting with the majority of students because of their underrepresentation and a lack of understanding from the native students (Endo, 2011; Fillmore, 2000; Ngo & Lee, 2007).

Several studies have suggested that Japanese sojourner students have limited social networks (Endo, 2011; Haneda & Monobe, 2009; Ileleji, 2008; Kanno, 2000, 2003; Toyokawa, 2005). While *hoshuko* (a supplementary Japanese school in the host country; detailed descriptions of this school are given later) is a good place to increase students' networks (Endo, 2011; Hasebe, 1987, Shibata, 2000), *hoshuko* is limited to Japanese people, which leads to a lack of interaction with people of different ethnicities and cultures. On the other hand, Japanese exchange students (as opposed to sojourner students) usually live with host families during their stay in host countries; therefore, the exchange students share a lot of time and social spaces with the host family. In fact, several exchange students have various opportunities to experience the social spaces of their host families (Ileleji, 2008). Some examples of social opportunities for exchange students are going to church with the host family, meeting relatives of the host family, attending host parents' company events, having parties with American friends, and hanging out with host siblings and their friends. As a result, many Japanese exchange students effectively expand their social network in the host country. Unfortunately, sojourner students do not typically have access to these kinds of opportunities.

First, the off-campus social network of Japanese sojourner students is relatively limited, although they may have opportunities to interact with other students at school through school-sponsored extra-curricular programs and student organizations. An example of the off-campus social network, going to church becomes one of the most important means of enlarging students' social connections. In certain regions, especially the Midwest, religion is a significant part of many residents' lifestyle (Endo, 2011, p. 176). Endo (2011) noted that many students in his observation school were Christian, and going to church became a common practice. In fact, some of his participants who were Asian immigrant students attended church, and they interacted with new people as well as their classmates who went to the same church. Also, several Japanese exchange students in the Midwest attended church with their host families and made new connections there (Ileleji, 2008). On the contrary, Japanese sojourner students and their families seldom have an opportunity to meet school friends and community people at church; I assume that this is because the Japanese sojourner families have trouble finding an appropriate church to attend because of the differences of faith and denomination.

Second, Japanese sojourner students' tight schedules often keep them from expanding their social networks. In addition to daily homework assigned at school, Japanese sojourner students also need to complete assignments from *hoshuko* each week (Akiyama, 2012-2014; Haneda & Monobe, 2009). Moreover, many Japanese sojourner students receive private tutoring lessons in order to improve their English skills and catch up on their schoolwork (Miyamoto & Kuhlman, 2001; Yashiro, 1995). One Japanese student hired two native English-speaking tutors and one Japanese tutor (who was bilingual with English and Japanese) when he started life in the U.S. (Akiyama, 2013). This student recollected his days in the U.S. as filled with intensive studying, but he did not mention other primary things (except playing soccer with his school friends) such as hanging out with friends on weekends.

Lastly, Japanese sojourner students often have tighter connections with their family members during their sojourn (Yoshida et al., 2002) because they live with their own families (Harkins, 2001; Hasebe, 1987; Kanno, 2000, 2003; Toyokawa, 2005). Spouses of Japanese sojourners (usually wives) cannot work due to their visa status, and so these wives usually socialize in a group consisting of other sojourner wives (Toyokawa, 2005); children of sojourners are more likely to participate in in-group events (such as home parties) and interact with peers within the group.

These facts reflect that Japanese sojourner students face an issue of narrower social networks in their communities. Inadequate opportunities of interacting with people of different ethnicities and cultures in off-campus settings can have negative impacts on the students' sense of belonging and cause further isolation and marginalization that results in lower self-esteem (Hamann, 2001; Iwamoto & Liu, 2010), which makes the students' school lives more challenging. Although exploring the correlation between students' sojourning lives and their social networks would be beneficial for an in-depth understanding of students' sojourning experiences, studies that focus on the students' social networks are seldom available. Thus, further research on the roles of sojourner students' social networks is required.

Preparation as Future Returnee Students
While acquiring their host country's language and culture, many adolescent Japanese sojourner students make extra efforts to maintain their first language fluency and the academic progress of their home countries because they are likely to be future returnees or *kikokushijo* (Endo, 2011; Haneda & Monobe, 2009; Kanno, 2000, 2003; Miyamoto & Kuhlman, 2001; Yoshida et al., 2002). This represents a unique challenge that Japanese sojourner students face: they are typically expected to return to their home country and resume their social and academic lives there after their sojourn.

Several scholars stressed that many Japanese sojourner students face culture and language shock not only in adjusting to their host country but also with their reentry—which is considered reentry shock, readjustment difficulties, and so on (Hasebe, 1987; Kanno, 2000, 2003; Koga, 2009; Miyamoto & Kuhlman, 2001; Takeuchi et al., 2001; Yoshida et al., 2002). Hasebe (1987) introduced several issues that Japanese returnees tend to face: clearly expressing their ideas in Japanese, getting re-accustomed to tight school rules, speaking and acting appropriately, and establishing friendships (p. 202). Kanno (2003) noted that several returnee students regarded themselves as "incomplete" because of their degraded Japanese language proficiency as well as their non-perfect English (p. 156). Also, several returnee students are considered disrespectful if they do not use honorific speech (speech that shows respect) when talking to older students at school (Kanno, 2000, 2003; Yoshida et al., 2002). These examples of reentry shock strongly reflect how Japanese sojourner students struggle in terms of linguistic, cultural, and social contexts after their return. Consequently, some students face identity issues (Takeuchi et al., 2001; Yoshida et al., 2002) or become targets of teasing, isolation, or bullying because of their "being different" or as a result of atypical manners, behavior, or speech that is different from Japanese social norms (Kanno, 2000, 2003; Koga, 2009; Yoshida et al., 2002). Furthermore, Rikyu (2009) and INFOE-USA (2011) learned that several *kikokushijo* had difficulty understanding Japanese literature, Japanese history, and advanced courses such as math. They also run the risk of feeling bored in English class because of their advanced linguistic ability.

These challenges often become major concerns for Japanese students and parents during their sojourn (Haneda & Monobe, 2009; Hasebe, 1987; Rikyu, 2009; Shidata, 2000). Therefore, many Japanese sojourner students prepare themselves for reentry—they try to maintain their Japanese culture, language, and socializing manners, as well as their academic skills.

One limited method of maintaining Japanese identity is by enrolling children in one of only three Japanese schools or *Nihonjin gakko* (a full overseas day school for Japanese citizens) in the U.S. (MEXT, 2009; Rikyu, 2009). Because there are so few of these schools, most Japanese sojourner students attend local schools with U.S. students (Hasebe, 1987; MEXT, 2009). In addition, a lot of Japanese sojourner students attend *hoshuko* on Saturdays or after school (Haneda & Monobe, 2009; Hasebe, 1987; Kanno, 2000, 2003; Shibata, 2000; Yoshida et al., 2002). *Hoshuko* is open to all students who have Japanese citizenship. This school follows the Japanese school curriculum and is a place where students can learn primarily Japanese, math, and social studies in Japanese (Hasebe, 1987; MEXT, 2009) so that the Japanese sojourner students can keep up with basic academic content that students in Japan learn.

Hoshuko has several functions for Japanese sojourner students. First, *hoshuko* enables Japanese sojourner students to maintain their home culture and language (Haneda & Monobe, 2009; Kanno, 2000, 2003; Shibata, 2000). Especially in the Midwestern regions, which have a smaller Japanese population, few Japanese resources are available in the community (Shibata, 2000); Shibata emphasizes that *hoshuko* can be an effective place to provide Japanese cultural and linguistic opportunities as well as resources. Second, Japanese sojourner students can receive emotional support (Endo 2011; Kanno, 2000, 2003; Shibata, 2000) from other sojourner students and Japanese teachers that they meet at these schools; thus they can make friends, share their culture and experiences, and communicate with each other in Japanese. Such an environment provides comfort as well as a sense of belonging for Japanese sojourner students (Endo, 2011; Hasebe, 1987; Shibata, 2000). Third, *hoshuko* is a place where students can effectively use authentic Japanese language and culture by interacting with Japanese peers and adults, which can foster Japanese identity (Shibata, 2000).

In addition to *hoshuko*, Japanese sojourner students try to maintain their Japanese culture, language, and identity in various ways. A Japanese sojourner student might use the Internet to speak with her relatives and friends in Japan (Akiyama, 2012-2014); some students enjoy recent Japanese dramas and music (Endo, 2011); and some students read Japanese magazines and comic books, while others keep diaries in Japanese (Haneda & Monobe, 2009).

Statistics from MEXT (2014) showed that the majority of returnee students every year consist of elementary and middle school students (8,554 out of 10,518 students were elementary and middle school ages in 2011). Although some private schools and public high schools provide special courses and support for *kikokushijo* (INFOE-USA, 2011; Hasebe, 1987), Yashiro (1995) criticized Japanese public schools' insufficient support. Because of the lack of support upon returning to Japan, Japanese sojourner students need to be well prepared in advance of reentry during their sojourn.

Conclusion

Few Japanese sojourner students are fully prepared to move to the U.S., and they are easily identified as cultural and linguistic minorities in mainstream classrooms at local schools. In particular, Japanese sojourner students are often an ethnic minority within certain regions such as the Midwest, which have smaller Japanese populations. In such situations, Japanese sojourner students face several challenges as previously discussed. These issues are interconnected, which causes other problems that negatively influence Japanese students' sojourning lives.

Although many studies on Japanese sojourner students are available, there are very few qualitative research projects focusing on Asians, including Japanese adolescent students, in the Midwest. Therefore, in addition to reviewing studies on Japanese sojourner students in general, reviewing the literature of actual recounts of the students that described bitter experiences or struggles that ethnic minority students face in the Midwest played a significant role in enriching our knowledge about these students residing in specific areas.

The findings from this chapter will prove the necessity of further research in this area in order to inform and strengthen teacher education research in majority contexts, particularly concerning issues that apply to sojourner populations, such as cultural and linguistic adjustment and limited social networks. These findings will also contribute to teacher preparation programs and help them better cater to the needs of culturally, linguistically, and ethnically diverse students to the extent that future educators will be fully aware of the importance of understanding experiences of different types of ethnic groups.

Notes
1. This governmental data consisted of students who were from 1st to 9th graders—high school students (10th-12th grades) were not included because they are not included in the compulsory education system in Japan.
2. Some of the research did not focus on students in the U.S.—Greenland and Brown (2005) conducted their study in the UK, and Kanno (2000, 2003) conducted her research in Canada. Their research is still useful and acceptable because there are has been limited research into my specific subset. As such, I use these resources as reference.

References
Abedi, J. (2004). The no child left behind act and English language learners: Assessment and accountability issues. *Educational Researcher, 33*(1), 4-14.
Akiyama, R. (2012-2014). *Cultural and linguistic differences: A Japanese student's life as a sojourner in a Midwestern school.* Unpublished manuscript, Purdue University, West Lafayette, IN.
Akiyama, R. (2013, April 28). *The meaning of leaning in culturally and linguistically diverse environments.* Paper presented at American Educational Research Association, San Francisco, CA.
Banks, J. A. (1991). Teaching multicultural literacy to teachers. *Teaching Education, 4,* 134-144.
Berry, J. W. (1995). Psychology of acculturation. In N. R. Goldberger & J. B. Veroff (Eds.), *The culture and psychology reader* (pp. 457–488). New York: New York University Press.
Causey, V. E., Thomas, C. D., & Armento, B. J. (2000). Cultural diversity is basically a foreign term to me: The challenges of diversity for preservice teacher education. *Teaching and Teacher Education, 16,* 33-45.
Cooke, P. (1995, February). *How sojourner students cope: When perceptions of teachers don't match expectations.* Paper presented at the Annual Meeting of the Western States Communication Association, Portland, OR.

Crosnoe, R., & Turley, R. N. L. (2011). K-12 educational outcomes immigrant youth. *The Future of Children, 21*(1), 129-152.

DebBurman, N. (2005). *Immigrant education, variations by generation: Age-at-immigration and country of origin.* New York: LFB Scholarly Publishing, LLC.

Endo, H. (2011). *Schooling experience of Asian immigrant high school students in the Midwest: Race/ethnicity, identity and culture* (Unpublished doctoral dissertation). Purdue University, West Lafayette, IN.

Fillmore, L. W. (2000). Loss of family languages: Should educators be concerned? *Theory into Practice, 39*(4), 203-210.

Greenland, K., & Brown, P. (2005). Acculturation and contact in Japanese students studying in the United Kingdom. *The Journal of Social Psychology, 145*(4), 373-389.

Hakuta, K., Butler, Y. G., & Will, D. (2000). How long does it take English learners to attain proficiency? *Policy Reports, University of California Linguistic Minority Research Institute,* UC Berkeley.

Hamann, E. (2001). Theorizing the sojourner students (with a sketch of appropriate school responsiveness). In M. C. Hopkins & N. Wellmeier (Eds.), *Negotiating transnationalism: Selected papers on refugees and immigrants* (Vol. 9, pp. 32-71). Arlington, VA: American Anthropological Association.

Haneda, M., & Monobe, G. (2009). Bilingual and biliteracy practices: Japanese adolescents living in the United States. *Journal of Asian Pacific Communication, 19*(1), 7-29.

Harkins, L. F. (2001). Understanding the acculturation process for Kaigaishijo. *The Educational Forum, 65,* 335-343.

Hasebe, M. (1987). *Kaigai shijo kyoiku manual: Kaigai chuuzaiin kazoku hikkei* [A manual for oversea students' education: A handbook for overseas resident employees and families]. Toranomon, Tokyo: Kaigaishijo kyoiku shinko zaidan.

Ileleji, R. H. (2008). *Go abroad, young women: A Narrative inquiry of Japanese female youth exchange students in the United States* (Unpublished doctoral dissertation). Purdue University, West Lafayette, Indiana.

INFOE-USA (2011, January 4). Jugyo chu no shitsumon, hatsugen wa seiseki no ichibu [Questions and articulations in class are sources for evaluation]. *Kaigaishijo, Kikokushijo* [Youtube video]. Retrieved from http://youtu.be/p9cIw0yXlh4

Iwamoto, D. K., & Liu, W. M. (2010). The impact of racial identity, ethnic identity, Asian values, and race-related stress on Asian Americans and Asian international college students' psychological well-being. *Journal of Counseling Psychology, 57*(1), 79-91.

Jones, N. A. (2012, May). *The Asian population in the United States: Results from the 2010 Census.* Paper presented at the 2010 Asian Profile America Event, Washington, DC. Retrieved from http://www.ssa.gov/aapi/2010census-data.pdf

Kanno, Y. (2000). Bilingualism and identity: The stories of Japanese returnees. *International Journal of Bilingual Education and Bilingualism, 3*(1), 1-18.

Kanno, Y. (2003). *Negotiating bilingual and bicultural identities: Japanese returnees betwixt two worlds.* Mahwah, NJ: Lawrence Erlbaum Associates, Inc.

Kinghom, M. (2011). *Census 2010: Children=diversity.* Bloomington, IN: Indiana University Kelly School of Business. Retrieved from http://www.incontext.indiana.edu/2011/july-aug/article1.asp

Koga, N. (2009). *Growing student Identities and school competences in sojourning: Japanese children's lived experiences across Japan and the United States* (Unpublished doctoral dissertation). Boston College, Chestnut Hill, Massachusetts.

Lucas, T., Villegas, A. M., & Freedson-Gonzalez, M. (2008). Linguistically responsive teacher education: Preparing classroom teachers to teach English language learners. *Journal of Teacher Education, 59*(4), 361-373.

Matsumoto, D., Yoo, S. H., & Nakagawa, S. (2008). Culture, emotion, regulation, and adjustment. *Journal of Personality and Social Psychology, 94*(6), 925-937.

Ministry of Education, Culture, Sports, Science and Technology. (2009). *Kaigai de manabu nihon no kodomotachi:Waga kuni no kaigaishijo kyouiku no genjou* [Japanese overseas students: The current situation of Japanese oversea students' education]. Retrieved from http://www.mext.go.jp/a_menu/shotou/clarinet/002/001.htm

Ministry of Education, Culture, Sports, Science and Technology. (2014). *Kaigai ni chokitaizai shita-ato kikoku-shita jidouseito no kazu no suii* [Transition of numbers about returnee students]. Retrieved from http://www.mext.go.jp/a_menu/shotou/clarinet/004/001/004/001.htm

Ministry of Foreign Affairs of Japan. (2012). *Kaigai zairyu hojinsu toukei* [Statistical data of Japanese overseas residents]. Retrieved from http://www.mofa.go.jp/mofaj/toko/tokei/hojin/12/pdfs/WebPrint.pdf

Ministry of Foreign Affairs of Japan. (2013). *Zairyu hojin shijo-su (choki taizaisha)* [The number of overseas resident students (long-term residents)]. Retrieved from http://www.mofa.go.jp/mofaj/files/000018782.pdf

Miyamoto, Y., & Kuhlman, N. (2001). Ameliorating culture shock in Japanese expatriate children in the US. *International Journal of Intercultural Relations, 25*, 21-40.

Moss, R. C., & Davis, D. (2008). Counseling biracial students: A review of issues and interventions. *Journal of Multicultural Counseling and Development, 36*, 219-230.

Murakoshi, Y. (1997). Shudan to ko no kankei ni kansuru bunkaron: Nihon bunka to America bunka [Cultural theory about groups and individuals: Japanese culture and the U.S. culture]. *Department Bulletin of Atomi University, 11*, 1-35. Retrieved from http://sucra.saitama-u.ac.jp/modules/xoonips/download.php/atomi-eibungaku-11-1.pdf?file_id=24186

Ngo, B., & Lee, S. J. (2007). Complicating the image of model minority success: A review of Southeast Asian American Education. *Review of Educational Research, 77*(4), 415-453.

Okazaki-Luff, K. (1991). On the adjustment of Japanese sojourners: Beliefs, contentions, and empirical findings. *International Journal of Intercultural Relations, 15*, 85-102.

Rikyu. (2009, October). Taikendan [Experiences] [Web log post]. Retrieved from http://kaigaishijo.com/experiences/

Shibata, S. (2000). Opening a Japanese Saturday school in a small town in the United States: Community collaboration to teach Japanese as a heritage language. *Bilingual Research Journal, 24*(4), 465-474.

Spring, J. (2008). *The intersection of cultures* (4th ed.). New York: Taylor & Francis.

Takeuchi, R., Yun, S., & Russell, J. E. A. (2002). Antecedents and consequences of the perceived adjustment of Japanese expatriates in the USA. *The International Journal of Human Resources Management, 13*(8), 1224-1244.

Takeuchi, S., Imahori, T. T., & Matsumoto, D. (2001). Adjustment of criticism styles in Japanese returnees to Japan. *International Journal of Intercultural Relations, 25*, 315-317.

Takeya, K. (1992). Culture shock: Schools in the U.S. and Japan. *Kaleidoscope, 3*. Retrieved from http://leo.stcloudstate.edu/kaleidoscope/volume3/cultureshock.html

Toyokawa, N. (2005). The function of the social network formed by Japanese sojourners' wives in the United States. *International Journal of Intercultural Relations, 30*, 185-193.

Tsuneyoshi, R. K. (2001). *The Japanese model of schooling: comparisons with the United States.* New York: Routledge Falmer.

Yashiro, K. (1995). Japan's Returnees. *Journal of Multilingual and Multicultural Development, 16,* 139-164.

Yee, A. H. (1992). Asians as stereotypes and students: Misperceptions that persist. *Educational Psychology Review, 4*(1), 95-132.

Yeh, C. J. (2003). Age, acculturation, cultural adjustment, and mental health symptoms of Chinese, Korean, and Japanese immigrant youths. *Cultural Diversity and Ethnic Minority Psychology, 9*(1), 34-48.

Yoshida, T., Matsumoto, D., Akiyama, T., Moriyoshi, N., Furuiye, A., Isii, C., & Franklin, B. (2002). The Japanese returnee experience: Factors that affect reentry. *International Journal of Intercultural Relations, 26,* 429-445.

Zeichner, K. M. (2009). *Teacher education and the struggle for social justice.* New York: Routledge.

Zhou, M. (1997). Growing up American: The challenge confronting immigrant children and children of immigrants. *Annual Review of Sociology, 23*(1), 63-95.

CHAPTER 14

EVALUATING CONCEPTS OF FACE

Lin Tao
Kanazawa University

Introduction

The concept of 'face' has been an important research topic since the first publication of politeness theory was presented by Brown and Levinson in 1978. It was Goffman (1955) who first introduced the notion. Goffman (1967) defined face as "an image of self delineated in terms of approved social attributes" (p. 5). However, it is Brown and Levinson's (1978) application of face in the context of politeness theory that has dominated much of the debate thus far (Haugh, 2010, p. 2073). Brown and Levinson (1978, 1987) further developed Goffman's notion of face and presented two additional foci. According to Brown and Levinson (1978, p. 61), face is "highly abstracted " and subject to "cultural elaboration." It is their dualistic notion of face, or public self-image, with matching positive and negative politeness behaviours, that is at the heart of their model and that departs most radically from both Goffman's elaboration of face (and "face-work") and Durkhaim's "positive and negative ritual" (Bargiela-Chiappini, 2003, p. 1460). That is, face constitutes the public self-image that every interlocutor wants to claim for himself or herself, and consists of two related aspects: positive face and negative face.

Positive face is the basic claim for the projected self-image to be approved of by others (crucially including the desire that this self-image be appreciated and approved of). Negative face is the basic claim to territories, personal reserves, and rights to non-distraction. Since the concepts of positive and negative face were introduced, research on face has often centered on the validity of Brown and Levinson's notion of "face" for explaining politeness across various cultural contexts (Gu, 1990; Haugh & Hinze, 2003; Haugh, 2005, 2007; Ide, 1989; Matsumoto, 1988; Pizziconi, 2003; Tao, 1998).

As Bargiela-Chiappini (2003) pointed out, "In particular, it is 'negative face' and, consequently, negative politeness that have generated the most criticism, usually on cultural relativistic grounds" (p. 1460). Whereas Goffman (1987) views 'avoidance' as a process whereby individuals avoid face-threatening situations, this is not reduced to a clear-cut distinction between "freedom of action and freedom from imposition" that characterizes Brown and Levinson's negative face" (p. 61).

According to Haugh (2010), the continuing controversy as to whether or not honorifics in Modern Standard Japanese are indeed examples of a failure of Brown and Levinson's politeness theory is a case in point. On the one hand, there is the often cited argument by Matsumoto (1988) that "what is of paramount importance to a Japanese is not his/her territory [negative face], but the position in relation to others in the group and his/her acceptance by others" (p. 405). On the other hand, other scholars have argued that Brown and Levinson's notion of face can in fact be applied to the study of honorifics, and thus politeness, in Modern Standard Japanese (Fukada & Asato, 2004; Fukushima, 2000; Ishiyama, 2009; Usami, 2002). In these latter approaches, however, Brown and Levinson's notions of positive and negative face are reduced to an undifferentiated notion that can be either "lost" or "saved" (Haugh, 2005, p. 44).

The collectivist/individualist issue also questions Brown and Levinson's model. For example, Gu (1990) declares that Brown and Levinson have focused too exclusively on a model of politeness involving two rational model persons, neglecting the wider social context. Gu points out,

> In the Chinese context, politeness exercises its normative function in constraining individual speech acts as well as the sequence of talk exchanges. A society, to be sure, consists of individuals, but it is more than a total sum of its individual constituents. Politeness is a phenomenon belonging to the level of society, which endorses its normative constraints on each individual. (p. 242)

As is well known, the notion of face attracted scholarly attention especially through Brown and Levinson's (1978/1987) politeness theory. Central to their politeness framework is the concept of face. One of the main goals in social interaction is to maintain and even enhance face during conversation, especially the East-West debate on positive face and negative face. Furthermore, the notion of face and politeness behavior can vary across contexts, groups and time in a cross-cultural perspective. As Spencer-Oatey (2007) has pointed out, "face is a complex phenomenon that needs to be studied from multiple perspectives" (p. 654) . It is very important and necessary to investigate face and politeness in different communities of practice and groups by means of the 'discursive' analytical framework.

In recent years, face theory has been reexamined by many researchers and scholars. Despite debates such as the previously mentioned issue, there has been relatively little research on native speaker beliefs about face, and a number of important questions remain. The present study aims to address the following questions in this regard:

1. Do Chinese and Japanese people regard saving face very highly?
2. Do Chinese and Japanese young people think that saving face is very important?
3. How do Chinese and Japanese young people perceive positive face and negative face?
4. Do Chinese and Japanese young people like to save their face in personal relationships?

I think that interviews and questionnaires focusing on native speaker beliefs about face are highly valuable sources of insight into the emic conceptualization of the face perspective. This study focuses on questionnaires and provides useful insights into the thoughts and traditional moral values of Chinese and Japanese young people, particularly Eastern cultures, on the basis of an analysis of questionnaire data. The data are also analyzed in terms of group and gender differences. The main purpose of this study is to discover how Chinese and Japanese young people evaluate the notions of positive and negative face (Brown and Levinson, 1987), the importance of saving face, and their conscious effect on the emic conceptualization of face in personal relationships. It is hoped that this study is not only important for reexamining values of notions of face for younger Asian generations, but also for increasing our understanding how face and politeness impact Chinese and Japanese culture and verbal communication, so as to promote intercultural communication.

Face in Chinese

The concept of face is Chinese in origin. Goffman (1955) acknowledges in a footnote that he read Smith (1894), Hu (1944), Yang (1947) and one other work on Chinese society that discusses the Chinese concept of face. As is well known, it is the great success of Smith's book (Hayford, 1985, p. 153), that the term face as an explanation for what is peculiar to the Chinese became more common. After that, MacGowan (1912), like Smith, contains an entire chapter on the term (pp. 301-312), and uses both the expressions 'save face' and 'lose face' in several other parts of the book (pp. 165, 189-90, 261, 297). Gilbert (1926, pp. 27-29) repeats many of the points made by Smith, and his examples also include those of a servant stealing and then needing to save face over the theft.

However, MacGowan is perhaps the first person to divide face into two different aspects. One he identifies as "honour, reputation", bestowed by others on the self; the other aspect of face is "self-respect, or dignity", which is more an inner feeling, but which in turn leads to an outward showing (hence the theatricality of face). The concept of face as the basis of the Chinese national character is most famously taken up in Chinese by Lu Xun in the 1920s. It is interesting that Lu Xun often employed the compound *timian* ('dignity'; 'face') and, less frequently, the term *mianzi* in his writings.

Hu (1944) locates the meaning of both terms within the English term 'prestige', a category which she claims is universal in human societies everywhere. She then makes the claim that *mianzi* is associated with "the kind of prestige that is emphasized in this country [the United States]: a reputation achieved through getting on in life, through success and ostentation. This is prestige that is accumulated by means of personal effort or clever maneuvering" (p. 45). *Lian,* however, is more of an "internalized sanction" and something that, although perhaps present in American society, is not "formally recognized." Three years later, Yang (1947) gave us his definition of face:

> 'Face' is a literal translation of the Chinese character *lien* or *mien*. Although *lien* or *mien* means just what the English word face does, the Chinese expression *tiou*

lien ('losing face') or *yao mien-tze* ('wishing a face') has nothing to do with face in our usual understanding of the term.... When we say in Chinese that one loses face, we mean that he loses prestige, he has been insulted or has been made to feel embarrassment before a group. When we say that a man wants a face, we mean that he wants to be given honor, prestige, praise, flattery, or concession, whether or not these are merited. Face is really a personal psychological satisfaction, a social esteem accorded by others. (p. 167)

In contrast to Goffman, who deracinates the term face, Ho (1976) begins by drawing attention to the Chinese origin of the concept, citing etymological dictionaries of English that identify it as a loanword. He says that the terms are often interchangeable in Chinese, even if there is a distinction in the way in which face is judged, either on character (*lian*) or on "amoral aspects of social performance" (*mianzi*) (p. 867). Ho also advances an extremely detailed argument to distinguish from prestige. He claims that while prestige is almost identical to face and the two are easily conflated, face is a broader and more basic category than prestige. He argues that face is useful in highlighting the problems of Western cultures that over-value the individual, and therefore tend to deny the importance of face in the maintenance of social structures (pp. 878-880).

In Chinese, however, there has always existed a variety of expressions relating to the concept of face, such as *lian, mian-zi, timain, qingmian, renqing, guanxi*. The terms *lian, mian-zi, timain, and qingmian* play important roles in the emic notion of face in Chinese. To sum up, the notion of Chinese face includes two aspects, namely *lian* and *mian-zi*. *Lian* represents the confidence of society in the integrity of the ego's moral character, while *mian-zi* represents a reputation achieved through success and ostentation.

According to Sueda's (1995) research, historical analyses of the Chinese concept of *mian-zi* explains how it differs from the honor of the Japanese samurai or warrior or the Western European knight.

Face in Japanese

In Japan and Western Europe, honor is not centered around social fame but around an individual's level of dignity under feudal systems. However, Chinese society has, since 200 B.C., been governed by civilians rather than by soldiers, and their sense of honor is traditionally different from that of Japan and Western Europe. Chinese society placed less value on a warrior's honor than did Japanese society, rather placing value on the reputation of an individual and family. With the increase of interaction between China and Japan, the word *mian-zi* was introduced to Japan and came to be realized as *mentsu*. According to Sueda (1995), *mentsu* was not regarded as seriously as a warriors' honor, for which a warrior could die. Because *mentsu* is but one factor contributing to an individual's reputation in the community in daily life, Sueda describes it as "little honor" as opposed to warriors' honor, which is described as "big honor." With the decline of the warrior class over time, *mentsu* or "little honor" became the more prevalent notion. Japanese *mentsu* encompasses an evaluation of not only the individual, but also the entire group or community to which the individual belongs (Inoue, 1977).

Haugh (2007) argued that

> in discussions of face in Japanese thus far, the focus has been primarily on how Japanese face differs in nature from that proposed by Brown and Levinson (1987), but little has been said about the actual constituents of face in Japanese. The lack of explanation about the nature of Japanese face is due in part to the lack of clarity as to the status of folk or emic notions of face. (p. 662)

It is true that in discussions of Japanese face, it is not enough to know about how Japanese face differs in nature from that proposed by Brown and Levinson. Most importantly, the actual constituents of face, the nature of Chinese and Japanese face, and status of folk or emic notions of face should be clarified.

Japan is a shame-sensitive society. According to Japanese dictionaries, the emic notion of face in Japanese is represented through a number of related lexemes; the terms *kao, menboku, taimen,* and *sekentei* play important roles in the emic notion of face in Japanese. For example, the term *kao* has the widest semantic field, encompassing face as representative of a person, both literally as an individual and figuratively as one's social image. The latter may involve the social image of individuals, groups or family. *Kao* also encompasses face as representing power, in terms of one's degree of influence in a group.

The term *mentsu* in Japanese is used to reflect one's social image (e.g., *mentsu o omonnjiru* ('hold face in esteem'). In Tao's (1998) investigation, it was also pointed out that *mentsu* has a more narrow conceptual field than *kao* and *menboku*.

As Haugh (2007) pointed out, the concept of face in Japanese as a kind of positive social image, representative of a person as an individual or of the group to which the person belongs, can be analyzed in terms of the notions of *menboku* and *taimen* (p. 663). According to the Kojien dictionary, *menboku* is defined as "the face with which one meets people" or "honor in the *seken*." Haugh suggested that *menboku* thus primarily involves external evaluations within a particular community of practice or wider society (the *seken*) of one's *meiyo* (lit. 'honour'), or one's own dignity/character (*jinkaku*), or that of one's salient in-group (*uchi*).

The notion of *taimen*, in contrast, is defined in the Kojien dictionary as "an individual's or group's appearance in public." Nevertheless, while the notions of *menboku* and *taimen* initially appear to encompass different aspects of face, they are arguably both related to the core notion of place, both in the sense of the place one belongs (*uchi*) and the place one stands (*tachiba*). According to Haugh, loss of face (*Kao o tsubusu*) may arise in situations where harmony within the place one belongs (*uchi*) is not maintained, while one can give face (*kao o tateru*) by allowing others to look good in the place they stand (*tachiba*) (Morisaki & Gudykunst, 1994, p. 56, as cited in Cole, 1989). The difference between the two appears to lie in the way they vary in their orientation to place. Many researchers point out that the notion of place underlying face in Japanese is also closely related to external evaluations by particular "imagined communities" (*seken*) that are perceived as constantly having the potential to judge one's actions as (in) appearance (Abe, 1995; Haugh, 2007; Inoue, 1977; Shiba, 1999). In sum, as many scholars have pointed out, particular definitions of face are culture-specific.

Research Procedures

The Questionnaire

Data was gathered by means of respondents completing a written questionnaire. The questions on the questionnaire aimed at gathering information on current conceptualizations of what constitutes Chinese *mianzi* and Japanese *mentsu*. The data allowed a comparison to be drawn between the concepts of communicative behavior concerning face (*mentsu*) of Chinese and Japanese young people, and other English concepts that assess human behavior. The questionnaire consisted of a total of 54 questions, including both multiple-choice and free-response questions. This paper focuses on the data drawn from the answers to the following four questions:

1. Do you think that Chinese/Japanese people regard saving face very highly?
2. Do you think that saving face is very important for you?
3. Which one do you think is considered most important in Chinese/Japanese culture, negative face or positive face?
4. Do you like to save your face in personal relationships?

The questionnaire was translated into Chinese and Japanese by the researcher, and the equivalence between the Chinese and Japanese versions was ensured through careful checking by three bilingual helpers.

Data Collection

The Chinese questionnaires were distributed at two universities in China. One- hundred-ten copies were given to a university in Shanghai; fifty copies were distributed at a university in Zhengzhou; One-hundred-fifty were returned, and of these, 137 had been fully completed and were included in the study. Fifty copies were distributed at universities in Japan for overseas Chinese university students; fifty-three were returned and fully completed and were included in the study. Thus 190 (96 males, 94 females) complete Chinese questionnaires were obtained overall, with participants ranging in age from 19 to 30 years.

The Japanese questionnaires were distributed at four universities in Japan. One-hundred-ten copies were given to two universities in Tokyo and Yokohama; One-hundred-five were returned, fully completed, and were included in the study. Ninety copies were distributed at universities in Toyama and Kanazawa; Eighty-two were returned, and fully completed and were included in the study. Thus 187 (94 males and 93 females) complete Japanese questionnaires were obtained overall, with participants ranging in age from 17 to 21 years.

As Yu pointed out (2003),

> Face is an individual trait, and there are many other variables, such as 'gender', 'status', and 'distance' that may affect speech act behavior; hence it seems very unlikely that we will be able to account for all speakers' politeness performance entirely from the perspective of cultural conditioning. (p.1703)

We certainly can expect to find individuals within the same culture oftentimes making very different types of responses. In order to examine differences between Chinese and Japanese young people, different features between Chinese male and female, and Japanese male and female, the data obtained from the written questionnaires were separated according to the gender of the Chinese group respondents and Japanese group respondents. Following this, qualitative differences among the different types of responses to each particular question were determined by grouping the responses into categories.

Results

As mentioned above, the data obtained from the questionnaires were separated according to the gender of the respondent. Following this, qualitative differences among the answers to each question were determined by grouping the responses into specific categories. Data were collected through an open-ended question. Each question presented two, three, or four options, and respondents were aksed to select one of the options based on their own opinion. The data below indicate the percentage of respondents selecting each option, and are not from the free-response questions. Below, similarities and differences in face described by Chinese and Japanese students are examined. Regarding Question 1, Table 14.1 classifies the types of responses by Chinese males and females.

Table 14.1
Responses of Chinese male and female respondents to Questions 1 and 2

Questions	Answers	Male	Female	Total
Q1. Do you think Chinese people regard saving face very highly?	Very highly	89 (92.7%)	87 (92.6%)	176 (92.6%)
	Not very highly	7 (7.3%)	7 (7.4%)	14 (7.4%)
Q2. Do you think saving face is most important for you?	Important	72 (75.0%)	77 (81.9%)	145 (76.3%)
	Not important	24 (25.0%)	17 (18.1%)	42 (23.7%)

As can be seen from Table 14.1, 92.6% of the Chinese respondents showed that Chinese people regard saving face very highly. In response to Question 2, 76.3% of the respondents indicated that saving face was most important for them, specifically 75.0% of the male respondents and 81.6% of the female respondents.

In the above answers, it is a fact that Chinese people regard saving face very highly. In summation, most Chinese males and females are fully aware that Chinese people regard saving face very highly and saving face is most important for themselves. On the other hand a few males and females also fully understand that saving face is not most important for themselves. In addition, the study shows that slightly more female than male respondents indicated that saving face was most important for them. Furthermore, the table shows that answer rate of Question 1 "Chinese people regard saving face very highly" is higher than Question 2 "Saving face is most important for you". This example clearly shows that cross-cultural variation is a complex issue.

Table 14.2
Responses of Japanese male and female respondents to Questions 1 and 2

Questions	Answers	Male	Female	Total
Q1. Do you think Japanese people regard saving face very highly?	Very highly	79 (84.0%)	82 (90.3%)	161 (85.8%)
	Not very highly	15 (16.0%)	11 (9.7%)	26 (14.2%)
Q2. Do you think saving face is most important for you?	Important	70 (74.5%)	75 (80.6%)	145 (77.5%)
	Not important	24 (25.5%)	18 (19.4%)	42 (22.5%)

As is clear from Table 14.2, 85.8% of respondents thought that Japanese people regard saving face very highly, specifically 84% of the male respondents and 90.3% of the female respondents. In response to Question 2, 77.5% of respondents indicated that saving face was most important for them, specifically 74.5% of the male respondents and 80.6% of the female respondents. Table 14.2 therefore shows that slightly more female than male respondents indicated that "Japanese people regard saving face very highly."

Likewise, slightly more female than male respondents indicated that saving face was most important for them. Like Chinese people, the table shows that the answer rate of "Japanese people regard saving face very highly" is higher than "Saving face is most important."

Table 14.3
Responses of Chinese male and female respondents to Questions 3 and 4

Questions	Answers	Male	Female	Total
Q3. Which one do you think is considered most important in Chinese culture, negative face or positive face?	Negative face	6 (6.3%)	10 (10.6%)	16 (8.4%)
	Positive face	24 (25.0%)	32 (34.0%)	56 (29.5%)
	Both of them	65 (67.7%)	50 (53.2%)	115 (60.5%)
	Neither of them	1 (1.05%)	2 (2.2%)	3 (1.6%)
Q4. Do you like to save your face in personal relationships?	Yes	75 (78.1%)	78 (83.0%)	153 (80.5%)
	No	21 (21.9%)	16 (17.0%)	37 (19.5%)

Table 14.3 presents data based on the Chinese respondents' answers to Questions 3 and 4 of the questionnaire. In response to Question 3, 29.5% of the respondents indicated that positive face is considered most important in Chinese culture, 60.5% that both positive and negative face are considered most important, and 8.4% that negative face is considered most important. Only 1.6% of the respondents indicated that neither positive nor negative face is important. In response to Question 4, 80.5% of respondents indicated that they like to save their face in personal relationships, while 19.5% of the respondents did not agree with this.

Table 14.3 separates the responses to Questions 3 and 4 on the basis of gender. More female respondents thought that positive face is considered most important in Chinese culture than did male respondents. Likewise, more male than female respondents indicated that both positive and negative face are considered most important in Chinese culture than did female respondents. In response to Question 4, more female respondents thought that they like to save face in personal relationships in Chinese culture than did male respondents.

In sum, most of the Chinese students surveyed in the present study thought that aspects of face are important, and liked to save their face in personal relationships. It would also appear that both positive face and negative face remain important and meaningful to Chinese students.

Table 14.4
Responses of Japanese male and female respondents to Questions 3 and 4

Questions	Answers	Male	Female	Total
Q3. Which one do you think is considered most important in Japanese culture, negative face or positive face?	Negative face	19 (20.2%)	21 (22.6%)	40 (21.4%)
	Positive face	36 (38.3%)	41 (44.1%)	77 (41.2%)
	Both of them	31 (33.0%)	29 (31.2%)	60 (32.1%)
	Neither of them	8 (8.5%)	2 (2.1%)	10 (5.3%)
Q4. Do you like to save your face in personal relationships?	Yes	74 (78.7%)	75 (80.6%)	149 (79.6%)
	No	20 (21.3%)	18 (19.4%)	38 (20.4%)

Table 14.4 presents data based on the Japanese respondents' answers to Questions 3 and 4 of the questionnaire. In response to Question 3, 41.2% of respondents indicated that positive face is considered most important in Japanese culture, 32.1% that both positive and negative face are considered most important, and 21.4 % that negative face is considered most important. Only 5.3% of the respondents indicated that neither positive nor negative face is important. In response to Question 4, 79.6% of respondents indicated that they like to save their face in personal relationships, while 20.4% of the respondents did not agree with this.

Table 14.4 separates the responses to Questions 3 and 4 on the basis of gender. As can be seen, there is no difference between male and female respondents, although more female respondents thought that positive face is considered most important in Japanese culture than did male respondents.

The responses to Question 4 indicate that 78.8% of male respondents and 80.6% of female respondents like to save face in personal relationships. On the other hand, 21.3% of male respondents and 19.4% of female respondents did not agree with this.

The data presented above suggest that Japanese young people regard saving face very highly. To summarize, most of the Japanese students surveyed in the present study thought that aspects of face are important and positive, and liked to save their face in personal relationships. It would also appear that positive face remains important and meaningful to Japanese students.

Discussion

The present study yielded valuable information on the emic conceptualization of face among Chinese and Japanese university students. The results objectively verify the awareness of face among younger Chinese and Japanese people, suggesting that most Chinese and Japanese university students regard saving face very highly and think that saving face is most important.

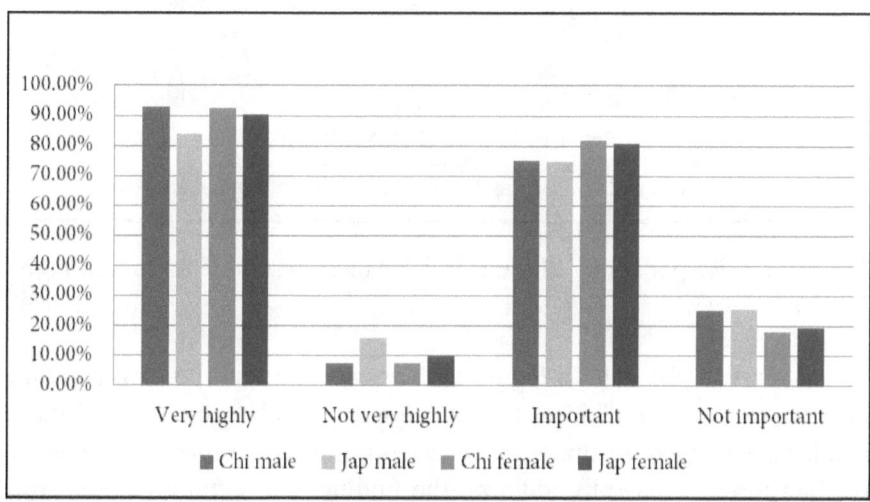

Figure 14.1. Responses of Chinese and Japanese respondents to Questions 1 and 2

The data from Figure 14.1 show that more Chinese and Japanese respondents are fully aware that generally, Chinese and Japanese people regard saving face very highly. But a few Chinese and Japanese participants indicated that they did not agree that "Saving face is most important" for themselves. The data also suggest that most Chinese and Japanese young people like to save face in their own communicative behavior. The results show that slightly more Chinese male responders regard saving face very highly than did Japanese male respondents. While Question 2 shows no significant difference between Chinese and Japanese respondents, more female respondents think that "Saving face is most important" in Chinese and Japanese culture than did male respondents.

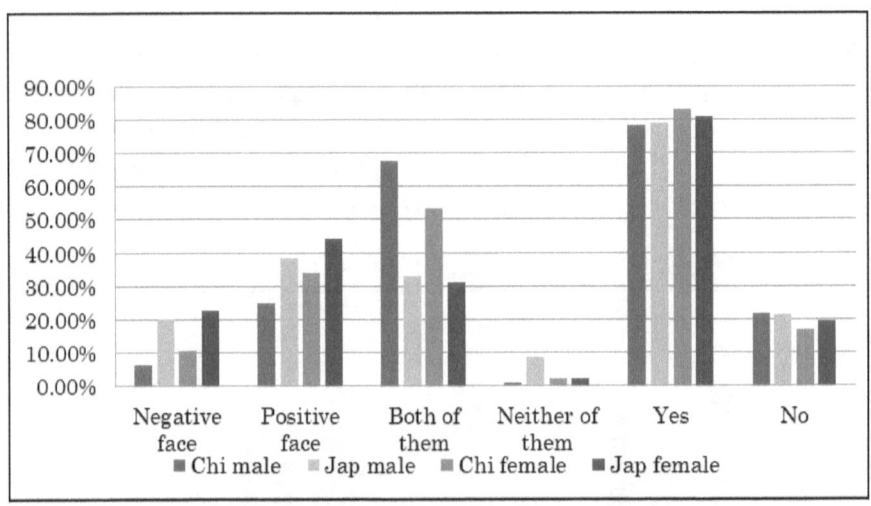

Figure 14.2. Responses of Chinese and Japanese respondents to Questions 3 and 4

As a result, the data in Figure 14.2 reveals that both positive face and negative face exist in Chinese and Japanese culture, but that more Chinese and Japanese students think positive face is important in their culture, more so than negative face. In addition, the findings show more Chinese and Japanese female respondents thought that positive face is considered most important than did male respondents.

On the whole, more Chinese respondents thought that both positive and negative face are considered most important in Chinese culture than did Japanese respondents. Meanwhile, more Chinese male respondents thought that both positive face and negative face (67.70%) are considered most important in Chinese culture than did female respondents (53.20%).

Mao (1994) argues that *mian-zi* and *lian* are distinct categories, as Hu (1944) and Ho (1976) have claimed, at the same time arguing that Brown and Levinson's negative face does not really apply to China. In my study, only 8.4% of Chinese respondents thought that negative face is considered most important in Chinese culture. This finding is indeed evidence that Brown and Levinson's negative face does not really apply to China. As Yu (2003) has pointed out, "Accordingly, the universality of negative face want does not appear to be substantiated, and even less so its mutual knowledge. In addition, as negative face plays a minor role in the Chinese conception of face, Brown and Levinson's thesis that Chinese society, due to its generally higher weighting of FTAs, is a negative politeness culture seems to be problematic" (p. 1697).

Unlike Chinese respondents, more Japanese respondents indicated that not only negative face, but also positive face are considered most important in Japanese culture. On this point, the data differ from Brown and Levinson (1978, 1987), namely that, in Japanese society, "the perceived evaluation of one's place by particular 'imagined communities (*seken*) has much to do with the loss, gain or maintenance of one's own face, or that of one's group. The kind of face that arises through interactions is thus dependent on what one thinks others in a wider 'imagined communities' (*seken*) show they think of one's conduct relative to the place one stands or belongs" (Haugh, 2007, p. 663).

Many scholars have pointed out what Matsumoto (2003) claimed, namely that there is not "enough evidence to support the universality of Brown and Levinson's definition of negative face" (p. 1516). In the present investigation, I also found that Brown and Levinson's negative face concept does not fully explain other cultural notions of face. This is particularly so in terms of the widely used Japanese formulaic expression *yoroshiku onegaishimasu*, which literally means "Please treat me favorably" or "Please take care of me," conveyed through an imperative structure that is typically used upon meeting someone for the first time in everyday living. This might be seen by an outsider an imposition, but it is not viewed as imposing by Japanese speakers, rather as a politeness token. This shows that Japanese politeness is different from Western politeness, which is seen as a means to avoid imposition (Ide, 1989; Matusumoto, 1988).

With regard to the concept of negative politeness in Japan, Takita (2012) analyzes the Japanese notion of *enryo* as face, and provides evidence for a common phenomenon observed in negative face, as suggested by Brown and Levinson. Takita (2012) argues as follows:

> The classic concept of *enryo* is described as an empathic orientation and hesitation of self expression by minimizing frank expression, which can be seen to protect the hearer's negative face. However, people nowadays, particularly the younger generations, are using *enryo* more conveniently and more as a means to show their refusal to an invitation. This might indicate that the younger generations in Japan are becoming more individualistic and less sensitive to empathic orientation toward others. Therefore, unlike looking at the collectivistic perspective of face argued by Japanese scholars in the past, the new concept of *enryo* can be said to be similar to the concept of negative face, since both negative face and *enryo* can be seen as the social contract that allows rejection to be expressed indirectly to others by satisfying one's desire to be unimpeded on an individual level. (p. 194)

This may explain why approximately one-third of the Japanese university students surveyed in this study also regard negative face as important. The results of the present study lead me to agree with Matsumoto's position in terms of the importance of a social perspective of face rather than individual autonomy in Japanese society. I also support Takita's idea that the new perspective of *enryo* as a desire not to be imposed upon by others is very similar to the concept of negative face proposed by Brown and Levinson.

On the basis of the data of Chinese young people, face is still important in Chinese society, although young people are greatly influenced by Western thought and sense of values now. Most importantly, we know that both Chinese culture and Japanese culture belong to Asian cultures and vary in their conceptualization of face and practice of politeness. Since the late 1980s, many students of sociolingustics, pragmatics have been seriously investing Eastern languages, particularly Chinese and Japanese. "In fact, there is little doubt that they are the best studied languages among all languages spoken in the entire continent of Asia" (Chen et al., 2013, p. 141). As seen above, my findings about these two cultures have provided scholars reasons to doubt Brown and Lenvison's notion of face.

There is a subtle difference in importance of positive face and negative face between Chinese and Japanese younger generations in the era of growth of intercultural communication. On the one hand, the results show that 60.5% of Chinese university students believe that both positive and negative face are considered most important. On the other hand, only 32.1% of Japanese university students indicated that both positive and negative face are considered most important. On the contrary, 41.2% of Japanese university students indicated positive face is considered most important. In addition, 29.5% of Chinese university students indicated that positive face is considered most important in Chinese culture. In other words, this study reveals the fact that the younger generations in China and Japan have different opinions on positive face and negative face. For example, as noted earlier, Japanese usually use an imperative form to express politeness when meeting someone for the first time; Chinese people, on the other hand, usually say *"Qing duoduo zhijiao,"* which literally means "Please teach me a lot." This self-humbling/self-abasement shows respect for others, demonstrating how a Chinese speaker will gain his or her positive face.

To summarize, issues around face tend to be vulnerable to subjective perceptions, and thus can never be judged in true versus false terms. This makes data informing perceptions of face both worthwhile and necessary (Spencer-Oatey, 2007). In other words, face is a very complex phenomenon, where different cultures have different value of the notion of face. The relationship between these two aspects of positive face and negative face and politeness need to be explored in more detail at a deeper level in order to fully understand what this relationship looks like. It is necessary to also examine cross-cultural comparisons of the actual constituents of face.

Concluding Remarks

The study of perceived face in Chinese and Japanese verbal communication is a very interesting theme. First, this study gives an overview of research on the status of face. Second, it provides further explanation around the different conceptualizations of face in Chinese and Japanese culture. Third, this research investigated the opinions of Chinese and Japanese students' own conceptualizations concerning face. Fourth, it discusses and analyzes the nature or emic notion of Chinese and Japanese students' conceptualizations of face, as well as considering the data in terms of respondents' gender. The results suggest that face is a universal construct in Chinese and Japanese interaction. Generally speaking, it appears that the notion of face is regarded as important, and that saving face is regarded as important in Chinese and Japanese verbal communication. While there is a difference between the two groups, sixty percent of Chinese consider that both positive face and negative face exist in Chinese culture. On the other hand, Japanese university students appear to consider positive face (41.2%) to be more important than both positive face and negative face (32.1%) and negative face (21.4%).

Yu (2003)argued "as noted before, the Chinese sociocultural context embraces a tradition according to which individuals should subordinate themselves to the group or the community, thereby downplaying the importance of self or ego (e.g., Mao,1994; Oliver, 1971; Tu, 1985). As a consequence, there has long been a high value placed on communal needs over individual preferences. In terms of Brown and Levinson's definitions of positive and negative face, Chinese sociocultural norms actually place much greater emphasis on positive politeness" (p. 1704). The present study has shown that 29.5% of the Chinese believe positive face exists in Chinese culture, and the Chinese regard negative face as irrelevant. In addition, the Chinese younger generations tend to deem positive face and negative face. This result shows the Chinese younger generations are changing their cultural norms, Western culture can have a major influence on younger lifestyles. In contrast, Japanese university students appear to consider positive face to be more important than negative face. Generally, the above discussion of the Chinese and Japanese concepts of face, as many researchers

> have argued that negative face desires, which attend to the interlocutor's territorial concerns for privacy and autonomy, derive directly from the high value placed on individualism in Western culture, and that such face needs seem to be irrelevant or negligible in societies such as the Chinese and Japanese with their collective orientation, and that therefore face needs cannot account for politeness behavior in those societies. (Yu, 2003, p. 1698)

This finding represents a divergence from Brown and Levinson (1978, 1987). This study makes a contribution to research on the concept of face among Chinese and Japanese younger generation, especially in Asian culture.

In discussion of face in Chinese and Japanese culture, we not only examine how Chinese and Japanese face differs in nature from that proposed by Brown and Levinson, but also analyze the actual constituents of face in Chinese and Japanese culture. In order to promote understanding of the notions of face behind the culture usefully. It is also useful and important to analyze how face emerges through communication in Chinese and Japanese. Because it offers an emic perspective which explicates emic notions of face. The concept of face is a complex and an interesting phenomenon, and it is necessary to develop in-depth studies of the conceptualization of face across cultures and societies.

Acknowledgments

This paper has been partially supported by the Grant-in-Aid for Scientific Research of the Japanese Society for the Promotion of Science (Scientific Research (C), Grant-Number 25370469).

References

Abe, K. (1995). *Seken towa nanika* [What is seken?]. Tokyo: Kodansha.
Bargiela-Chiappini, F. (2003). Face and politeness: New (insights) for old (concepts). *Journal of Pragmatics, 35,* 1453-1469.
Brown, P., & Levinson, S. C. (1978). Universals in language usage: Politeness phenomena. In E. N. Goody (Ed.), *Questions and politeness: Strategies in social interaction* (pp. 56-289). Cambridge, MA: Cambridge University Press.
Brown, P., & Levinson, S. C. (1987). *Politeness: Some universals in language usage.* Cambridge, UK: Cambridge University Press.
Chen, R., He, L., & Hu, C. (2013). Chinese requests: In comparison to American and Japanese requests and with reference to the "East-West divide." *Journal of Pragmatics, 55,* 140-161.
Cole, M. (1989). *A cross-cultural inquiry into the meaning of face in the Japanese and the United States cultures.* Paper presented at the Speech Communication Association Convention, San Francisco, CA.
Fukada, A., & Asato, N. (2004). Universal politeness theory: application to the use of Japanese honorifics. *Journal of Pragmatics, 36,* 1991-2002.
Fukushima, S. (2000). *Requests and culture: Politeness in British English and Japanese.* Frankfurt: Peter Lang.
Gilbert, R. (1926). *What's wrong with China.* London: John Murrag.
Goffman, E. (1955). On face-work: An analysis of ritual elements in social interaction. *Journal for the Study of Interpersonal Processes, 18,* 213-231.
Goffman, E. (1967). *International ritual: Essays in face-to-face behavior.* New York: Pantheon Books.
Gu, Y. (1990). Politeness phenomena in Modern Chinese. *Journal of Pragmatics, 14,* 237-257.
Haugh, M. (2007). Emic conceptualizations of (im)politeness and face in Japanese: Implications for the discursive negotiation of second language learner identities. *Journal of Pragmatics, 39,* 657-680.
Haugh, M., & Hinze, C. (2003). A metalinguistic approach to deconstructing the concepts of 'face' and 'politeness' in Chinese, English and Japanese. *Journal of Pragmatics, 35,* 1581-1611.
Haugh, M. (2005). The importance of 'place' in Japanese politeness: Implications for cross-cultural and intercultural analyses. *Intercultural Pragmatics, 2,* 41-68.

Haugh, M. (2010). Jocular mockery, (dis)affiliation, and face. *Journal of Pragmatics, 42,* 2106-2119.
Hayford, C. (1985). Chinese and American characteristics: Arthur Smith and his China book. In S. Barnett & J. Fairbank (Eds.), *Christianity in China* (pp. 153-174). Cambridge, MA: Harvard University Press.
Ho, D. Y. F. (1976). On the concept of face. *American Journal of Sociology, 81,* 867-884.
Hu, H. C. (1944). The Chinese concepts of "face." *American Anthropologist, New series, 46,* 45-64.
Ide, S. (1989). Formal forms and discernment: Two neglected aspects of universals of linguistic politeness. *Multilingua, 8,* 233-248.
Inoue, T. (1977). *Sekentei no kozo* [The structure of sekentei]. Tokyo: NHK.
Ishiyama, O. (2009). A note on Matsumoto regarding Japanese verbs of giving and receiving. *Journal of Pragmatics, 41,* 1061-1065.
MacGowan, J. (1912). *Men and manners in modern China.* London: Unwin.
Mao, L. R. (1994). Beyond politeness theory: 'Face' revisited and renewed. *Journal of Pragmatics, 21,* 451-486.
Matsumoto, Y. (1988). Reexamination of the universality of face. *Journal of Pragmatics, 12*(4), 403-426.
Matsumoto, Y. (2003). Reply to Pizziconi. *Journal of Pragmatics, 35,* 1515-1526.
Morisaki, S., & Gudykunst, W. (1994). Face in Japan and the United States. In S. Ting-Toomey (Ed.), *The challenge of facework: Cross-cultural and interpersonal issues* (pp. 47-93). New York: State University of New York Press.
Oliver, R. T. (1971). *Communication and culture in Ancient India and China.* Syracuse, NY: Syracuse University Press.
Pizziconi, B. (2003). Re-examining politeness, face and the Japanese language. *Journal of Pragmatics, 35,* 1471-1506.
St. André, J. (2013). How the Chinese lost 'face'. *Journal of Pragmatics, 55,* 68-85.
Shiba, R. (1999, Feb 19). *Seken ni tsuite* [About seken]. *Shukan Asahi,* 50-55.
Shimura, I. (Ed.), (1998). *Kojien.* Tokyo: Iwanami Shoten.
Smith, A. H. (1894). *Chinese characteristics.* New York: Fleming H. Revell Company.
Spencer-Oatey, H. (2007). Theories of identity and the analysis of face. *Journal of Pragmatics, 39,* 639-656.
Sueda, K. (1995). Differences in the perception of face: Chinese mien-tzu and Japanese mentsu. *World Communication, 24*(1), 23-31.
Takita, F. (2012). Reconsidering the concept of negative politeness 'Enryo' in Japan. *Foreign Language Research and Education, 20,* 189-196
Tao, L. (1998). The linguistic expression of politeness: "Face," "mianzi and lian," "kao and Menboku" in cross-cultural perspective. *Socio-Environmental Studies, 3,* 209-223.
Tu, W. (1985). Selfhood and otherness in Confucian thought. In A. J. Marsella, G. DeVos, & F. L. K. Hsu (Eds.), *Culture and self: Asian and Western perspectives* (pp. 231-251). New York: Tavistock Publications.
Usami, M. (2002). *Discourse politeness in Japanese conversation: Some implications for a universal theory of politeness.* Tokyo: Hituzi Syobo.
Yang, M. (1947). *Chinese Village: Taitou, Shantung Province.* London: Kegan Paul, Trench, Trubner.
Yu, M. (2003). On the universality of face: Evidence from Chinese compliment response behavior. *Journal of Pragmatics, 35,* 1679-1710.

Appendix 14.1

Questionnaire

This questionnaire is to be used in my research on the cross-cultural comparison of polite language. I will investigate the politeness phenomena in English, Chinese and Japanese. I am collecting data about the characteristics of *face*. I want to compare the characteristics of *face* in Chinese and Japanese with Brown and Levinson's (1987) conceptualization of *face*, identifying their major difference. Here, I would like to know how you think face and polite language.

Sex: F / M   Age: _____   Nationality: _____

Major: _____ Profession:_____

Q1.   Do you think that Japanese people regard saving face very highly?
      A. Japanese people regard saving face very highly.
      B. Japanese people do not regard face very highly.

Q2.   Do you think that saving face is very important for you?
      A. Yes B. No

Q3.   Adapted from *Goffman* (1967), *face* is a universal (albeit culturally elaborated) notion, a public self-image that every member of a society wants to claim for himself (p. 61). Brown & Levinson (1987) characterize two types of face in terms of participant wants rather than social norms:

<u>Negative</u> *Face*:
"the want of every 'competent adult member' that his action be unimpeded by others" (p. 62).

<u>Positive</u> *Face*:
"have to do with one's want to be appreciated and approved of by others" (p. 61).

Which one do you think is considered most important in Japanese culture, negative face or positive face?
      A. Negative face B. Positive face C. Both of them D. Neither of them

Q4.   Do you like to save your face in personal relationships?
      A. Yes B. No

INDEX

A

Ainu 174-178, 185, 193-197
autoethnography 219-221, 230-232

B

Bakhtin 69, 70, 72, 74, 76, 79, 81, 157

C

Common European Framework of Reference vii, xii, 151-154, 158-167
communities of practice 233, 235-236, 243, 247, 271
community vii, x, xi, xiv, 45-67, 71-74, 76-77, 79-81, 89, 97, 105, 135, 143, 177, 180, 182, 187, 189-190, 192, 194-196, 198, 201, 207, 223, 233-240, 243-246, 252, 254, 259-260, 262, 266, 274-275, 286
community-based pedagogies x, 45, 47, 62
conflict xii, 25-26, 56, 147, 180, 200, 206, 209, 211, 213-214
critical discourse analysis vii, xii, 90, 98, 101, 137, 152, 154, 157, 165-166
critical literacy 45-48, 51, 56, 62-63

critical pedagogy vii, 64, 67, 69-70, 72-73, 77-81, 223
cultural adjustment 233, 235, 252, 255-256, 267

D

desire xi, 17, 68, 73, 76, 79-81, 86, 113, 180, 232, 244, 269, 284
discourse xi, xii, 21, 31, 39, 69, 70, 83, 86, 90-95-105, 127, 130, 137, 152, 157-159, 162-163, 166-167, 170, 191, 221-222, 229, 238, 246-247, 288

E

education ix, xii, xiii, 5, 17-21, 26, 39, 51, 63-65, 67, 69-72, 80-82, 84-85, 89, 92-93, 99-101, 104-105, 139, 146-149, 151-154, 159, 161-167, 170-174, 180-181, 183-184, 187-198, 201, 223, 232-234, 238-239, 245-246, 249-251, 253, 264-267, 288
English vii, x, xi, 4, 8-11, 13-14, 17, 20, 24, 29-38, 40-43, 45-46, 49, 56, 61, 65-82, 95-102, 104, 110-113, 115-118, 124-127, 151-152, 154, 158, 161-163, 165-167, 169-170, 178, 187-188, 192, 199-203, 205, 212, 215,

222-227, 229-230, 232-234, 237-243, 245-247, 255-258, 260-262, 264-266, 272-273, 275, 287, 289
English as a foreign language x, 8, 20-22, 24-26, 28-30, 32, 36, 38, 42-43, 45-51, 64-65, 67, 69-70, 73, 76, 80, 127, 151, 154, 165, 237, 245
essays xi, 9, 18, 63, 77, 79, 81, 83, 89, 109, 114-120, 123-127

F

face xiii, 23, 25, 29, 39, 58, 138, 174, 183, 211-212, 230, 236, 250, 252, 255, 258-261, 263-264, 269-289
Fairclough xii, 58, 100-101, 103, 104, 152, 154, 155, 157, 166
France vii, xii, 133, 138-140, 143-145, 147, 148
Freire x, 45, 46, 63-64, 67, 70, 72, 80-81, 90, 104, 170, 196

G

gender 31, 78, 82, 104, 149, 219, 222, 225-226, 229, 232, 271, 276-277, 279-280, 285
grassroots movements xii, 170-171, 174, 191, 193-196

H

Halliday xii, 8, 20, 152, 155-157, 167

I

identity ix, xi, xiii, 21, 23, 27, 29, 43, 47, 62, 68-82, 91, 93, 97, 99, 101, 104, 135, 141, 143, 145-146, 148, 173, 175-176, 179-180, 183, 187, 192-193, 196-197, 211, 222-223, 226-227, 229, 232-238, 241, 246-247, 250, 252, 261-263, 265, 288
immigrants 96, 170-171, 174, 180, 185, 190, 192, 196-197, 246, 249, 258, 260, 265, 267

J

Japanese vii-viii, x-xiii, 4, 8-10, 11, 13, 17, 20, 68, 70, 72, 74-78, 80-81, 111-120, 123, 124-126, 127, 151-152, 154, 156, 160, 163-164, 166-167, 170-185, 187, 191-198, 209-220, 222-226, 228-230, 232, 249-267, 270-289, 298

L

language barriers 249, 252, 255-258
language ideology xii, 133, 137-138, 152, 165-166
language rights 148, 170, 196
linguistic politeness 24, 38, 288

M

Mexico 24, 29, 32, 36, 39, 56, 84, 200
motivation 26, 68, 198, 233, 235-237, 240, 243-244, 251
multiliteracies vii, 46-47, 63, 105

N

narrative vii, xi, 62, 69-70, 72-73, 75-77, 79-80, 82-83, 87, 89-92, 94-96, 102-103, 105, 174, 176-177, 221, 225-226, 229, 231-232, 236, 246
nation-state xii, 133-134, 136-137, 147, 191
negotiating 102, 110, 223

P

peace xii, xiv, 38, 199, 201, 206, 210, 212-215
peer review vii, x, 3-21
policy xii, 81, 84, 97, 104, 133-134, 137-138, 140-141, 144, 147-148, 151-152, 158, 161-167, 176, 180, 191, 196-197, 246
policy borrowing 151
preservice teachers xi, 83, 87-89, 93-94, 96-98, 104, 249

R

revitalization 177-178, 186-197

S

Slovenia xii, 133, 140-141, 145, 147-149
social justice xi, 83-84, 86-87, 90, 97, 103-104, 267
society iv, vii, ix, xii, xiv, 3, 17-19, 22, 39, 45, 49, 55, 60-61, 67-71, 73, 80-81, 97, 101-102, 123, 126, 139, 143-144, 148, 152, 162, 169-170, 172, 175-177, 183, 195-196, 199, 209, 213, 222, 229-230, 245, 254, 256, 270, 272-275, 283-284, 289
Society iv, vii, ix, x, xi, xii, xiv, 39, 148-149, 196-197, 215, 287, 301
sociolinguistics 91, 134, 186
sojourner viii, xiii, 249-266

T

teacher xi-xiii, 3, 5-7, 10-13, 16-19, 21-24, 27-38, 41-43, 46-47, 49, 53, 63-65, 67-68, 70-74, 76, 78-80, 82-84, 86-90, 92-102, 104, 115, 151, 160, 163, 166, 188, 199, 209, 223, 230, 249-250, 252-258, 262, 264, 266

U

unification 133, 139-147

V

violence xii, 171, 199, 201-204, 212-215

W

writing x, xi, xiii, 3-22, 46-47, 61, 64, 66, 73, 79, 83, 86-97, 99, 102-104, 109, 111, 114, 116-118, 126-131, 183, 191, 220, 222, 226-229, 234, 239-243, 246, 255-256

ABOUT THE EDITORS

Paul Chamness Miller, Ph.D., is Associate Professor in the English for Academic Purposes program at Akita International University in Akita, Japan. His research interests include instructed SLA and social justice issues of English Language Learners and LGBTIQ teachers and students.

Hidehiro Endo, Ph.D., is Assistant Professor in the Teacher's License Program at Akita International University in Akita, Japan. His research interests include social justice issues in education, English language teaching and learning, and teaching and teacher education.

John L. Watzke, Ph.D., is Professor and Dean of the School of Education at the University of Portland. His research focuses on beginning teacher pedagogical development and teacher professional identity formation.

Miguel Mantero, Ph.D., is Professor of Educational Linguistics and Director of the program in Second Language Acquisition and Teaching at the University of Alabama. His research focuses on cognition in second language acquisition, and identity and discourse processes in language education.

ABOUT THE CONTRIBUTORS

Reiko Akiyama, Ph.D. Candidate, Curriculum Studies, Purdue University, Indiana, USA

Tamara M. Chung Constant, Doctoral Candidate in Language, Literacy, and Culture in the College of Education, University of Massachusetts-Amherst, USA

Amparo Clavijo-Olarte, Ph.D., Associate Professor of the Master's program in Applied Linguistics to TEFL, Universidad Distrital Francisco Jose de Caldas, Bogota, Colombia

Takayo Kawabe, M.A., Instructor of English to EFL Students, Kobe University, Kobe, Japan

Shinji Kawamitsu, Doctoral Student in the College of Education, University of Massachusetts-Amherst, USA

Aya Kitamura, M.A., Assistant Professor, Department of English, Tsuda College, Tokyo, Japan

Charles Kowalski, Associate Professor of English and Peace Studies, Tokai University, Kanagawa, Japan

Heejung Kwon, Ph.D. Candidate, Second Language Studies/ESL, Department of English, Purdue University, Indiana, USA

Kazumi Matsumoto, Ph.D., Assistant Professor of Japanese, Ball State University, Muncie, Indiana, USA

Rosa Alejandra Medina-Riveros, Doctoral Student of Language Literacy and Culture, University of Massachusetts-Amherst, USA

Gerrard Mugford, Ph.D., Lecturer at the Modern Languages Department, Universidad de Guadalajara, Mexico

Luz Maribel Ramirez-Galindo, M.A., Lecturer of the Master's program in Applied Linguistics to TEFL, Universidad Distrital Francisco Jose de Caldas, Bogota, Colombia

Brian G. Rubrecht, Ph.D., Associate Professor, School of Commerce, Meiji University, Tokyo, Japan

Lin Tao, Ph.D., Guest Researcher of Human and Socio-Environmental School, Kanazawa University, Kanazawa, Japan

Anton Vegel, M.A., Kent State University, Kent, Ohio, USA

Nancy Wasser, Ph.D., Multicultural Curriculum Design/Instruction, New Mexico State University, Las Cruces, New Mexico

Also Available from ISLS!

READINGS IN LANGUAGE STUDIES
VOLUME 1
Language across Disciplinary Boundaries

Edited by
Miguel Mantero, University of Alabama
Paul Chamness Miller, Akita International University
John L. Watzke, University of Portland

Available at all bookstores and online vendors:
ISBN-10: 0977911411
ISBN-13: 978-0977911417
Paperback: 652 pages; 35 Chapters
Average price: $39.00 paperback; $55.00 hardcover

READINGS IN LANGUAGE STUDIES
VOLUME 2
Language and Power

Edited by
John L. Watzke, University of Portland
Paul Chamness Miller, Akita International University
Miguel Mantero, University of Alabama

Available at all bookstores and online vendors:
ISBN-10: 097791142X
ISBN-13: 978-0977911424
Paperback: 466 pages; 23 Chapters
Average price: $45.00 paperback; $60.00 hardcover

READINGS IN LANGUAGE STUDIES
VOLUME 3
Language and Identity

Edited by
Paul Chamness Miller, Akita International University
John L. Watzke, University of Portland
Miguel Mantero, University of Alabama

Available at all bookstores and online vendors:
ISBN-10: 0977911446
ISBN-13: 9780977911448
Paperback: 467 pages; 32 Chapters
Average price: $50.00 paperback; $63.00 hardcover

READINGS IN LANGUAGE STUDIES
VOLUME 4
Language and Social Justice

Edited by
Miguel Mantero, University of Alabama
John L. Watzke, University of Portland
Paul Chamness Miller, Akita International University

Available at all bookstores and online vendors:
ISBN-10: 0977911462
ISBN-13: 9780977911462
Paperback: 348 pages; 18 Chapters
Average price: $30.00 paperback; $60.00 hardcover

Publications of the International Society for Language Studies, Inc.
To learn more about ISLS and its mission, visit their website:

www.isls.co

ISLS retains a low membership fee that includes:
a quarterly journal, monthly newsletter, and a reduced conference rate.

www.ingramcontent.com/pod-product-compliance
Lightning Source LLC
Chambersburg PA
CBHW032051220426
43664CB00008B/949